BUMPS

IN

THE

ROAD

Part One

By

D.J. Sweetenham

PublishAmerica
Baltimore

First printing

ISBN: 1-60441-453-7
PUBLISHED BY PUBLISHAMERICA, LLLP
www.publishamerica.com
Baltimore

Printed in the United States of America

BUMPS

IN

THE

ROAD

Part One

By

D.J. Sweetenham

To my wife, Millie and our two four-legged children, Sam and Dee, with love.

Thanks, guys, for allowing me the time and space to work on this project.

Acknowledgments

I would like to thank the following for their encouragement and support:

Durant Godwin, Diane Holmes, John and Dee Pina, John Winstead, and Ashley Brannen.

Particular thanks go to Chad and Benita Hardy of 911 PC Repair, Inc., without whose help I would still be writing this with a pencil!

Introduction

The following is a collection of anecdotes, in roughly chronological order, dealing with events that occurred during my life. Almost every time I retell one of these stories, a listener will comment, "You should write a book." And I wonder if anyone else would be interested.

So, here it is.

All the events described are based on fact, but names have been changed to protect the innocent—and sometimes, the guilty!

I was born in Portland, Dorset, England, at the end of 1934, an only child. My father was an officer in the Borstal Service, a part of the British correctional system between Reform School and Prison. My wife and I and our two little dogs, now live on a small lake within half an hour's drive of Atlanta, Georgia, U.S.A. These stories represent some of the "bumps in the road" on the journey from there to here.

The Journey

Part One: To Africa and Back

Part Two: The Rest of the Journey
COMING SOON

1.

Portland, Dorset was about as far South in England as you can go. It was a huge rocky outcropping joined to the mainland by a shingle strip known as Chesil Beach. It held a small village and a collection of buildings and houses which comprised the Portland Borstal Institution. The other structure of note was the Portland Bill Lighthouse. Nearby Weymouth Harbor, on the mainland, was clearly visible on most days from the top of the cliffs. The date was early in 1942, just two years into the second World War.

It was a brisk, cool spring morning as the school children gathered on the corner of High Street and Evans Road. There was a certain comfort in doing what we had practiced so often, the formation of the "squad" for the walk to school. A formation of twos, four senior students in the lead, followed by the smaller children, with a teacher bringing up the rear. It was a little over a mile to school, along a country lane leading out of the village and with the birds in full song in the hedges lining the ditches on either side of the lane, we were soon under way, keeping up a fairly brisk pace. For a crowd of young school children we were surprisingly well disciplined in our morning march to school, trying to emulate the military marchers we had seen in newspaper photographs. Occasionally, the teacher at the rear of the column would shout an instruction to keep us in line and to remind us that this was not playtime.

The sun was shining brightly but the weather was cool with a promise of summer holidays not very far away. It was a beautiful spring day, and thoughts of "The War" were far from anyone's mind as we made our way to another day of lessons and learning. Chattering quietly amongst ourselves as we walked along, we paid little attention to our familiar surroundings, wrapped up in our own childish concerns. Gradually I became aware of a humming noise in the distance, which was rapidly getting louder and, somehow, threatening. Just at that moment the teacher at the rear of the column screamed out, "Everyone—get down in the ditch—NOW!"

The seniors at the front of the column whipped round and immediately started pushing and herding the younger children into the ditch where we huddled face down with our hands clasped over our heads, as we had been taught. It was just a bit muddy and something wasn't really fresh there in that ditch but nobody seemed to notice the smell. Everyone was too scared. The approaching humming noise increased to a thunderous roar as the German fighter plane swept down with wing guns blazing, spraying the lane with shells and scattering dirt and shattered stones over the terrified children, screaming and crying in the ditch. As the roar of the plane faded, I cautiously peeped over the bank and saw the plane climbing away. The German insignia on the wings showed clearly against the metallic glint of the airframe as it gained altitude and turned, heading back towards the sea, back towards Europe.

As the plane approached the coast line, a recently established anti-aircraft battery opened up with a pounding barrage. Innocent seeming little black clouds of exploding shells surrounded the fleeing attacker and in a matter of seconds the plane was headed back towards land in a shallow dive, with black smoke streaming behind like a dark comet. I watched the plane disappear behind the tree line and became aware of the acrid smell of gunfire and hot stones and the cries of relief from the senior members of our party. The ground shook with the impact and the column of black smoke rising from behind the trees indicated where the plane had crashed to earth. I knew that area well, it was a solid limestone plateau, so there was no chance that much would be left of the plane or the pilot.

After what seemed to be an eternity, but was really only a couple of minutes, the teacher called out to ask if anyone was hurt. A few of the younger children had suffered some minor abrasions, from diving into the ditch so rapidly, but thankfully, nobody had been hurt by the gunfire. Slowly we climbed back onto the road and stood huddled together in a state of fear and shock, like a small herd of sheep waiting for and needing some instruction. Gradually the tension lessened and the crying of the younger children eased. As soon as she was able, the teacher called us to order and we resumed our walk to school. What had been quiet chatter in the ranks before the attack, was now much louder and more excited. We really had a story to brag about to the other children already at school.

We couldn't help but cast occasional glances between the trees at the black smoke rising into the otherwise clear blue sky. We knew that it represented the end of the attacking aircraft but few seemed to realize that it also meant the death of the pilot who had fired on us. But I knew it and felt that it was a well-deserved end for a man who would fire on a group of school children for no reason. If he hadn't broken off his escape run to the coast to make the attack, he might have still been alive. *Too bad. Serves you right,* I thought, but I kept my thoughts to myself. I had heard the arguments that arose amongst grownups when war subjects were raised, and I didn't want to get involved.

As I followed along with the rest of the group, I was planning how to get away from the squad after school was finished for the day. I wanted more than anything at that moment to see, up close, where that plane and pilot had met their end. I felt that I needed to see the crash site to assure myself that it had happened and that the incident was over. I was really too young to understand the compulsion, I just knew I had to see for myself. I didn't learn much that day at school. All the talk was of the attack and about all I could think of was how I was going to get away from the group "march" home. In the afternoon a police sergeant and a civil defense officer came to the school and asked a lot of questions of the children and teacher involved in the incident. We all did our best to remember the details, it was not something any of us would soon forget. They filled out their reports and then left.

At this time of the year it would start getting dark around 7.30 p.m. so I reckoned I would have plenty of time to get to the crash site and back home before my parents would start to be concerned. Coming up with nothing better, I finally told the teacher in charge of the march that I wanted to stop off to visit with my aunt, who lived close to the route home. As usual I got away with it, after all it wasn't a lie. Of course, Aunt Doris had heard of the attack and was relieved to see me.

"Did you get hurt?" she asked. "Are you okay?"

"Of course I'm okay, although it was a bit scary—all the noise and smell, and everything. A lot of the younger kids were crying, after it was all over, but they were just frightened. No one got hit, just a few bruises and scratches from jumping down in the ditch. In a way it was kind of exciting!"

"Exciting!" exclaimed Aunt Doris. "We don't need any more of that kind of excitement around here. This war is getting too close for comfort. Your Mum and Dad and me were just talking about that a few days ago. They're thinking about moving away from the South Coast. Your Dad has been offered a transfer to a new Borstal on the East Coast—something like a farming area, I believe. No doubt they'll tell you about it when you get home. At least it should be quieter there; there's nothing there for the Jerries to attack!"

"Anyway," I replied, "I've got to get going. I just wanted to let you know that I'm okay before I go home, so give us a kiss, and I'll be gone"

Leaving my aunt's house, I walked quickly around the first corner and then broke into a run as I reached the line of trees bordering an adjacent field. Easing my way between the strands of the fence wire surrounding the field, I sprinted across the field and into the cover of the woods on the other side. Knowing that the authorities would be nearby, as the crash site was in a shallow valley just a few yards ahead, I carefully crept between the trees and undergrowth, moving as silently as possible. My pulse was racing and the adrenalin was flowing, and I knew what the consequences would be if I was caught. I remembered an occasion, not too long before, when my Dad had chastised me for some indiscretion. I never would forget the sting of that little split bamboo cane on the back of my legs. Doing my best to control my breathing and to stay as quiet as I could, I finally made it to the edge of the woods. Peeking out, I could see several policemen and a couple of men in white coats, standing together at the far side of the shallow depression in the ground. Close to where they stood, the ground was all torn up with pieces of metal scattered around the point of impact.

So far, so good. My presence had gone unnoticed, and a quick scan of the area from my hiding place showed me a piece of the aircraft wreckage lying on the ground, a hundred yards or so off to the right of the crash site. The woods in which I was hiding, circled the area and I made my way quietly, along the edge of the trees until I was directly opposite the aircraft fragment. It was a jagged piece of aluminum, which until that morning, had been part of the rudder assembly of one of Germany's finest fighting planes. It even had part of a swastika painted on it, and I knew that this was going to be a great souvenir of the whole incident, and I just had to have it. The officials on the other side of the crash site were too engrossed in their discussions and paper work to notice a small boy crawling furtively through the grass a hundred yards away. Making no more disturbance than a scared rabbit, I eased through the tall grass towards my prize. It was just a bit bigger than I had originally thought, but grasping it firmly with one hand I backed slowly and carefully into the cover of the woods. Once out of sight of the officials I sat down on the ground beside my treasure, back against a tree and let my breath out. It felt as though I had been holding it in for ages.

After a few minutes, I had calmed down enough to be able to make my way quietly back to the other side of the woods and once through the fence, I was off and running the rest of the way home. Arriving at the narrow alley between our back yard and the neighbor's back yard, I found the two loose slats in our fence and crawled through, still clutching my prize. This placed me behind the garden shed where several pieces of scrap wood, leftovers from some of Dad's various carpentry projects, leaned up against the shed wall. I wasn't sure how I would ever be able to show off my trophy so I hid it amongst the wood, hoping that when the dust settled I would be able to bring it out into the light. The sun was well on its way to the horizon by the time that I eased out of the alleyway and into the house by way of the front door.

Glancing at the kitchen clock and then at me, my Mum said, "You're late again. What was it this time? Chasing rabbits or bird nesting? I was beginning to worry, especially since that air raid this morning, but Ron called out as he went by and said that you had stopped off at your aunt's. How is she? I haven't seen much of her for several days now...."

As Mum chattered on my thoughts were all of my little adventure that day. Suddenly I realized that Mum had stopped talking and was looking at me, waiting for a reply.

"I'm sorry, Mum, I was thinking about something else—what did you say?"

"I said that Dad and me had something important to tell you, but it can wait until he gets home. Shouldn't be long now."

I had a good idea what it was about—Aunt Doris had given the game away—but I said nothing about that, just, "Okay, Mum."

Dad came home a few minutes later and the three of us sat around the dining table as he told us about the upcoming move. It was exciting news for me; I had been born in Portland and had never been anywhere else. To move across the entire country of England to a new house and meet new people was going to be a major change in my life. I never suspected that this sort of thing would turn out to be a pretty routine event during the rest of my life. And to move from Portland, Dorset, on the South Coast to Hollesley Bay, Suffolk on the East Coast would be a very small step for me, compared to the moves that I would make in later years.

As far as my souvenir of the day's events was concerned.... Early the next morning, before the march to school started off, the local policeman propped his bicycle up on the curb outside our house and rang the doorbell. I answered the door, surprised and a little scared when he growled at me, "All right, young fella, where is it?"

I gulped. "Where's what, sir?"

"You know what I'm talking about. Where's that piece of German airplane you stole yesterday? And don't deny it—you were seen bringing it home."

By this time I was trembling a bit and very shakily I told the policeman where I had hidden it. He ordered me to go and bring it to him, which I did, quickly. He tied the piece of metal on the carrier of his bike, and before he set off he gave me one more piece of advice. "Don't ever touch anything like this again. Apart from the fact it might be dangerous, it doesn't belong to you, and you have no right to it."

"I'm very sorry, sir. I didn't know I was stealing—I'll never do it again, I promise!"

"Okay, then, just remember what I said. I don't want to have to come round here again. I may have to take you to the police station if I do."

With that he pedaled away, while I stood stunned, on the front doorstep. I was still a bit shaky when I joined the squad to march to school, but I didn't speak about the incident to anyone.

I never did find out who turned me in, but Dad told me much later that he had set up that little "meeting" with the local Bobby to teach me a lesson! It worked—for a while, anyway.

I have always had a love for boats and the sea or any body of water big enough to float a boat and this I'm sure, was passed on to me by my father. A couple of weeks after the airplane attack, Dad asked me if I would like to go eel fishing with him. He and several other fishermen had boat sheds on Chesil beach where they kept their wooden rowboats. Normally around fifteen feet long, clinker built, they were driven by manpower on two oars; no outboard motors there. It was impossible to get petrol for boat use anyway and the rowing exercise was very beneficial. I remember my Dad going for a physical exam for some life insurance and the Doctor remarked that he had never seen such a fine set of abdominal muscles. Dad was not a big man, only about five feet nine inches and around one hundred and sixty pounds but he was as strong as an ox and tough with it. Dealing with the young thugs and criminals who were the inmates of the Borstal, being a "hard man" was a necessity.

Naturally I jumped at the chance to get out in the bay in the boat. This was on a Saturday morning and my Grandmother, Dad's mother, was coming to visit and stay the night. We would be back from fishing before she arrived.

All the fishing gear was stowed in the boat shed, so we only had to carry our lunch: a couple of sandwiches and a thermos of tea, on our bikes. This was the easy part of the ride, all downhill to the beach.

There were some greased boards lying in the shingle leading from the boat winch beside the shed to the high tide mark on the beach. Dad unlocked the boat from the winch and after loading up the fishing gear, lunch and the oars, we pushed it down to the water's edge. I climbed aboard and sat on the stern seat while Dad jumped in and pushed off at the same time. The weather was a little rough with gray skies and patches of drizzle. Sea swells were running at around two feet, just enough to make rowing a heavy wooden boat interesting. That didn't concern me too much. Just being out in the boat on the sea was magic to me. With all the rocking and pitching the boat was doing, it could be expected that I would be a bit "queasy," but I wasn't sick then, and I have never suffered any kind of travel sickness in my life.

After a short while we arrived at an area which Dad knew to be a good spot for catching eels. We didn't use rods or poles for this type of fishing. Just hand lines wound on a simple wooden frame. Baiting the hooks was a bit of a smelly business—we used old, stale fish heads which had been saved from Dad's fishing expedition a couple of days before. They had been kept in a bucket in the boathouse and left to get "ripe." Nobody had refrigerators then. But, apparently, that was how the eels liked them.

During the morning we had several bites but nothing latched onto the bait and I was beginning to get bored.

I commented, "You know what, Dad, I think these eels must have known we were coming and they moved away. They'll probably come back after we move to the East Coast."

Dad said, "You could be right; let's give it one more try, and then we'll go in. We want to get back home before Nan arrives, and it's a hard push up the hill with or without fish to carry."

Almost before the words were out of his mouth, there was a violent tug on the line and the bait was taken. The line was tied off to an anchor point in the boat so we just sat and let the fish, or whatever it was, pull the boat wherever it wanted to go. It must have taken about ten minutes or so before Dad was able to pull in any line and retie it to the anchor point and then we waited some more. This routine continued for almost an hour before Dad pulled the head of the conger over the side of the boat, followed by six feet of writhing, lashing, angry eel. It was a monster to me, crouching as I was, on the stern seat keeping my feet and legs as far away from the creature as I possibly could. Dad was also struggling to keep clear of the snapping jaws and the wildly lashing body. Beating the fish on the head with a wooden club, kept in the boat for this kind of thing, did little to slow the eel down. Somehow we managed to get the hessian bag out from the hatch under the seat on which I was crouched. It was on old coal sack, which Dad used to haul his catch ashore. After a lot of maneuvering, we finally bagged the eel. It still had the hook in it; Dad cut the line rather than try to get the hook out. Once our catch was in the sack, I felt confident enough to stand up in the boat and stretch my legs but I made sure I didn't get too close to the bag!

When we reached the beach, it was with a shout of relief that I jumped over the side of the boat and ran up to the winch to fetch the hook to attach to the boat. As we were cranking the winch handle another fisherman, walking along the beach towards his boat shed, called out to us, "Any luck today, Joe?"

"Just one conger, Bill; but he's a big one—about six feet, I'd say."

"Is he in a bag? If so, just keep him there; I'll believe you."

"Don't worry, Bill, he's going to stay in the bag until he's dead. I told Don just how dangerous these things can be. Come on over and show him."

He put out his hand to shake hands with Dad and then me. When I reached for his hand I noticed there was no thumb, and he smiled when I asked him what happened to it. Apparently, the fishermen along that stretch of shingle beach had a habit of cutting off the head of their biggest eel catch and nailing it to the side of their sheds. Something to do with bragging rights.

"One day last year," said Bill, "I had been out early in the morning and caught a big eel, an eight-footer, and when I brought him ashore, I cut his head off and nailed it to my shed. The next afternoon, some visitors were walking along the beach and they asked me about the eel head, the biggest they had ever seen. Of course, I had to show off a bit, and trying to show them the teeth inside the skull, I levered open the mouth with my thumb. And that's when the bloody thing got its own back on me. It snapped my thumb clean off! I never believed it was possible for anything to live without its body. The Doctor said it was possibly some kind of nervous reaction. Whatever, it taught me a lesson, and I hope you remember it, too."

Lashing the bag with the eel inside, to the crossbar on Dad's bike, we started up the hill pushing our bikes to our house in the officer's quarters. Mum wasn't home when we arrived; she was meeting Nan at the bus station. We dropped the bag in the washhouse, a building in the back yard which housed the concrete boiler for laundry. No washing machines in those days. We knew Mum wouldn't be doing any laundry while Nan was there, and knowing Nan's fear of snakes and anything else "creepy, crawly" as she used to say, Dad said we shouldn't even tell them about the day's catch.

Early the next morning, Sunday, we and half the neighborhood were awakened by a piercing scream which kept on and on. Dad and I both dashed out into the back yard in our pyjamas to see what had happened and found Nan, standing outside the washhouse in an apparent state of shock. She had awakened early and decided to go for a stroll in the yard before breakfast. Being a little nosy she had opened the door to the washhouse and peeped inside. The lighting wasn't very good in there and she thought she saw a large log lying in the shadows. The eel had torn its way out of the coal sack, which lay in tatters in the corner. She was going to go in and look around, but the "log" suddenly lurched towards her, and she immediately supposed that it was a huge snake coming for her. She literally leapt back out of the washhouse, slamming the door behind, screaming her head off!

Several cups of strong tea later, she calmed down enough to tell Dad and me, just what she thought of our fishing expedition and our catch.

We left the eel in the washhouse the rest of that day and in the evening, Dad went in with a hatchet and decapitated it before chopping it up into meal-sized steaks. The whole neighborhood enjoyed conger eel for dinner the next day. It was delicious.

We never did nail the head up to the boat shed, and it wasn't long before we were too busy with moving to the other side of the country to think any more about catching the big conger.

2.

Coming from a normally quiet, reserved type of life in Portland to a somewhat rambunctious countrified existence in Suffolk was quite an experience in itself. The Colony, as it was called, was a large farming estate which was manned by Borstal Boys living in separate camps named after the Saints of Britain. St Andrew's House, St George's, St David's and St Patrick's. These "Houses" were really large barracks type living accommodations for the boys who worked the land, the orchards and tended the livestock. There were strict rules for them to obey but very little security. It was very much an open prison where a lot of trust was placed in the inmates. Not that an escape would do a prisoner much good. Everyone who tried it was caught within a day or so and then transferred to a real prison with real security in the form of cells with bars and an extended sentence. Not many tried it.

The quarters provided for the officers were really nice, three-bedroom, semi-detached, brick-built two-story houses, with small front gardens and large back yards. They were situated in a large circle on the top of a hill known as "Oak Hill." The circular road running in front of the houses was exactly one quarter of a mile long with one exit/ entrance road leading to the highway. The main offices and administration buildings were located about a mile away with a company store where staff could purchase, at very cheap prices, produce grown on the estate. All other essentials were available in the local village but that was two and a half miles away and only a couple of the officers had cars. This created an ideal situation for pedlars and regular delivery services and we had all kinds of services on wheels, from the usual milk man, baker, butcher, paper boy to the more exotic like the paraffin man, (kerosene) and the mobile scissor, knife, hatchet and saw sharpener. All of these people drove vehicles of some sort which provided the local children who owned roller skates, with free rides around the circle, knowing the vehicle would stop somewhere before it exited onto the main road.

Except for one occasion when I hitched a ride behind a delivery van after he made one delivery. The driver must have forgotten something or was late for a delivery somewhere else. He took off at what seemed to me to be light speed with me hanging on, too scared to let go and yelling my head off to get him to stop. As he swung round the final curve to the exit street, he took the turn very close to the sidewalk and my skates hit the curb. Although my feet had stopped the rest of me hadn't. I flew straight through the fence and hedge of the adjacent house and ended up on the lady's front lawn in a pile of tangled rose bushes and broken fence slats. I wasn't really hurt, just scratched and bruised, but I looked worse than I was and the officer's wife who helped me stand up obviously felt sorry for me. After I apologized to her, I staggered off home to clean up. In a small community like our's, every little thing was news, and Dad knew all about it by the time he came home. Fortunately he saw the funny side of it but he made me promise, there and then, that I would not do anything stupid like that again. Of course, I promised!

The Colony had its own landfill, known locally as "The Dump." Few of the neighborhood boys could afford to buy bicycles so we made our own from old pieces of bikes we found at the dump. Brakes were not considered important and we soon learned how to fix punctures. There was a short-lived fad amongst the kids for a while of trying to copy the local heroes of the speedway track in Ipswich. Oak Hill was the name of the officer's quarters, but the road which led down the hill on the opposite side was called Tank Hill, for the large water tank situated on top. It was a long, fast hill with steep wooded banks on both sides. Two thirds of the way down, a gravel lane led off to the left in the direction of St Andrew's House. On the downhill side of the junction of Tank Hill and the gravel lane was a thatched cottage with a beautiful rose garden, cut into the side of the hill. The drop from the gravel lane to the garden was about fifteen feet. It was the perfect place to practice our speedway skids, as far as we were concerned. Not so the lady of the cottage, though. While we would come flying down the hill on our old wrecks of bikes, sliding into the corner on the gravel lane, she would stand outside her front door with a first-aid kit in her hands, waiting for one of us to come flying through the hedge. Several of us came close at times but we always managed to get caught up in the hedge and never made it all the way through.

Another of our hobbies was what we called, "Dilly-carts." Tank hill was the perfect venue for those. The cart consisted of a wooden plank with an axle clamped on one end with two wheels and a movable axle with two wheels on the other end. A length of rope provided steering. The deluxe models had a wooden box or crate to hold the driver. Few of them had brakes; the cart stopped when it ran out of speed or hit something solid. All the materials for these machines came from the dump. We let the Borstal boys who worked at the dump know what we needed and they would save parts for us in exchange for cigarette butts.

For a brief period of time I had the biggest cart in the group. The wheels were bigger than any others, having come from an old twin-size baby carriage and it sported a box big enough for two kids. It picked up quite a bit of speed down Tank Hill and could almost make it to the Colony buildings, a mile away. This was the main road to the colony so we had to keep watch for regular road traffic. Our antics weren't popular with adult road users and of course, now I can see why.

One day, after I had made a good run down the hill in my cart, a boy who didn't own a cart asked me for a ride. It would be his first time, and my cart was big enough to carry both of us. He was the local vicar's son, and his Dad wouldn't let him have a cart of his own. For some reason the vicar thought they were too dangerous! I had just about recovered my breath after hauling the cart back up to the top of Tank Hill, so with two other kids holding the cart back, I sat in front and the vicar's son sat behind me, holding onto the sides of the box.

I shouted, "Let go!" and we were off, rapidly gaining speed with the extra weight on board. We were at maximum velocity as we approached the gravel lane junction, when a large dog dashed down the bank, through the trees, and out onto the road in front of us. There was no way I could have stopped, even if the cart had been equipped with a brake, and I couldn't hit the dog. I jerked the rope steering to the right and, leaning over on two wheels, the cart shot up the bank, coming to a sudden halt when it demolished itself against a tree trunk. Fortunately, the passenger and I had been thrown clear before the impact, and we came crashing through the bushes and grass onto the road in a heap. Both of us carried signs of an accident such as bruises, skinned knees and elbows, but no broken bones. Looking back, it could have been a lot worse. Perhaps the fact that the passenger was the vicar's son had something to do with it, but that day we were both truly blessed!

The officer's quarters were quite close to the coast, about one and a half miles from the nearest beach. The first thing Dad did, as soon as we were settled, was to get another row boat like the one he had in Portland. Fishing was still his passion although here the fish of preference was cod, not conger eel. One time I went with him, on our bikes, during the winter when the water was just too rough to get the boat out and he spent the whole day, in his rain gear, sitting on the beach holding his fishing rod, waiting for "the big one." After an hour or so of complaining about the cold and how boring this was, I left him there and rode off home. When he came home later that afternoon he emptied his catch bag in the back yard and he had caught, amongst others, a beautiful ten-pound cod.

Summer holidays from school lasted six weeks, plenty of time to get into all sorts of mischief, but one summer I decided I needed a new, drop-handlebar, lightweight bike, so that at least I could look like a serious cyclist. A cycling club had formed in the area, and I wanted to join in the weekend rides. The bike I wanted occupied the window of a shop in Woodbridge. It had a green frame, a three-speed hub and drop handlebars. The price was fifteen pounds. I had asked Dad for the money but he just couldn't afford to give it to me, he said. He was only earning nine pounds a week at that time as a Borstal officer, but he said he would lend it to me. I had to agree to pay it back by the end of the year. This meant finding a job for the summer.

The area surrounding the colony's property, which was very extensive, held several privately owned farms, the closest being at the far end of the gravel lane which led off Tank Hill and past the cherry orchard. On the first Sunday afternoon of the summer holiday in my fifteenth year, I rode down the lane and knocked on the farmer's door. When he answered the door, as tall as I was, he still looked down on me. He was a large, muscular man, with mutton-chop whiskers and a red, sunburnt face.

"What d'ya want, son?" he asked, gruffly.

"I'm looking for work," I replied. "Anything will do."

"You ever worked on a farm before?" he asked.

"No, sir," I answered, "but I'm a quick learner, and I'm sure I could be useful to you, given the chance. You see, I need to earn enough money to pay my Dad back for the bike he's going to buy me. He's only lending me the money if I can pay him back, and I really want that bike."

He looked at me for a few minutes, then said, "You're one of those Borstal officer's kids, aren't you? This kind of work might be a bit tough on you, but harvest is coming up, and I'll need all the help I can get then. It might only be for four or five weeks. You'll be looking at ten hours a day, six days a week, minimum, and I can't pay more than a shilling an hour. And if you are late or can't stay the course, you'll be out on your ear, no arguments. If that's okay with you, I'll see you at seven in the morning."

"That's fine with me, sir. I won't let you down, and I'll be here bright and early!" I promised.

Dad wasn't too sure that I could handle it when I told him. "Let's see how the first week goes, and then we'll have a better idea of what you've let yourself in for." Dad was always very cautious in any new situation.

I was up, dressed and ready to go at six the next morning, with my sandwiches for lunch in the saddle bag on my old bike. Mum and Dad had just got up and were sitting at the breakfast table when I told them "Goodbye," and they wished me "Good luck!"

It was a beautiful morning for a bike ride, but I didn't take the time to appreciate it fully; I had a job to go to! I was really excited about getting the job and I was determined to keep it and get my new bike. It was six thirty when I knocked on the farmer's door. The farmer's wife answered the door and directed me round to the barn at the rear of the house and across the yard.

When he saw me, the farmer commented, "Well, you're early, but there's nothing wrong with that. I thought you could start with loading hay on the cart with the land girls; we've got six of them, and they've been cutting and baling hay the last week. Now we need to get it brought to the corner of the field and stacked." He added, "They'll be here soon; go and wait for them over there in the tractor shed, and they'll show you what to do."

"Land girls" were part of the government's plan to keep agriculture alive and well in the farming communities, which were short of farm workers, with most of them fighting in the army in Europe. These "girls," or young women, usually in their twenties and thirties, were a special breed. They could tackle any job on the farm as well as any man. They were rough and tough, and their language was often just as bad as any other farmhand. Being the only male in their crew, and a kid at that, I had to stand for a lot of teasing. Much of it could have been called sexual harassment or even child molestation these days but none of it was malicious, and I took it as it was intended, just good-natured fun.

The girls arrived at seven and after introductions were made, we set off on a hay cart, pulled by a small Fordson tractor. I rode standing up beside the girl who was driving the tractor, watching what she was doing. She said that I needed to learn how to drive it as that would free her up to pitch hay bales with the other women. When we arrived at the field, I could see what she meant. The bales were laid out in rough rows and the driver had to keep getting down off the tractor to pitch bales on the cart and then get back on to move it. Once the cart was loaded we drove it to the corner of the field where a haystack had already been started. Off-loading the bales, I learned that they had to be stacked in a particular pattern which would make the stack stand firm against the gales and winter storms to come.

We had all brought our lunch sandwiches with us when we left the barn and at noon we took a half hour lunch break. Sitting on hay bales, we were eating lunch and chatting when I came up with a suggestion.

"How about this?" I said. "I've just had an idea how we might get this job done a little easier. If we had two hay carts, we could load one, bring it to the stack, unhitch it and take an empty one back to the field right away. Three of you could build the stack while the other three could be loading the empty cart. Then, after lunch we could switch teams. Those who had been loading could switch to stack building, and vice versa. What do you think?"

"Sounds like we've got ourselves a foreman here, girls," said one of the older ladies. "Let's see if he can take a tickling."

And with that I was buried under a mass of female bodies, being tickled all over. I was always ticklish as a youngster, but no one had tried that on me in years. By the time they let up on me, I was gasping for breath, covered in hay and almost wetting myself with laughter. I had been tickled in places I didn't even know were ticklish, but I did get in a few tickles back, which were quite enjoyable. This could be even more fun than rugby, I thought!

There was no more talk about my master plan, but the next morning before we left the tractor shed, the girls hitched up a second wagon behind the first. As the plan hinged on having someone to drive the tractor. I was nominated and quickly learned how to handle the Fordson. At age fifteen, being able to drive any mechanical machine was an achievement. Dad was really impressed when I told him about it; I neglected to tell him about the tickling incident though, he might have wanted some of that for himself!

Once the field was clear, we had two haystacks in the corner of the field, which needed to be thatched. Thatching was a dying art and there was only one man in the area who specialized in that kind of work. Toby was a thatching genius and was always in demand by the local farmers at this time of the year When I met him, he was in his nineties and still thatching stacks, cottages and anything that required his services. The day after we cleared the hay field, the farmer told me to work with Toby on thatching the stacks. My job was to fetch the thatching straw up to Toby who was working on top of the stack, when he called for it. It wasn't too high up so I wasn't bothered by the height. And Toby liked to talk. While he was placing the straw and securing it, he would tell me tales about his navy experiences. He was in the Navy as a boy and even served on one of the last Naval sailing ships. He was a very interesting old man to listen to and I must admit that I didn't do much to earn my shilling per hour while he was around.

There were no giant harvester machines in those days although the combine harvester was just evolving. Grain fields were cut with a tractor powered machine which produced bundles of oats, wheat or barley, tied up in sheaves. These were left scattered on the ground behind the machine. Corn fields in England were generally very small and after the field was cut, usually only a day, the field crew would come in and arrange the sheaves into tent-like piles which we called "shooks." This allowed the grain to dry out before being picked up and stacked. Once stacked, Toby would be called to thatch it.

When harvesting began, the work day on the farm for me extended from dawn until dark. If I wasn't driving the Fordson, I was pitching sheaves, making shooks or helping Toby.

The days flew by, and it seemed that summer was over really fast that year. It was hard work, but it was also enjoyable. Each new task was a challenge and I had to push myself hard to overcome some of them but there was a great deal of satisfaction in being able to say that I had done, or could do, a particular job. When I left work to go back to school, the farmer invited me to return the next year but that didn't happen as that was my last summer before I left school and joined the East Suffolk County Constabulary as a Police Cadet.

I had earned my new drop-handlebar bike, with a few pounds to spare and, as a junior member of the cycling club I was covering a lot of miles at weekends. We toured all over the county of Suffolk in day-long rides, that autumn. Cycling became a big part of my life and one weekend my Father had a few vacation days due to him and we decided to ride to my Grandparents' house in Gillingham, Kent. He rode his old sit-up-and-beg bike, which he rode to work every day, and I rode my new machine. It was eighty miles, one way and we made it in one day. We visited with family for a couple of days and then rode back. Neither Dad nor I had much built in padding in the seat area, and it was a couple of days after we arrived home before we could sit down in comfort or even walk properly.

During the summer holidays from school, most of the kids with road-worthy bikes would ride down to a beach known as Shingle Street. This was about two and a half miles away from Oak Hill but on tarmac roads all the way. As its name implied, the beach was all pebbles and was a source of aggregate for the concrete used in coastal defense structures. The removal of all this shingle left two huge elongated pits on the inland side of the beach, which were full of sea water. The water was changed daily as it seeped through the beach with the tides. Swimming in sea water, without the waves and currents was perfect. As long as a person could swim, it was perfect, but the bottom was very uneven. That was how I taught myself to swim, by stepping into a deep hole in the bottom of what we called "the lagoon." It was a case of swim or drown, and I learned quickly! The beaches along this part of the east coast of England were all shingle and not easy to walk on with bare feet. A little uncomfortable for us but at least we didn't have to put up with too many tourists.

One of the local landmarks at Shingle Street was a Martello Tower. This was a stone built circular structure about fifty feet high, once used for coastal defense. The walls were six feet thick and the only entrance, a small arched doorway, was about fifteen feet up on the side of the tower. Climbing that ladder was an achievement for me but I did it several times, one summer, when the local Air Cadets, of which I was a member had a weekend camp on top. The small arched doorway opened into a passage through the wall and then into a large circular room. Steps at one side led up to the roof which was an open, stone, circular area surrounded by a six-foot-high wall. It was perfectly sheltered from the wind and an ideal place for our tents. In the main room below we had a long wooden table with bench seats either side and a stone fireplace where we could boil a kettle for tea.

At the time, I was smitten by a young girl whose brother, Ben, was also a member of the Air Cadets. He was present on that camping trip and was sitting across from me at the table. About the same age as me, but a few inches shorter, he had a loud and dirty mouth. We were all enjoying our mugs of hot tea, after breakfast one day when the subject of girl friends came up. Sometime during all the teasing, Ben started picking on me and his sister. He was calling her all the dirty names he could think of and I took exception to it. I told him to shut his mouth or I would have to do it for him. I had a reputation for having a short fuse, and he should have been warned. His answer to me was to throw half a mug full of hot tea all over me. I was told later, by the other boys present, that I jumped up, knocking the bench seat backwards and throwing a couple of boys on their backs. I threw the table over onto Ben and the others sitting on that side, then I jumped over the table, dragged Ben up into a fireman's lift, and headed through the passageway towards the door. I had kicked the door open and was about to toss Ben out when the officer in charge, Flight Lieutenant Easton, caught up with me. He wrapped his arms around both of us and dragged us back into the room. That was when I started to become aware of what was going on. I was acting out of pure temper, and if someone hadn't been there to stop me, I would have probably killed Ben. A head-first fall from fifteen feet onto a pile of rocks below might well have proved fatal.

Once the room was in order, benches and table back in place, we sat down to regain our composure. Nobody said anything for a while, and Ben and I were surrounded by wide-eyed stares. Still in a state of shock, Ben finally managed an abject apology, at Mr Easton's suggestion and I accepted it on condition that he never spoke of his sister, or any other girl, that way again. After that, the impromptu meeting broke up and we all went our separate ways, some to sun bathe on the roof, others to go to the lagoon to swim.

When I stood up to leave the table, Mr Easton said, "Wait a minute, Don; I'd like a word with you before you go." He waited until we were alone and then said, "You know you could have killed Ben, don't you?"

"I do now," I replied, "but I didn't know what I was doing. I was so mad with him I don't remember a thing until you pulled us both inside. I'm still having trouble believing it."

"Well, you'd better believe it, young man, Ben could have been dead by now, and you would be in prison. Just remember this: it's okay to play and fight hard as long as you keep your wits about you, but when you lose it, as you did just now, you're an easy target. If Ben's feet had been on the ground, he could probably have taken you. Fighting when you are that mad makes no more sense than fighting when you are drunk. It's just plain stupid. Just remember that for when you are old enough to drink!"

It all made sense, and I apologized to Mr Easton and thanked him for his advice.

He then added, "Whatever you do, you need to start working on controlling that temper. If you don't, it's going to get you in more trouble than you can handle."

And that was the last time he mentioned the incident. I took his advice about the temper and made some progress in that direction. The fighting-when-drunk part I only remembered much later, as I was being patched up in sick bay after a brawl in a north of England pub while I was in the R.A.F.

This was during the war, and other than the inconvenience of rationing on everything, we were blessed not to have the air raids that were a nightly event in the big cities like London and Liverpool. There was very little on the East Coast to interest "Jerry," but it was the way home for the German bombers after raiding London. We quite enjoyed watching the shore line gun emplacements sending up their streams of anti-aircraft shells, interlaced with tracer shells, at the fleeing planes. Every so often they would score a direct hit and the whole neighborhood would cheer as the German plane exploded. It was even more exciting when the Germans started sending over the V2 unmanned "Doodle-bugs" or "Buzz-bombs" as we called them. This time it was the other way around. The flying bombs were incoming, headed towards London. The exhaust flame on these was clear to see from the ground and it was a thrill to see the tracer shells rising up from the shore and homing in on the target. When the hit was made, an enormous explosion resulted and standing on the front steps of our house, we could feel the hair on our heads raise up from the shock wave.

Although this nightly activity wasn't really dangerous to us, it did provide a lot of interesting debris in the area. One interesting item I found in a nearby field, was a German parachute. The pilot had been caught a few miles away the previous day. Of course, we had to give it up to the authorities, but not before Dad had secured a good stock of "rope" for the boat, and I even had a couple of shirts made from one of the panels. Mum was a seamstress before she was married.

As this was a farming area, it was usual for the local children to roam the woods and fields, looking for bird's nests or chasing rabbits, or just looking to get up to some kind of mischief, to pass the time during the long summer holidays. Trying to prevent accidents, the local civil defense officer often gave talks and presentations at school, showing various types of enemy bombs and ammunition that might get dumped when the Germans were returning home. Apparently they had to get rid of their loads for a number of reasons. One was to lighten the aircraft so that it could flee faster and another was the pilot would not be believed by his superiors that he had reached his target if he still had munitions on board. From these talks we soon determined that the least dangerous souvenirs we could find were the unexploded incendiary bombs, which were quite common. They were small and easily carried, and we found that by carefully removing a couple of screws, the nose piece came off and exposed the black powder inside. This, of course, was strictly against the law, and we turned in a few to the local Bobby just to show good faith. A few more were emptied of the powder and then hidden in the woods. The powder, in very small quantities, when wrapped up tight in newspaper with the ends screwed up like a toffee wrapper, made a very acceptable firework. And November the 5th, Britain's big bonfire and fireworks celebration of Guy Fawkes' attempt to blow up the British Parliament in 1605, was only a couple of months away. We hadn't been able to celebrate the 5th for a number of years because of the war and there were no fireworks to be had anywhere.

Except for those we made ourselves! We only tested a couple of bangers and then stored the rest away for later use.

It was around the middle of September when Dad suggested a trip to our local beach again to go fishing. It was a Saturday and I had nothing planned. We set off early in the morning and rode our bikes along the path through the marshes, to the shore. The tank traps, which had been set up at the beginning of the war to deter an invasion, were visible from a long way off sticking up out of the shingle. We had told Mum that we would be home for lunch, so it didn't seem to be worth while taking the boat out and we fished from the beach. Sitting quietly, waiting for the tug of a bite, my eyes wandered sideways along the water's edge. About two hundred yards away, I noticed what appeared to be a large crate on the high-water mark.

"Dad, there's something on the beach down there. Maybe something got washed up."

"Okay, son, I didn't think you could sit still too long; go and take a look, and I'll mind the rods."

Leaving my rod in the holder, I got up and walked towards the find. It could have been anything. Items of salvage were often found on the beach; resulting from the war at sea. As I got closer, I could see writing on the side of the box and when the words were legible, in big letters I could read the name "Aspro." Not a very interesting find, but if there was anything left in the crate, at least we could cure a few headaches! I was concentrating on the crate when I reached it and found that it was indeed, intact and shouted back to Dad, "It's a crate of Aspros"(the British version of Aspirin), and then I looked further up the beach and noticed what looked to be a bundle of rags. While Dad was securing the fishing poles and making his way towards the crate, I decided to take a quick look at the rags. I stirred them over with my foot and found a dead German sailor looking at me. That was the first dead person I had ever seen, and it gave me quite a shock. I remember the smell wasn't too pleasant, either.

That, of course ended our fishing trip, and after extracting a few large packets of Aspros, which were, fortunately, in waterproof wrappings, we set off home. Dad stopped off at the Colony to report our findings, while I carried our loot home in a sandbag, tied to the crossbar of my bike. We distributed the Aspros around the neighborhood later that day.

That was one time I was able to reduce headaches, instead of causing them.

One other source of materials for firework manufacture was a huge aircraft dump located on Sutton Heath. This was part of the USAF base, about five miles from home. The remains of German, British and American aircraft which had crashed or been shot down in the eastern counties of England, were piled up with everything including ammunition, radios, cameras, etc., still inside. Some of the local officer's sons including me had worked out a system to get into this treasure trove. The heath was a huge, wide-open expanse of wasteland with the base at one end and a pine forest at the other. The aircraft dump was about one hundred yards from the trees with one American airman on guard patrolling the circumference armed with a rifle. It took him anywhere between thirty and sixty minutes to encircle the dump, depending on the number of cigarettes he smoked on the way.

By riding our bikes into the forest, we were able to follow trails through the woods which placed us in the closest position to the dump. The ground beyond the tree line was covered with heather and bracken, about two feet high, and by observing the location of the guard from the trees, we were able to crawl through the ground cover to the dump, undetected. Once inside the twisted and torn aircraft wreckage we were fairly safe, at least from the guard. The whole dump was creaking and groaning from the wreckage moving in the wind and settling. The little noise we made as we scavenged for interesting items was negligible. And there were plenty of interesting things to be found if we ignored the obvious blood stains.

Aside from electric motors from cameras and various radios we found a plentiful supply of cannon shells. Those that had the bullet tip colored pink or red were considered particularly valuable. These were the tracers, the bullets were hollow and contained a hard substance which, when ignited would erupt with a huge jet of fire. Once we had collected all we needed, we found a suitable hole in the airframe where we could insert the bullet and by wiggling the casing back and forth the bullet would come loose from the casing. Emptying the cordite from the casings into small flour sacks which we carried for that purpose, we stuffed as many of the tracer bullets into our pockets as we could. On a whistled signal from our lookout, left behind amongst the trees to observe the guard's movements, we crawled back through the bracken to our bikes. When we arrived home we stored our treasures in a rabbit burrow; the entrance hidden with a rock. So now we had bangers and fountains for our bonfire night, but we still lacked rockets.

One early morning, after collecting a large basket full of the mushrooms which grew in the horse pastures adjoining the marshes close to the beach, a friend and I decided to see what we could see at the beach. If nothing else, I could watch the waves for a while; I've always been in love with the sea. We left the bikes leaning up against Dad's boat shed and strolled along the high water line kicking at the flotsam as we went. As we approached the area where I had found the German sailor, I noticed a cylinder about two feet long and maybe three inches in diameter amongst a bunch of seaweed. I pulled it out and could hardly believe my eyes. It was a military issue distress signal rocket. All we needed was the stick, and I had no doubt Dad could take care of that. He had a shed full of wood and carpentry tools. When I told him about it, he took charge of the rocket and promised we could be with him when he set it off on bonfire night. He said it might be too dangerous for us to play with as it needed a flare to set it off. And he just happened to have a few flares that he had found on previous fishing trips that he hadn't told me about!

Any German airmen flying home over that part of Suffolk on the 5th November that year must have wondered what on earth was going on down there. We had a huge bonfire in the middle of the circle, the area surrounded by our circular road, and had home-made bangers, erupting volcanoes (tracer shells stuck in the ground with a trail of cordite to ignite them), flares, and to top it off, a brilliant rocket. In addition to all of this we had the usual airborne activity and the response from the shore batteries. All in all, it was one of the most interesting nights of the war for us, and the spuds (potatoes) roasted in the embers of the fire were delicious.

During the autumn, when the apples were ready for picking, "scrumping" was a common activity amongst the officer's children. Everyone knew about it, and it was an accepted fact by the colony authorities that a certain portion of the apple, pear, and plum crops would be stolen by the kids. It was such a small percentage that nobody really cared. It was just regarded as a bit of fun by the powers that be. All the orchards were surrounded by wire fences but there were so many and they were so large that it was impossible to keep watch over all of them. The only orchard which had a fairly constant watch was the cherry orchard. This was located half way down, on the right-hand side of the gravel lane which led off Tank Hill. On the opposite side of the lane the colony's only gamekeeper lived in a small, thatched cottage. During the cherry picking season, the old gamekeeper would often patrol through the trees carrying an ancient shotgun, loaded with rock salt. I never felt the sting of it myself, but several of my friends said that they had experienced it and it was quite painful. My main interest in the cherry orchard was the "bird-chasers." These were long strings of bangers, suspended from the tree branches, which had slow-burning fuses. The gamekeeper would tie them to the trees at intervals and light the bottom fuse. When the first banger exploded, all the birds in the surrounding trees busily eating cherries, would scatter. By the time they had regained their taste for the fruit the next banger would explode and so on. With two dozen bangers in a string, the old gamekeeper's legs were saved a lot of walking. These bird-chasers were not intended to be used for entertainment, but they made an excellent substitute firework. The fuse of each banger was woven into the main fuse which was a very slow-burning type of cord and spaced so that there was about a minute interval between explosions.

Scrumping cherries was more of a challenge than the other available fruit, knowing that the gamekeeper could appear at any moment. The possibility of getting our hands on some of the bird-chasers was even more attractive. My best friend at that time was a boy named Dave. He was the same age as me and equally as mischievous. Together, we came up with a plan that would give us both some cherries and some fireworks.

We walked along the gravel lane, passing two fenced in horse paddocks before reaching the cherry orchard. As we walked we could hear the occasional bang of a bird-chaser explosion, and we knew the gamekeeper would be somewhere in the vicinity. We carried on past the orchard and I had spotted the smoke from his pipe, in the near corner of the orchard. We could both smell it as we walked by. After another hundred yards or thereabouts, we turned around and headed back for the orchard. We knew that the gamekeeper was at the other end, close to the road, so we slipped through the fence and quietly started filling a large paper bag with cherries. Once we had enough, I took my pocket knife and cut down three strings of bird-chasers which we found hanging from branches. The old man had hung them there ready to light later. We had just finished and I had stuffed the bangers inside my shirt, when we heard the old gamekeeper approaching. I guessed that all the bangers where he had been, were finished and he was coming to set off the others which he had left behind. Dave and I crouched over, crept silently through the cherry trees towards the far corner of the orchard where I stopped. Dave turned to his right and followed the rear fence towards the first horse paddock. So far, so good.

When Dave cleared the hedge and fence at the paddock, he let out a loud yell, as if he had been hurt, and kept on running across the field into the next where he was supposed to wait for me. I was crouched down in the ditch which lined the fence when Dave yelled and the game-keeper came crashing by, running and cursing to himself, hot on Dave's trail. I waited a couple of minutes and then backtracked quietly to the gravel lane. Once I was clear of the fence and standing in the lane I let out a yell, trying to copy Dave's and took off running towards the second horse paddock. The sounds of pursuit on the other side of the orchard stopped and I could hear the gamekeeper puffing, panting and swearing like a drunken sailor, heading in the direction of my yell. By the time he reached that spot I was already through the fence and into the second horse paddock, looking for Dave. There was no sign of him, only three trees which stood close together in the middle of the field. One was a very large oak tree, next to a chestnut and a wild pear tree.

I called as loudly as I dared, "Where are you?"

He answered from the clump of trees, "Over here!"

I ran across the field to the trees, and Dave called, "Here," from the pear tree.

"What are you doing up there?" I asked.

"Look behind you," he replied. At that moment a horse suddenly whinnied down the back of my neck, it seemed. I turned and nearly jumped out of my skin. It was the governor's personal mount, Satan. He was pitch black all over and had a nasty gleam in his eye. Before he could blink, I was up in the pear tree with Dave, and I wasn't a good tree climber! How I had missed seeing him when I came into the field, I'll never know, but there we were, stuck in a tree. Up until then, the caper had gone pretty much as planned, but neither of us wanted to come down from the tree with Satan still in the field. He had a bad reputation with the local kids.

All we could do was wait. We knew the governor would come along eventually for his evening ride, and hopefully, he wouldn't notice us in the tree with our stolen cherries and bird-chasers. While we waited, we climbed higher into the tree, trying to put as much foliage between us and anyone standing on the ground. Satan, of course, decided that the best grass in the paddock was directly under our tree, and quietly grazed away while he waited for his master.

At last the governor drove up and parked his car at the gate. Satan spotted the car and trotted over to meet his master. His saddle and gear were in the car and it didn't take the governor long before they were off across the paddock to the path which led to the marshes, down by the beach.

Once they were out of sight we scrambled down from the tree with the bangers and what was left of the cherries. We had eaten almost half of them while stuck in the tree. It was a relief to be back on solid ground again and we ran most of the way home, laughing at ourselves.

I intended to save the bangers until Guy Fawkes day on November the fifth and, when I arrived at the house, I left my share of the remaining cherries in the kitchen while I went into the yard to hide my treasure. I wrapped the strings of bangers in an old sack and placed them under a galvanized pail which was lying behind the garden shed.

When Dad returned from work, the next day, he said that the word was out about several people who had raided the cherry orchard. He said that the gamekeeper did all he could to chase them, and they got away with nothing. "Nice cherries," he commented, as he took one from the bowl on the sideboard and popped it in his mouth.

The following year, I won a scholarship to attend a secondary school in a town named Leiston. There were four of us, all officer's sons, who would be going to this new school, I was third in seniority, by age. This was going to be a big change for me. The school was far enough away from home that I would have to stay there all week; only coming home at weekends. All four of us had obtained lodgings in the same boarding house, run by a Mrs Smith. We had the attic in her house for a dormitory and the run of the house and garden, which was very big, for our recreation time. There wasn't too much spare time during the week as we had to cope with quite a large amount of homework and of all things, my Mother had signed me up for piano lessons with a teacher who lived just a couple of streets away. Our neighbor at home, a Mr Perry, played piano, and he had taught me a few tunes on his piano. Encouraged by this, Mum bought a used piano for me, and during the summer months when the weather was dry, Mr Perry and I had our pianos in the bay window areas of our houses where, with open windows, we could play duets of a lot of the current pop and "boogie-woogie" pieces. "Fats" Waller was our hero. Not so with my new piano teacher, an old spinster in her sixties, Miss Greene. Everything had to be by the music, and it had to be classical. If I hit a wrong note I was rewarded by a sharp rap across the knuckles with a wooden ruler. It didn't take long for that part of my education to come to a grinding halt. I soon informed Mum that she was wasting her money on music lessons for me, and that if I couldn't be allowed to play what I wanted to then I'd find something else to occupy my spare time. She understood and agreed to stop the lessons if I would still go on playing the piano my own way. This I did for several years, which made me quite popular at parties and barrooms in several different countries. But that's another story.

As Leiston was quite a distance from Hollesley, the most economical way to get there was to catch a bus from home to the nearest train station at Melton, six miles away. After that it was just under an hour's ride on the train to Leiston station, followed by a fifteen minute walk to Mrs Smith's house. Monday mornings were always a rush, to catch the early bus. There were no such things as tardy notes at that school, and no acceptable excuses. Caning was the normal punishment, and it didn't take long for me to learn the meaning of the expression, "Six of the best!"

This didn't mean that we were all little angels. We soon realized that it wasn't the prank that was important, it was the ability not to get caught!

Leiston was a large town which was well off the beaten track of the war and there were no interesting finds to be made. The nearest thing we had to open country, within walking distance, was an old abandoned brick quarry at the bottom of Mrs Smith's back garden. It looked to be an interesting place; we couldn't see to the bottom for all the brambles and bushes. But there were animal tracks of some sort, running along the slopes. Along the far side of the quarry, the rail tracks ran to the station; we could see Mrs Smith's house from the train, on Monday mornings. Several times we had tried scrambling down the quarry side but the bush was impenetrable and, scratched and torn, we had given up. Until I had a bright idea!

The following Monday morning, when we had all settled down in the train compartment, I opened my school satchel and showed the others, two hand-held signal flares, which I had found on the beach at home. They had wooden handles and a tear-strip on the top for ignition. I had tried one out when I had found them. They had five "shooting stars" each, like a "Roman Candle." My idea was to wait until we were approaching Leiston station, then as we were alongside the quarry, we would shoot the flares into the brambles and bushes and maybe that would clear them out. Of course we would do that from another part of the train and then return to our compartment before it arrived at the station in case anyone saw us.

We eagerly awaited our target arrival, having moved into the next carriage, by the adjoining corridor. I held one flare and Ken, the oldest boy there, held the other. As the train worked its way around the final bend past the quarry we lowered the window, aimed the flares, and pulled the tear strips. We hadn't allowed for the commotion that would be caused by the loud bangs that preceded each shooting star and, after the second shot we let go of the flares and slammed the window shut. People had started to emerge from behind their newspapers, and looking out their compartment doors were asking "What happened?"

"We didn't see anything," I called as we pushed past on the way to our compartment. I just knew we had been spotted and fully expected to be met on the platform by a policeman. But we were in luck. When we arrived, all attention was being paid to the local fire brigade rushing past the station, sirens blaring. Talking nervously amongst ourselves as we ran, we hurried to Mrs Smith's house where everything was in an uproar. Mrs Smith and the maid were both in tears and were being consoled outside by the neighbors. A fire engine was at the curb in front of the house with hoses running along the ground to the back yard. The air was thick with smoke and ash, but, apparently no actual damage was done to the house or the adjoining properties. The fire had taken a good hold on the dry vegetation in the quarry and as it was doing no harm the authorities decided to let it burn itself out. They couldn't reach it, anyway.

The story was written up in the local newspaper as a freak accident. It was reported that a spark from the train's wheels had caught some dry grass alongside the tracks, on fire and this had spread rapidly into the quarry. This was a blessing in disguise, according to the reporter as the quarry had become an overgrown nuisance, and an unofficial dump. After the ash was washed away by rain, perhaps some use might be made of it.

I didn't get to explore the bottom of the quarry. After the fire it was ankle deep in black ash and the sides were too slick to climb down without a lot of trouble. By the time that it was accessible, I had obtained another scholarship to attend The Woodbridge Grammar School, an upper-crust type of learning center, only eight miles from home.

The town of Woodbridge was almost half way between Hollesley Bay and Ipswich, the county capital of Suffolk. There were several schools located there, but no other could compare to The Woodbridge School. Most of the students were boarders who lived in any of the three residential halls scattered across the extensive grounds. There weren't many "Day boys," as those of us who lived locally were called and I was very fortunate to have been chosen to attend there. I was reminded of this on several occasions, by the authorities!

Transport to Woodbridge from home was provided by the colony, in the form of a converted three-ton lorry, or truck. The conversion was only to fit wooden benches, one on each side and it carried about ten school children. With the tailgate lowered, we had to climb up and position ourselves along the seats, with nothing but the seat to hang onto. The bigger boys sat near the tailgate to grab anyone who might otherwise fall out. On several occasions, climbing up the dropped tailgate my foot slipped on the sometimes-wet wood, and I cracked my kneecap on the metal hinge. That and a pretty tough school career as a rugby forward probably accounts for the arthritis which I have to put up with now.

Although fighting at school was frowned upon, it was never considered to be the sin that it is these days. Boys were expected to stand up for themselves. Because of my somewhat sheltered early years in Portland, I was a little slow in developing an aggressive nature and was often teased about this, particularly when I first came to the area. I had made up my mind that this was going to change at this posh new school, where nobody knew me. The grounds of this school were enormous by any standards of that time, with a swimming pool and tennis courts in "the valley," cricket pitches, rugby and field-hockey fields beyond the Great Hall, which housed meeting rooms, the auditorium, and an extensive gymnasium. Leading down to the main gate was a wide, winding, gravel pathway bordered on each side by beautifully manicured high laurel hedges

It was a custom at this school for senior "men" to be assigned to meet newcomers at the main gate on their first day at school, to greet and help them get their bearings. It would take several weeks to get to know the place thoroughly. On my first day it was cold, damp and drizzly, typical English weather, when I left the colony lorry at the town square under the town hall clock and walked the half mile to the school.

I had been told to wait at the gate for my escort, should he not be there. I was a few minutes early, so I idled away some time, polishing my new shoes on the back of my socks and trying to straighten out my new school uniform from the early morning lorry ride from home. I was determined to make a good first impression, as my parents had instructed.

At last I saw the escort strolling down the path, obviously in no hurry, and I made a move to walk up the path towards him.

"Stay where you are, newby," he shouted, with an educated English accent, and kept on strolling, making me wait.

This struck me as being rather impolite, but I said no more and waited until he finally reached me at the bottom of the path. He was at least three years older than me, I guessed, and a few inches taller. His school uniform looked very smart and his attitude was extremely condescending. After all, I was just a scruffy, newby day boy. A local, no less. I could almost read his mind by just watching his expression.

Finally, after giving me a good lookover, he opened his mouth to introduce himself, and without thinking about it, I decided to alter his self-important, haughty expression by planting my right fist with all my weight behind it, into the space between his upper lip and nose. He went down like a ton of bricks, and for a moment I felt a twinge of panic, thinking I may have killed him, until he groaned and rolled over with blood running from his nose and his split lip. Slowly he sat up, his uniform all grimy from the path, tears running down his face. I felt a little sorry for him then, but I recalled being in similar circumstances myself, when I first came to Suffolk, and I soon got over it.

"What was that for?" he spluttered, as I stood over him.

"That's just a reminder," I said. "Don't ever speak to me first, do not call me 'newby,' and don't look down on any boy who is not a boarder. Now get up and clean yourself up and keep your mouth shut about this. I'll find my own way around, thank you." I turned away to leave as he was getting to his feet and added, "Oh, by the way, my name is Don, not newby, and don't you forget it."

He must have told someone about the incident, as I was treated with a great deal of respect by the other boys and this had never happened to me before at a new school. It felt good.

It didn't take too long for me to familiarize myself with my new surroundings and to make new friends. Eventually one of them asked me if it was true that I had hit my greeter on the first day, and I dodged the question, neither confirming nor denying it. I really enjoyed the little air of mystery this created and it made me realize how important it is to throw the first punch—and make it a good one!

Both the greeter and I learned a valuable lesson, that first day for me at The Woodbridge School.

One aspect of school life which I didn't find appealing was cricket. It is hard to imagine, in my opinion, a more boring waste of time than a game of cricket and I did anything I could think of to avoid it. From early spring to early autumn, we were required to play cricket every Wednesday and Saturday afternoon, unless a very good excuse was provided. I used up all the standard reasons for not being able to play until all I was left with was "personal sickness." It had become a bit of a joke amongst my pals to see how far I would go to avoid cricket. One particularly pretty Saturday afternoon I decided I would rather take an early bus home, than waste the time standing in the outfield on the cricket pitch all afternoon.

The previous day had been payday, when Dad gave me my weekly allowance of one shilling so during lunch break I broke rules and ran to the nearest grocer's shop outside the school grounds, and bought two cans of Nestle's condensed milk. I ran back to school and arrived just in time to get changed into "whites" for the game, or "match," as it was called. Before going out onto the field, I hid in one of the changing-room stalls, opened the cans with my pocket knife, and swallowed the contents of both cans. The sweet, sticky stuff took a lot of swallowing, but I suspected it wouldn't be inside me for very long. With one hand over my mouth and the other clutching my stomach, I staggered onto the field.

Immediately, the closest umpire to me called out, "What's the matter with you, Sweetenham?" I couldn't answer, so I just took my hand off my stomach, waved weakly at him, turned away and threw up. Big time! Projectile vomiting, I think is the correct term.

There was a distinct tone of disgust in his voice when he ordered me to leave the field and if I didn't feel better soon, to go to the infirmary. That was all I needed and I was soon riding the bus home, using the remains of my pocket money for the fare. But it was worth it. I spent the rest of the day, down at the beach, alone.

I wasn't against all sport at school. My favorite game was Rugby and I eventually made the First Fifteen. This was the team which represented the school in competition with other schools from all over the county. It was a fairly rough game, something like American Football, but without all the protective padding. Injuries were common, but it was a mark of pride to be able to say that it had happened playing "Rugger, you know." One of the rugby coaches was also one of my favorite teachers—Mr Applegate. He was only about five and a half feet tall, and not heavily built, but he was as hard as nails. He taught that the best way to avoid being hurt was to play as hard as you can and make sure it was the other chap who got hurt! And he was right. Every time I entered into a tackle half-heartedly, I was the one who regretted it afterwards. Sometimes he would actually take part in a game to show us what he was talking about. Tackling him was like running into a brick wall. The only way to get him down was to throw caution to the winds and to put every ounce of power into it. Anything less and I soon found myself limping off the field, with permission, of course.

During one particular game, I remember having broken the middle finger on my left hand. I raised the hand for the referee to see the finger bent backwards at right angles to the rest of the hand and asked permission to leave the field. He shouted back that I should wait until the next scrum down before leaving the field to get attention.

One big event of the year, at home, was the annual rugby game between the officers and their charges, the Borstal boys. My Dad didn't play rugby, soccer was his game. He played goalie for the officer's team. In my last year at school, I was asked if I would like to play against the "boys" for the officer's team. Although I played for the first fifteen at school, this was a real honor and my parents were very proud.

I knew most of the opposing team members; many of them over the years, had worked in our garden on Saturday afternoons for a couple of shillings and had been the targets of my teasing many times. I knew they particularly hated me calling them stupid, not for being criminals but for being caught. It really wasn't fair to them but they would give as much as they got, verbally and I always thought of it as good-natured fun, on my part, anyway!

The big day finally arrived and the match was to be held at the rugby field near St David's house. When I rode down to the field on my bike, I was already in my rugby gear and joined the rest of the officer's team. I was the only officer's son to be playing. I was surprised at the number of spectators on the side lines, my parents among them. I was playing in my usual position, second row forward. That meant I was in the second row of the scrum. Once the game was under way everything was going fine until I received a pass close to the side line and continued my run up the field towards the opposing goal line. Normally I would have expected no more than two men to tackle me but I was suddenly submerged beneath a pile of bodies, all trying to get as many cheap shots in as possible. I wriggled my way out of it as quickly as I could, getting in a few shots of my own.

Standing up I said, "Okay, chaps, I see your little game now. This is payback day for you, right? Well, all right. If you want to play hard, that's fine, but if you want to play dirty, someone's going to get hurt. It's up to you; I don't care."

The next play, which gave me the ball, followed a similar pattern, but with only four or five men after me, leaving a large part of the field undefended. I was ready for them this time and was easily able to pass the ball back to one of the officers who was unmarked. Without the ball I couldn't be tackled, so I made it a point to get the ball as often as I could, so that I could get in as many hits as possible before passing the ball. When I got the chance to tackle, I hit the target just as hard as I could. I may have been a couple of years younger than most of the boys, but I had been trained hard in rugby at school and I was as big and strong as most of them. The end result was that the officer's team won the game, and I thoroughly enjoyed myself. Not so some of the boy's team, who were limping dejectedly from the field back to their barracks.

Eventually, it was time to leave school; final exams were over and the results made known. I had earned a passing grade in seven subjects out of a possible eight. The eighth was advanced math which had been forced on the class during the last year. I never expected to pass that; I never even tried to understand it. Advanced Math was a three-year course that we were expected to cover in one. Only one student passed all eight subjects and he was a young genius, the son of a teacher at a different school.

I had no idea of what I wanted to do when I left school. I looked into several possible careers but nothing seemed to pique my interest. Following my Dad would have been too boring; I didn't even want to stay in England if I could avoid it. I didn't enjoy the weather, which was miserable most of the time, and the occasional days in summer when the sun shone and it was warm enough to go swimming at the beach, just made me wish to be in other places in the world where that kind of weather was the norm. I never had any great desire to be wealthy, just as long as I had enough to get by.

I felt sure that some day I would get an opportunity to travel but until that day came along I needed something to do to help with the family budget, if I was going to stay at home. At that time I was a keen cyclist and would regularly ride into the county town of Ipswich, some twenty miles from home, just for something to do. One day Dad mentioned an advertisement he had seen in the newspaper. County Police H.Q. in Ipswich had an opening for a Police Cadet. He thought I might be interested. I cut the ad. out of the paper and the next day I rode my bike into town and applied for the job. It was to be in the Traffic Department, run by a Sergeant Fanwell, a rather overweight, bad tempered man who barely made the five feet eight inches height requirement for the Force. I held my feelings in check when he interviewed me, literally biting my tongue on occasion. The interview with the Deputy Chief Constable went much better and I was given the job. My starting wage was three pounds a week, about five dollars U.S., and I gave half of it to Mum. I would be wearing a police uniform with a cap instead of the "copper's" helmet. I wouldn't be able to afford the bus fare, but a twenty mile bike ride to work in the morning and back home again in the evening was no problem for me.

It wasn't a very exciting job but I kept telling myself that it wasn't going to be forever. My prime duty was to keep records of all the traffic accidents in the county, indicating the severity and location of each one on a large scale map, using color-coded flags. Copies of the original police reports had to be filed in a bank of large steel cabinets, along one wall of the traffic dept office. It was a simple enough task but Sergeant Fanwell, or "Fanny," as I dubbed him, got into the habit of criticizing just about everything I did. He was lecturing me one day for some minor thing that displeased him, banging his fist on the desk for emphasis, swearing and raising his voice so that the switchboard operator, in the adjoining office could hear, when I decided that I had heard enough.

I stood up and, with my six-foot-two-inch height, glared down at him and said, "Now you listen to me, Sergeant; I'm not going to take any more of this shit, do you understand? If you don't like what I do, just say so, but be careful how you say it. I don't know who you think you are, but to me you're just a fat little freak with a really bad attitude. Now, if you don't want me to take this any further you'll go out to your patrol car, get in it, and keep out of my way."

I was shaking with anger, and it would have taken very little, at that stage, for me to punch his lights out. All the color had left his face; he stared at me for a few seconds, then turned and left the office. I sat back down at the desk and a few minutes later, once he was sure that the coast was clear, Bruce, the switchboard operator from the neighboring office came in.

"Well, done, Don!" he said, "Fanny's been asking for that for years, and no one has spoken back to him. I doubt if you've heard the last of it, though; I just hope the Old Man doesn't get to hear of it"

Well, of course, the deputy chief did get to hear of it, and I was summoned to his office. "Enter!" he called, when I knocked on his door. I stood at attention in front of his desk, and he told me to relax and sit down.

"Now then, young man, I have had a report from your sergeant that you were rude to him and called him a 'fat little freak.' I find that hard to believe, but I would like to hear your side of the story."

This was going a lot better than I had expected. I thought I would have been fired by now. "Sir, that's exactly what I called him but, I believe I had a right to, after the way he was speaking to me. I won't take that sort of abuse from anyone, and if you want me to quit my job, then that's it. I'll return my uniform tomorrow."

"Now calm down, Don. That won't be necessary. Let me tell you this, and it's not to go outside of this office. Sergeant Fanwell has cost us several good recruits in the past because of his sour disposition, and no one has ever stood up to him before. I've spoken to him about it, but it hasn't done any good. Perhaps, coming from you this time, it might make a difference. I'm prepared to overlook it if you are willing to give him another chance." I couldn't believe it! The Old Man was actually smiling while he was talking, and I was getting away with it.

"Thank you, sir," I said. "As long as Fanny...er, er, I mean, Sergeant Fanwell stays out of my way, and keeps a civil tongue in his head, we should get along just fine."

He smiled, stood up and put out his hand. We shook hands, and as I turned to leave, he said, "And, by the way, don't forget, not a word about this to anyone, okay?"

"Yes, sir," I replied.

"Fanny" was a changed man after I told him his fortune. Every morning after that he would wait for me to come into the office and then he would inform me that he would be going out on patrol, probably for the rest of the day, unless he had a meeting or some other commitment. He left me alone to do my work and never criticized me any more or questioned my work. It was very peaceful in the office, and Bruce commented on it, as did several other police officers. Headquarters was a better place to visit when Sergeant Fanwell wasn't around.

Although I enjoyed the little bit of notoriety this gave me, the work had become very routine and monotonous. There was no challenge and I could see no future in what I was doing. To succeed in the Force it would be necessary not only to be well informed about police methods and the law but also to be a politician of sorts. I quickly learned that I was not interested in office politics. I would always speak my mind rather than keep my mouth shut if I saw something that wasn't quite right, regardless of whose feelings might get hurt. I still had the idea in the back of my mind that I would like to see more of the world, and I couldn't see that happening if I spent the rest of my life pounding a beat in Ipswich or patrolling the county in a police car.

I was two month's short of my eighteenth birthday when I finally decided to make a move. With my parents' permission I volunteered for the Royal Air Force pilot training program. With the war being over, they assumed that service life in peace time would be a good experience for me. At eighteen I would be called up anyway, for two years National Service, or "conscription" as it was called.

3.

I had no trouble passing the physical exam and my educational standards were acceptable but when I arrived at the R.A.F. station that housed the pilot training program, I found that most of the other so-called officer cadets were from a much higher social class. I suddenly found myself amongst the sons of Members of Parliament, Lords, famous scientists at Harwell, Barristers, Professors, etc. and I was completely out of place. This was peace time, and the R.A.F. was considered to be an acceptable place for the sons of the upper crust to spend their mandatory National Service years.

I made only one friend there. He was trying to get out of the Service, having already spent two years with a Guards regiment and had obtained a transfer to the R.A.F. pilot program for that purpose. Neither of us was happy with our situation and we were sick of all the upper-class English being spoken there. I suppose we were like two "Rednecks" in a room full of "Yankees."

It didn't take too long to find out that we could ask to be released; my friend because he had already completed two years with the guards. I could leave due to the fact that I had yet to reach the age of eighteen. However, if I chose to transfer to a different branch of the R.A.F., the six weeks I had already served, would count towards my two-year commitment for National Service. Not wanting to waste six weeks, (it seemed such a long time, back then), I opted for the transfer.

When my final interview took place the sergeant asked me what did I want to do in the Air Force. I replied, "Well, Sergeant, I don't really know. All I know is, if this is the upper class of the Air Force, where are the men? I'm used to working with more down-to-earth kinds of people than these. I enjoy playing rugby, and I enjoy a good scrap now and then, but the most I can expect from these officer cadets would be a game of gin rummy and a round of ping pong."

He laughed and said, "Don't be too hard on them, lad. They'll get the polish knocked off them sooner or later. But I understand your feelings. It says in your file here that you spent a year with the East Suffolk County Constabulary. How did you like police work?"

"Okay, I suppose, although I didn't get to see much of it outside of the office. The people were regular chaps, though, and I could relate to them."

And that was when I decided to become an R.A.F. policeman. The sergeant explained that I would still have to go through basic training, or "square bashing," before going to Netheravon in Wiltshire for basic police training, but he promised that, if I was looking for some tough guys to work with, I'd find them there. He was right! But first, square bashing.

This was supposed to be the equivalent of boot camp in the American services, basic training with an emphasis placed on discipline and drill. Eight weeks of marching in formation on the square with a rifle, while being verbally abused by a young drill instructor, finding out first hand what it feels like to be gassed with teargas, extreme physical training, firing range drills, cross-country runs in full gear and other such fun. Those who appeared to be pulling less than their weight, were constantly screamed and shouted at by the sergeant in charge and the D.I. No matter how hard I tried to do what they ordered me to do, I always ended up paying penalties. The stigma of having been an officer cadet, was indelible, and I had to pay dearly for that. If an offense incurred other men a run around the drill ground with the rifle held overhead, I had to do it twice. I also had to suffer the gas treatment twice as long as anyone else and pushups seemed to be my favorite pastime. After eight weeks of this, it was suddenly all over. We were leaving for a 48-hour pass, going home for a weekend before taking up our various postings. I was last in line to get on the bus taking us to the local rail station and the D.I. was standing there, shaking hands with everyone as they climbed aboard. When it was my turn, I gripped his hand and pulled him up close to me.

He stuttered, "No hard feelings, Sweetenham?"

"None at all, Corporal," I snarled. "Just don't ever let me catch you when I get through with police school."

He turned pale as I held his hand in a fierce grip and finally I let him go.

Netheravon, a village on the edge of Salisbury plain, in Wiltshire, England was the center of a farming area, with an old World War 1 aerodrome as its claim to fame. No longer used for a flying base, the aerodrome had been converted into a Royal Air Force Police Training establishment. Here we faced yet another eight weeks of basic training, considerably harder than square bashing. Emphasis was placed on strength training, firearms use, hand-to-hand combat and elementary judo. We still had the cross-country runs in full gear but now we also had to carry a rifle. A seven-mile run under these conditions was hard enough, but we also had to do it, several times, in a foot of snow during the winter.

When I first arrived at the Police school, the barracks had yet to be built. Our living quarters were in an old WW I aircraft hanger which had been cleaned out and lined with beds. About fifty trainees were housed in that hanger and during the winter, the number one rule was to keep all kit particularly the parade boots, under the bed. The curved roof of the hanger was so high that during the night, condensation froze inside the hanger and fell down as snow. Many mornings I woke up to find a couple of inches of snow on top of the blankets. Showers, hand-basins, and toilets were situated in a partitioned-off section of one wall. There was no hot water and nobody rushed to be first in the showers. Not because of the water temperature but because of the ice on the floor. It took a couple of brave souls, skidding around on the miniature ice rink to wear away the slippery surface which formed in the night.

Three weeks into basic police training, a squad of trainee Army police arrived. They were supposed to learn how Air Force police were trained, and to work alongside us but their main interest was in the dog-training methods employed at Dog School. They only lasted a couple of weeks and they were recalled to their own training establishment. Just before they left, one of them tried to get a date with one of the WRAF girls who worked as kennel maids at the Dog School. She was a pretty little blonde and to look at her you would think that butter wouldn't melt in her mouth. That is until she was hit on by a trainee M.P. It happened when the two squads, RAF and Army, were lined up to march to the parade ground for drill practice and she was walking by with one of the other girls The RAF squad was silent, but several whistles came from the army boys and one of them asked the little blonde to go out with him that night. The vitriolic stream of comments relating to him, his ancestors and his service that he received in reply was staggering. From that angelic little face, that could easily be imagined singing carols on a Christmas card, came a stream of cuss words worthy of half a dozen drunken sailors.

There was no doubt in anyone's mind that it would be a really cold day in hell before she ever went out with him, but it broke the tension, when after she finally wound down, he replied, "Shall I take that as a no, then?"

About three weeks before the end of the basic police course, we received a surprise, three-day pass with travel vouchers. It was an unexpected chance to visit with my parents. One day to get home, one day to visit and one day to return. The reason for the pass was to get us all out of the way during the final stages of construction of the new barracks. This was a series of dormitories consisting of two large rooms joined in the center by two bathrooms. Each bathroom consisted of two baths, four hand basins and two toilets. Each of the large rooms contained beds, bedside cabinets, and lockers for ten men.

They were a huge step up from the hanger but there was still no running hot water. The only hot water available was outside, between the buildings, and we had to heat it ourselves. Forty-four-gallon steel drums had been set in bricks on top of brick built fireplaces, one for each barracks building. Fuel for the fire was gathered from the mess hall nearby. It was a way for them to dispose of their empty crates and boxes and anything else which would burn. Fire extinguishers were available in the common hallway of the barracks. The drums were filled from a hosepipe early in the morning before parade, and the fires were lit immediately after class in the afternoon. That meant there would be warm water at least for those taking a bath that evening. It had to be carried into the bathroom in buckets, and that's where the controversy started. Hot water raids started between barracks, and it wasn't long before we had to post guards on our respective boilers. Besides Billy, my best friend at police school, I was also friendly with a young man named Rob, who in civilian life was training to be a professional wrestler before he was called up. Rob was a really rough diamond, and never turned his back on a fight. He taught me a lot and the two of us would stand guard on our hot water supply most evenings, until it ran out. We didn't lose much but we paid for it with the occasional black eye and bruises. That was all part of the fun.

Back to my three-day pass. I had no trouble getting home on the first day, even though it took nearly all day to do it. The journey consisted of a bus ride from camp into Salisbury, a train ride to London, a bus across London to another train station, a train ride to Ipswich followed by another bus ride home, to Oak Hill. It was tea time when I arrived, and of course, Mum had baked some of her special jam tarts with the burnt edges that I liked. It was fun catching up with all the news about the Colony and the kids and the weekend flew by. In the blink of an eye it was Monday morning and I was waiting at the bus stop, when Dad stopped his bike on the way to work. He propped it up against the curb and stood with me a while. He didn't say much but I sensed something was on his mind. Finally he came out with it when he took a packet of Woodbines out of his pocket and offered me a cigarette. I didn't know what to say. Although he smoked, he had always told me when I was growing up, that he would kill me if he ever caught me smoking.

I didn't know how to react, but he put me at ease a little when he said, "Come on, now. I know you smoke. You've been smoking since you were in the county police. I could smell it on you. I don't approve, mind you, and I think you're stupid for doing it, but I suppose I can understand. Everyone else does it, so you have to, right?"

I took one of his cigarettes and lit his and mine with my lighter. "You're right, Dad, I suppose. Maybe one day I'll stop." Just then the bus came, and I told him "Goodbye," again, and climbed aboard.

The bus ride to Ipswich was taken up with thoughts of home and what was happening in the lives of my friends who still lived there. Somehow I had grown away from them and had tasted life away from the security of the Colony. There was a lot more to this world than Hollesley Bay, and I wanted to see more of it. I didn't know it then, but I felt I was on the right track to do just that.

I caught the train to London, with plenty of time to spare. It was late and while I sat in the waiting room, I overheard talk of a possible railway strike. I didn't pay it much attention, feeling sure that it wouldn't affect me. As usual on a British train, once settled into their seats, everyone became engrossed in their newspapers and they had no time for small talk with strangers. By the time we reached London, I had been totally ignored and hadn't had an opportunity to speak to anyone. It wasn't just the uniform; it was the normal reserved British attitude towards strangers. Not exactly unfriendly but insular by nature.

When we arrived in London, the railway situation had deteriorated. Some kind of labor dispute had developed into a "Go slow," in preparation for a strike. This meant that many trains out of London would be either delayed or canceled. I hurried to catch a bus across town to the other London station from which my train to Salisbury would, hopefully, run. As soon as I arrived at the station, I made a dash for the Booking Office and was told that the next train leaving for Salisbury would not be until the following morning. This was something I had not anticipated.

Being stuck in London, one of the largest cities in the world, with very little money and no place to stay was not this country boy's idea of a lot of fun. Particularly as this was in November and the weather was cold and damp. On top of that, I might be considered "Absent Without Leave" if I was late arriving back at camp. The best thing I could do, I thought, was to phone the Guardroom at Netheravon and ask them what to do. At least it would be on record that I was trying to get back.

When I called, the duty-station policeman told me that several others from my class had already called in and the Station was aware of the train delays. No action would be taken against any of us providing we were signed in at the guardroom the next day, before six p.m.

"Well, that's a relief," I said, "But what do I do about somewhere to spend the night? I don't have any money for a hotel room." He told me my best chance would be at the Army and Navy Club, and he gave me the address. It wasn't too far away, and I should have no trouble finding it. How many times I have heard those words since and ended up hopelessly lost in a town. Off the beaten track, in a forest, desert or a jungle, I can find my way with relative ease, but not in a man-made environment.

Days are short in England during winter, and by late afternoon it was already dark when I arrived, at last, at the steps of the Army and Navy Club. Making my way through the front door, I noticed all the servicemen crowding the lobby. Obviously my problem wasn't unique that night. When I finally attracted the clerk's attention, I was informed that there were no more vacant rooms or beds, but I could spend the night in the lobby with all the other troops. I looked around and spotted one chair at a small round table, just inside the front door and made tracks for it. At least I could sit down. I put my small suitcase on the table and my uniform pack on the floor, between my feet. I had no intention of being robbed, if I went off to sleep.

I quickly found out why the chair had not been occupied before. All night long, people were going in and out of that door. Every time the door was opened, I experienced a blast of icy cold air down my back. Cat naps between door openings was the best I could manage, with my head on my crossed arms, supported by the suitcase on the table. That was a very long night and I left there at daylight, tired, stiff and aching. I vaguely remembered the way back to the station and by the time I arrived, I felt really sick. I was flushed and feverish and couldn't stop shivering. The train was at the platform and I found an empty compartment. When other passengers thought about joining me, they quickly changed their minds and moved on, when they saw and heard me sneezing and coughing. That suited me just fine. I was in no mood for company, anyway.

The Netheravon bus was waiting outside the Salisbury train station, when the train pulled in and I dragged myself and my luggage up the stairs of the double decker. The sneezing and coughing had settled down a bit and I was able to catch a short nap on the way to camp. I felt slightly improved when I entered the Guardroom, inside the camp's main gate, and signed in. It was only twelve thirty but I felt like it should have been much later. The corporal on duty informed me that I was the first of the latecomers to check in and then, taking a harder look at me, told me to report to sick bay before going to the barracks. It was only about two hundred yards to the sick bay from the Guardroom, but it felt more like two miles.

As soon as I was seen by the medical officer, I was put in quarantine with influenza. This meant a private room with a cute little WRAF nurse to take care of me! I thought I had died and gone to Heaven! I couldn't even have visitors for a week and it was ten days before I got out of there. With all that rest and lack of exercise, I had a lot of work to do, to catch up with my colleagues back in the barracks, but it was worth it.

It didn't take me long to fully recover from my night in London. The tough training had made all of us very resilient and we bounced back quickly from any infection or injury. I had missed a few morning parades, being in quarantine and one of my biggest concerns was having my kit up to standard. I spent several hours polishing boots, pressing my uniform. Brushing the black tie was also important but had to be done no more than ten minutes before parade time. Somehow the inspecting sergeant could tell if it had been brushed earlier than that. Any infringement was subject to a "252," which was the name for a formal charge. Penalties included extra drill sessions or "jankers," which consisted of all free time for a given number of days to be spent in the mess hall doing menial jobs such as pot cleaning, spud peeling, floor polishing, etc. I was determined not to be booked on my first parade back, after being sick, when someone called out in the barracks, "Hey, it was snowing last night," and when I looked out there was about six inches of the white stuff on the ground. That wouldn't do my highly spit-polished boots any good, I thought. I waited until the rest of lads had made a path, high stepping to try to keep the snow off their boots, then boots in hand, pants legs turned up, wearing only socks on my feet, I ran and caught up with them at the parade ground. By the time I had my boots on and pants legs turned down, I couldn't feel my feet, but I didn't get put on a "fizzer," the common term for a 252.

I always enjoyed the physical training sessions at the police school. In addition to the seemingly endless pushups and squats, we were taught unarmed combat methods and basic judo. This would be very useful in the future when I found myself in some rather tense barroom situations in various parts of the world. At police school, I thought I was quite proficient in the self defense area until, one day, the P.E. instructor introduced a new man to the squad. Lenny was about three inches shorter than me and quite a few pounds lighter. The instructor told us that he was a good boxer and invited anyone to go three rounds with Lenny, in the ring. I knew nothing about boxing but it was the opportunity for a scrap, as I saw it, so I immediately put my hand up. We both put the gloves on, and the P.E. instructor acted as ref and timekeeper. There was no bell, so when the ref called, "Fight!" we both went at each other. Lenny spent the first round dancing around the ring, dodging everything I threw at him. It was like trying to hit a shadow, and I was getting more and more frustrated. By the second round, I was getting angry, not only with Lenny but also myself. I hadn't laid a glove on my opponent when he started to score on me.

When we stopped for a couple of minutes' break between the second and last rounds, I said to the ref, "What kind of a fight is this? Make him stand still so I can hit him. This is really pissing me off!"

"This is what real boxing is all about," he replied, "It's no good being able to give a punch; you've also got to be able to avoid one. Lenny might be about to teach you a valuable lesson."

The ref called, "Fight!" and we started the third round. I rushed at Lenny, hoping to gain an advantage, and once more he dodged me, and I ran into his corner post. As I passed him, I received his fist in my ear. Now I was mad. I swung round and went for him with both hands. It didn't matter how hard I tried to hit him, he avoided every punch and found the time and space to get one back at me every time. By the end of the round, I was bruised, battered, and out of breath while Lenny had hardly broken into a sweat. He sat quietly on the stool in his corner while the ref came over to my corner to hand out some advice.

"So you're not as good as you thought you were, are you? I'd say Lenny won that bout outright. What would you say?"

"I suppose you're right, ref. But if we could just take these gloves off and forget about the rules, I still think I could take him," I said.

"Perhaps," he said, "But the lesson here was that the angrier and more frustrated that you became, the easier it was for him to hit you. If you can't stay calm and focused you'll get a beating every time, whatever kind of fight you're involved in."

It was a good lesson, and I recalled one other particular incident when I had lost my temper. I wouldn't have lost that fight, but I could easily have lost my life as a consequence.

"How would Lenny like to take me on without gloves?" I asked.

The P.E. instructor laughed and said, "I don't think so, son. This wasn't a fair fight really; he was just here to teach everyone a lesson. He's actually the South of England, R.A.F. lightweight boxing champion. You just gave him a little workout."

Well, that made me feel a lot better. When the gloves were off I shook Lenny's hand and thanked him for not knocking my head off.

I also enjoyed firearms training at the range. The sergeant in charge of the shooting range was an expert with a handgun but he didn't have a lot of time for the sten gun, which was to be our second choice weapon. Sten- and Bren-gun training had been covered in square bashing; he said that anyone could shoot a sten gun. It was a bit like a hose pipe. Spray it around and you're bound to hit something! The revolver, on the other hand, took a lot of skill to master and he let it be known that he had that skill. He was a cockney from London—a peculiar breed of Englishman not known for their lack of self confidence and temerity. He taught us the use of the revolver by the book, using the standard R.A.F. issue webbing holster, but his own rig was a custom built, hand made leather belt and holster complete with leather tie-down thigh straps. He was a serious cowboy and Western fan. The instructors at the police school had a lot of freedoms not enjoyed by the students. Occasionally he would like to show off his fast draw and empty his gun at a target, fanning the hammer. It all looked very impressive but we were not allowed to copy it. We had to stand sideways on to the target, arm straight out, sight down the barrel and squeeze the trigger slowly. After a lot of practice, some of us were able to hit the target pretty consistently but it was one of those things where almost daily practice was needed to maintain proficiency.

Normally when we had a range session, our class sergeant in charge would leave us in charge of the range Sergeant. He would go off and do admin. work and return for us after shooting class. He was a large man in all senses of the word, but quiet, and very direct with his orders. Every one of us respected him and behaved ourselves mainly, I suspect, because nobody knew how to take him. His uniform was always immaculate with badge, buttons and belt brasses gleaming. One day he arrived at the range early, before the class was over, just as the range sergeant was doing one of his shooting demonstrations. When he had finished, our sergeant took a matchbox out of his pocket, walked over to the target area and placed it on the sandbank. Coming back to the firing line he indicated to the range sergeant to shoot at the box. The "gunslinger" snatched the gun out of his fancy holster and rapidly fired off six shots at the matchbox. All of them were close but none actually hit the box. Our sergeant then stood in his place. He drew his gun out of the holster, took up the official stance, with arm straight out, and fired one shot.

The matchbox disintegrated, and we all stood with our mouths open as he calmly announced, "There, see? It can be done!"

After completing the first eight weeks, we had one of three options. Those passing out high enough in the class could go on to become Provost Police, the rest went on to become Station Policemen, who guarded the gates of all R.A.F. establishments. The third option was Dog Handler which could only be obtained by volunteering. No dog-related injuries received compensation, other than normal sickbay treatment. The Provost Police section was the elite of course. They provided the mobile patrols outside the boundary fence of R.A.F. stations, they did all the crime investigations and were much closer to the civilian police force in their activities. I was selected for Provost Police training, but I decided to go for Dog Handling, the dog school being located at the other end of the aerodrome. As a boy, I had always been a little apprehensive around strange dogs and I thought this may be a good chance to get over that. It worked and I have been a firm dog-lover ever since.

So began another eight weeks in Dog School. The school consisted of an old aircraft hanger containing the C.O.s office, the vet's office, several store rooms, a small bed room for use by the on-duty handler at night and kennels in individual wire cages housing ninety two assorted German Shepherds. Some of them were newcomers, some trained and the others under training. There was also another large kennel area outside the hanger, where the dogs were kept on run-lines.

Inside the hanger one of the dogs was known as Mad Rex. He had been there the longest and had never been rematched with a handler. His first handler had finished his time in the Service. I met Rex on my first day at the dog school, as did every new recruit. The custom was for a group of "old hands" to grab the new lads and to introduce them, one at a time, to Rex. While some handlers were at the back of the cage teasing Rex to keep his attention, the new lad was thrown into the cage and the gate slammed shut. Rex would spin around and charge the intruder, all teeth and saliva, in an apparently savage attack. The result was always the same. Automatically, the new lad would raise his arm to protect his face and Rex would fasten onto it. And every time the newcomer would pass out from shock. Rex never did any real damage, just a couple of holes in the arm and as soon as the body went limp and fell to the floor, Rex lost all interest in the "game" and returned to being teased at the back of his cage. This was the opportunity to drag the body out of the cage and to revive him by throwing a pail of water over him. It may seem a bit brutal now, but I have never suffered from shock after being bitten by a dog since then. And dog bites were a very common occurrence during training.

The dog I was eventually matched with, named Valdi, had no idea of his own strength. When we first met, during my initial two weeks at dog school cleaning kennels, he was quite timid but after basic obedience and attack training, he developed quite a knack for police work. It was an important part of establishing a bond between dog and handler to spend part of each day in play. This was always fun for us but Valdi just didn't know how to squeeze gently when he gripped my arm in play. He ruined a fancy stainless steel watch, given to me by my Grandmother, when I graduated from The Woodbridge School, by sinking one of his large canine teeth through the center of the face. It completely pierced the watch, through the backplate, just breaking the skin on my wrist. For a couple of weeks after he became my dog, both my arms were in bandages from our "play" sessions. He was a tough one to handle during attack training, nobody really enjoyed playing "criminal" for him, even with the padded suit.

After passing the dog-training course there was a wait of two weeks for posting orders, during which time, qualified handlers were sent on dog-collection trips around the country. All R.A.F. police dogs were donations from members of the public who could no longer care for a large German Shepherd (Alsation) in their home. One such trip was to Gillingham, in Kent, the home of both sets of Grandparents. I visited with them for a couple of hours before taking a bus to the part of town where my "collection" lived. Walking to the house, I noticed that it was fairly small, semi-detached, with a bay-window looking out onto a pocket-handkerchief-sized front lawn. It certainly didn't look to be roomy enough for a large Alsation, and as I approached the front door, I could see this huge dog's head in the window, barking, snarling and showing off a really nice set of teeth! The lady of the house came to the door and, as I was in uniform, she knew exactly what I wanted.

"Come in," she said. "My name is Mrs Weston, and I suppose you have come for Elsie. You can see why we can't keep her here anymore, she was such an adorable little puppy when our son gave her to us Christmas before last, but she has become more than we can manage now. We hate to lose her, but she needs more than we can give her in the way of exercise, and she is really hard to control."

"I can understand that, Mrs Weston, and you have made the right decision to give her to the Air Force. I'm sure she will make a great police dog, and I know she will be well looked after but from her antics at the front window, it looks as though I'm going to have a fun trip back to Netheravon."

She smiled and said, "I already thought of that, and I've given her two sedative pills, prescribed by the vet, and there are another four left for you to take with you. I don't think you will need them; the vet said just one should make her quiet down."

That took a weight off my mind, except I had a quick vision of myself carrying this huge dog in my arms through London when I had to change trains. It didn't come to that, though.

"Well, I'd better get started back. It's a long trip, and I don't want to get stuck somewhere overnight." It only took a split second after we opened the front room door and let Elsie out, for me to realize that the pills had not started to work. It was a major struggle to get a service issue leather muzzle on her and a standard choke-chain. All the time she was snarling and fighting to get at me, I had to hold her off with the choke-chain to save my "Best Blues" uniform pants.

After the sad farewells, Elsie and I made our way to the nearby bus stop in a running battle. When the double-decker bus arrived, the conductor directed us to sit upstairs. Getting Elsie up that narrow, winding, steel staircase to the upper deck while she was doing her best to take me apart through the muzzle was interesting, to say the least. We had no trouble finding a seat. There were only four other people up there, and they left as soon as we joined them.

Elsie and I were not getting on well at all, by the time we arrived at the train station. The London train was waiting when we arrived at the platform and I soon found an empty compartment. With the doors firmly closed, we settled down for the 45-minute ride to London. The pills must have kicked in at this point, as Elsie relaxed a little with her efforts to destroy me and sat on the seat opposite, glaring and occasionally showing me her fine set of teeth. Several passengers made as though they were going to come into the compartment, but when they saw Elsie, they moved on along the corridor. At that stage, I thought, *Well, she's good for something!*

Arriving in London, the struggle started all over again. She was as fresh as a daisy. This time we had to find a bus that would take us across

London to a different station, to get to Salisbury, Wiltshire. Once again we had the top deck of the bus to ourselves and by the time we found the correct platform at the train station, Elsie had, somehow, managed to chew through the muzzle. Our relationship, not good from the start, was deteriorating rapidly. And then I got the break I needed.

"Hey, Don. Having a little trouble there, I see." It was my best friend at the dog school, Billy Williams. He had been sent on a collection which had fallen through. The owners had changed their minds and decided to keep their dog.

"Billy!" I shouted with relief, "You're a sight for sore eyes. Here, hold onto this monster for me for a few minutes while I go for a pee and get something to eat and drink. And if you have your muzzle with you, help me while I put it on Elsie."

Between us we soon had Elsie secure again in a new muzzle, and Billy sat on a bench with Elsie still tugging at the leash, trying to get at me. I headed for the snackbar, still keeping Elsie and Billy in sight except for when I went to the "loo." I didn't want to leave them too long in case Elsie decided to turn her attention on Billy, so I gulped down a cheese sandwich and a cup of tea and hurried back to the bench. Elsie greeted me like a long-lost hambone, but the new muzzle frustrated her, and she was reasonably quiet after a short while. Finally we climbed aboard the Salisbury train, once again having no trouble finding and keeping an empty compartment. She finally dropped off to sleep on the seat opposite me and I managed to catch a couple of winks too. I was really tired, but Billy kept an eye on things while we dozed.

It was after eight p.m. when we finally arrived at R.A.F. Netheravon main gate. Stepping down from the bus, which ran between Salisbury rail station to Netheravon village, Elsie hardly had a growl left in her, for me. I left her in the charge of the corporal on duty in the quarantine kennels; she made one last charge at me, all teeth and saliva and then I hurried off to the barracks to get a good night's sleep.

I was up early the next morning, fully refreshed after the previous day's ordeal when a trainee brought me a message from Quarantine. They needed to see me immediately. Naturally, I thought something had gone wrong with Elsie and quite honestly, at that stage I didn't really care. She wasn't my responsibility anymore. I was glad to get rid of her. But I thought I had better go and see what was going on. When I arrived at the Quarantine area, I was met by the sergeant in charge.

"What kind of wild beast did you bring in here, yesterday, Corporal? She won't let anyone near her—it's like she's crazy or something!"

"I know what you mean, Sergeant. I had to fight with her all the way from Gillingham, Kent. That was a trip I wouldn't want to repeat for anything. You know, I'll be quite happy if I never have to see that dog again!"

"Well, that's too bad, son. So far none of my people can get near her, and you are the only one with any experience with her. You brought her in; now you can take her out."

"Okay, Sergeant, but I sure hope this is going to be the last time. My posting should be coming through in a week or so, and I'd prefer not to be wearing bandages when I leave."

He opened a door for me and, not too gently, shoved me inside, slamming the door shut behind me. Crouched in the corner, glaring at me, was Elsie.

"Okay, girl," I said, "Just what kind of trouble have you been causing now?"

As soon as she heard my voice, her tail started wagging, her ears went down, and she almost crawled across the room towards me. I bent down with one hand out to welcome her and she nuzzled it and pushed up against my legs. No sign of the "Hound from Hell" that had terrorized countless British citizens on the journey from Gillingham to Netheravon the day before. I petted her for a while and she let me put the choke collar and lead back on her with no trouble. Within just a few minutes we were the best of friends and when I opened the door to take her out we found some of the kennel hands waiting to see if I was going to come out of there in one piece. Elsie was the perfect lady and greeted everyone like family. Of course, I had to get in a dig at the sergeant.

"I don't understand what was troubling you, Sergeant. She's just a quiet little lap dog. I should have thought that a big man like you could have handled her. I'd like to take her for a walk around the area before I go, okay with you?"

"Go ahead, Corporal, but watch your mouth, son. You just got lucky this time, that's all."

I took Elsie for a walk every morning after that until my posting came through, and by the time I left dog school she had been assigned to a handler and was doing very well in her training. She would make a fine police dog.

Billy and I got our posting notices at the same time. He was destined to go to Egypt which was considered by all to be a rough deal. My posting was to Germany, where I could even get home on the occasional weekend. But wherever I went, I would have to go without my dog, Valdi. He would be retrained with another handler. There were several dogs being held overseas, whose handlers had finished their time with the Air Force and because of England's strict quarantine laws, the dogs were unable to return. New handlers were required to take them over and I would be assigned a new dog when I transferred to my new station.

I wasn't too happy with the way things were turning out. Billy and a couple of other friends were leaving for Egypt in a few weeks for active service in the Canal Zone. This was at a time when England was defending her interest in the Suez Canal against the locals. On the other hand I would be patrolling a British installation somewhere in Germany, probably bored out of my mind. It didn't take too long for me to open my big mouth again and I went to see the C.O. of the dog school, Flight Lieutenant Smith.

"At ease. What can I do for you, Corporal?" he said, when I was shown into his office.

"Sir, I wish to request a change of posting."

"Oh, really?" he said, looking up from the papers on his desk. "And what did you have in mind?"

"My posting is to Germany, Sir, and I would like to change that for Egypt."

"You realize what you are asking for, do you? Germany is a cushy posting, with a good social life and all the amenities. You'll even be able to fly home on R.A.F. transports every other month or so, on 48- or even 72-hour passes. And the beer is the best in the world, I'm told."

"I'm sorry, sir; I can't believe that. No beer is better than British beer," I said, and was rewarded with a smile. "The thing is, my friends are going to Egypt, and I'd really like to go with them. I realize it's not going to be a picnic like Germany, but I believe it will be more interesting. And in any case, I want to get my knees brown."

"Well, Corporal, this is the first time anyone has asked to trade Germany for Egypt, but there's a first time for everything, I suppose. Actually, thinking about it, we do have one old dog there at R.A.F. Kasfarit, who needs a handler. He's been in the Air Force much longer than you, and he outranks you. Do you think you might want to work with him?"

"If he is senior to me, he may be able to teach me something, sir," I said. My rank was leading aircraftman, acting corporal. The C.O. told me Rex's rank was senior aircraftman. It seemed strange for a dog to have a rank, but that was the Service way. Rex had earned his rank by the level of training he had achieved.

After further discussion, the C.O. said he would see what he could do to get my posting changed with some other handler, who as yet didn't know how lucky he was going to be! The next day it was confirmed. I was going to Egypt with my pals.

Before we finally said goodbye to England, we had to spend a few days waiting for Air Force transportation to the Middle East. This we did on an embarkation station located near Blackpool, a seaside town on the west coast of England. There really wasn't anything to do there except wait; no drills, no parades, no inspections, nothing. It could have been boring if we hadn't decided to take a chance and sneak off into Blackpool. This was late summer time and the beaches were full of vacationing mill hands from the textile areas of northern England. Pretty girls in swimsuits were a big attraction to young service men about to go over seas. Billy and I had no trouble picking up a couple and we soon spent all we had on fairground rides, junk food and booze. The girls' drink of choice was gin and tonic, and we sank quite a few of those. The legal age in England to buy alcohol was eighteen, so we were already used to the effects, and the hangovers. We had a great time, that day, and after leaving the girls at their hotel, we walked to the bus station, hoping to get a late night ride back to camp

The office at the bus station was closed when we arrived, but there was a phone box outside, and we decided to call the camp guardroom to try to get a ride with their police provost patrol. Being service policemen ourselves, we thought this should not be expecting too much. Wrong! The corporal on duty told us in no uncertain terms, that if we were not signed in by midnight, we would both be considered to be "Absent Without Leave," and that their provost patrol was not there to provide personal transportation for the likes of us! With less than an hour to go to midnight, we were in a bit of a bind. I suggested we try calling the sickbay on camp to see if by chance, they had an ambulance they could send out for us but when I called, I was told that they could do that only if there was a medical emergency.

It was beginning to look as though we would be spending the next day and some time after that, in jail and we were wandering around the bus station trying to come up with a plan when I noticed a light at the back of the bus service area and the faint sounds of a radio.

"Hey, Billy," I said, "maybe someone back there can give us some advice, other than 'Get lost!'"

"It's worth a try," he replied, and I led the way across the service area. I should have gone around the line of parked busses, but going between them seemed to me to be a much quicker way towards the light. With my eyes on the light I stepped into the shadow between two busses, and with a loud expletive, disappeared from Billy's view.

"Don, where the hell are you?" Billy shouted, his voice echoing around the huge workshop.

Momentary silence, until a mechanic, working on a vehicle in the far corner of the place shouted back, "Who's there?"

"We need a little help over here, and please bring a light," Billy called, and, before long a mechanic in greasy overalls appeared with a large flashlight.

It turned out that when I stepped between two busses, I had fallen down a six-foot deep inspection pit. These pits, four feet wide, ran the full length of the service area, and busses were parked over them at night. Previously this bus station had housed electric trams before the city was "modernized" with the operation of busses.

After stepping into that very deep shadow, I knew nothing for a while. I woke up with a pounding headache and my right leg on fire, or so it felt, as I lay on the ground beside the pit. When I felt I could move, the mechanic and Billy helped me hobble over to the nearest bus, and I gingerly lay down on the back seat. I was still seeing a few stars and the effects of the last gin and tonics were fast evaporating when Billy commented, "Well, at least we can truthfully say we have a medical emergency now. So they ought to come and pick us up," and he went off to make another phone call to sick bay.

According to Billy, he had a hard time convincing them of the seriousness of the situation but they finally agreed to send an ambulance to pick us up. When he told me how they had reacted, he suggested that I "lay it on a bit" when the ambulance arrived. I really didn't have to do a lot of acting. I wasn't feeling at all well!

When the ambulance arrived, we thanked the mechanic for his help, and I was lifted onto a stretcher by two male medics and put inside. A nurse, a member of the W.R.A.F., took my pants off. I was hurting too much to enjoy that. She cleaned up the wound. She suspected a fracture, but the doctor would get x-rays. She also thought I might have a concussion from the crack on the skull I had sustained dropping down into the pit.

So ended our day out in Blackpool. By two a.m. I was all cleaned up, x-rayed, examined, bandaged up and in a ward with half a dozen or so other patients. The ambulance driver took Billy back to the barracks, where of course he had to relay the day's events to the rest of our group. We got away with that escapade without any formal charges, other than a good ear bending from the corporal in charge.

The next day, early in the morning, Billy came by the ward to say that they were leaving at 11 a.m. for the airfield to catch the plane. I was in a panic. I didn't feel too bad and I did everything I could to convince the duty nurse and doctor that I was fit enough to get out of there and be on my way. They wouldn't hear of it so Billy left and I said I would see him and the others as soon as I possibly could. When the chief medical officer made his rounds of the ward at 10.30 a.m I was fully dressed and ready to go.

"So where do you think you're going, Corporal?" he asked.

"I'm sorry, Sir; I know it looks like I'm in a hurry to get away from here, and I thank you and your staff for the treatment I've received, but I have a plane to catch to Egypt, and I don't want to miss it."

"We'll see about that, Corporal. First I want to see what you have done to yourself. It wouldn't make much sense sending a cripple overseas, now would it? So just calm down, take your pants off, and lie down on your bed. Nurse, fetch his x-ray file, please."

After what seemed an age, the examination was finally over.

"That scrape down your right shin went to the bone, Corporal, and will take quite some time to heal over, but luckily, there was no damage to the bone. You may also have a slight concussion, but I suspect your head is hard enough to take it. I'm going to release you, but I want you to take things easy for a while. No excitement and no physical activity until you've settled down in your new posting. Do I make myself clear?"

"Absolutely, sir," I replied. "May I leave now?" and I saluted.

He half-heartedly returned my salute, said, "Go ahead, Corporal," and turned to his next patient.

I had been given a crutch to use, and I hobbled out of that ward as fast as I could go. Outside an ambulance was at the curb, engine idling, but no driver in sight. Time was wasting. It was eleven o'clock already. The driver, an AC1, the lowest rank in the Air Force, finally came back. By then I was already sitting in the passenger seat. He climbed into the driver's seat before realizing I was there.

"What's going on, Corporal?" he asked, "I'm supposed to be waiting for the M.O. to take him to the Officer's Club for lunch."

"That's right, Airman, but while you are waiting, you can take me to my barracks first. I have a plane to catch."

"I'm sorry, Corp., I can't do that. I'll be in all kinds of trouble if the Old Man comes out and I'm not here waiting for him."

"And do you know how much trouble you will be in if I miss my plane?" I said, pointing at the two stripes on my arm. "I'm heading for Egypt today, with the rest of my police squad, and I would be most unhappy if I don't make it!" It was the first time I had used rank on anyone but, at the time, I could think of nothing else.

"Okay, Corporal, I'll do my best. If we speed a little I might get back before he knows I've been gone."

"Try speeding a lot, man. I've got to get that transport to the plane!"

It didn't help much; the bus with my pals on board was leaving by the main gate as we pulled into the barracks.

"Well, you tried, kid," I said as I clambered down from the ambulance. "Now hurry on back so the M.O. can get his lunch, and thanks for the ride."

He must have made it in time to pick up the M.O., as I didn't hear anything about taking the ambulance.

4.

I was stuck on camp for another two weeks, with nothing to do but heal up after our day in Blackpool. It really wasn't time wasted; my leg had healed nicely and the headaches were gone by the time I was advised that I would be aboard the next R.A.F. transport plane to Egypt, the following morning. It was a long, boring, overnight flight, and I wasn't ready for the climate change when we arrived. England never was a hot place, not like Egypt, even though this was early in the morning. Two other passengers on the flight were destined for R.A.F. Kasfarit, in the canal-zone area, and we soon located the camp transport, an open, three-ton truck with bench seats in the back. After we climbed aboard, the driver, also a corporal, handed me a sten gun.

"Hope you don't mind, Corp," he said to me. " We have to have an armed guard on all transports. There have been quite a few attacks on single service vehicles in the area where we will be going, and for a while we won't be driving on any main road, just a desert track. You might want to keep your heads down, too. The Wogs have come up with the idea of stretching wire across the road at about head height, and some of our lads have been decapitated. Particularly on motorbikes."

"Sounds like fun, Corporal," I replied. "We'll keep our heads down below the cab height. Just don't back up anywhere in a hurry."

The sun was well up when we started off to camp. Perched on the bench seat in the back of the truck, it wasn't easy staying awake and alert. The other two lads crashed out in the bed of the truck. As we traveled through the desert, I remembered what I had told the C.O. back in dog school when I asked for a posting transfer. I had told him I wanted to get my knees brown. This seemed to be a good time to start working on that, so I rolled my long woolen, R.A.F. issue, socks down, and hitched my khaki shorts up, exposing two large, lily-white knees. With the sten gun cradled in my lap, well clear of my knees, I tried to keep awake but I kept dozing off, jerking awake every time we hit a larger than usual bump in the road. There was nothing to be seen, anyway. Just sand and rocks as far as the horizon, all round. Eventually, the path smoothed out, and soon we were at the main gate of R.A.F. Kasfarit. One of the station policemen was coming off duty and, as my barracks was located next to his, he showed me the way. Billy, Ron, and Mick, my pals from dog school, were there to meet me. Someone brought out some Stella beers from hiding, and we drank a toast to our reunion. It was good to be back amongst people I knew.

That first night in Egypt I went on patrol with Billy, after briefly meeting with my new dog, Rex. I didn't take him out that first night— I had a week to get used to him and that would be best done during daylight and not in a working environment. At the end of a week, I was supposed to be acclimatized, and we should be familiar enough with each other's ways to be able to perform our duties properly. There was no set patrol route; a tall barbed wire fence surrounded the camp which contained medical facilities, a transit camp, bomb dump, various storage buildings, a NAAFI building and a tent storage area. Offices and mess halls were situated closer to the main gate. We were free to patrol where we wanted to; this way it was difficult for anyone watching to predict our actions. It also meant that we had to really keep our eyes open as surprise encounters could and did, happen. By the time that first shift with Billy was over, I could barely walk. My knees were killing me! My lily-whites were now a glorious shade of purple! The sun had almost cooked them on the truck ride from the airport. I staggered into the barracks, when the shift was over, and headed for the showers. All I could think of was cold water, to douse the fire flaming in my kneecaps. It was agony getting under the spray of the shower, but after a while a certain numbness set in, and I got out to dry off. Working my way down my body with the towel I reached my knees, where the pain seemed to have eased off, and I wiped the towel across both legs. Immediately the pain was back with a vengeance, as the skin on both knees came off in the towel, leaving a bleeding mess. Somehow I managed to get back in the barracks, grunting and cursing in agony.

Billy had a silly grin on his face but didn't say anything; he knew what was wrong. Ron said, "What's up, Don? You don't look too happy. The first patrol too much for you?"

"Not exactly," I snarled, through gritted teeth, and I pulled back the towel to expose my knees.

"Good God!" Ron blurted out, "What the hell did you do?"

I explained what had happened while Mick ran over to sick bay to get a couple of bandages. When he came back I bound up my knees, but not too tightly, so that I could still walk. During this time, Ron explained that getting sunburn was considered to be a punishable offence, and if it became known, I could be on a 252. That was the common name for a charge. As a policeman, that wouldn't look too good on my record.

Having that first week to get to know Rex was a blessing. We took it very easy, and by the time we were required to start patrolling properly, I was able to walk with no really noticeable hobble, and Rex and I were firm friends. Not only was he a very clever and well-trained dog, he was senior to me in age as well as rank, if you count one dog year being equal to seven human years. He was twelve human years old when I met him, and I wondered how long we could be together.

After the sunburn incident I made sure that I never stayed out in the sun for more than ten minutes at a time if I wasn't fully covered up, at least, until I had a tan. By the time I left Egypt, six months later, I looked like a wog, myself! With jet black, short-cropped hair and a black mustache, I only needed to wear a long white nightshirt to really look the part. And my knees were as brown as the rest of me.

On my second night on patrol with Rex, I decided to include a visit to the tent storage area. That was where military tents were precisely folded and stacked up to eight feet high. There was room to walk between the stacks and it was rather like being in a maze. This was a favorite spot for intruders to hide and to steal the tents. Egyptians were extremely clever thieves, almost invisible against the desert at night. There was a story going round camp that, just before Billy and Ron arrived, a group of a dozen newcomers stayed overnight in the transit quarters, on their way to a different location. They were tired after their long, uncomfortable flight from England and they turned in early, to get a good night's sleep. In the morning they woke up to find they were sleeping on bedsprings, with no bed clothes. During the night, local thieves had silently invaded the camp, evaded all security patrols and had entered the transit quarters. Not only did they take away all the occupants' belongings but they also removed the sheets, blankets and mattresses. Without making a sound and without arousing anyone! Now, I can't vouch for the truth of that tale, but the person who told me swore that it was a fact.

I must have had thoughts of this incident on my mind as Rex and I made our way, as quietly as we could, in between the tent stacks. Security lights on high poles, outside the tent area, threw strange shadows on the stacks and I kept my free hand on the butt of my service revolver, with the holster flap undone. Suddenly Rex froze. He was signaling me that we were not alone. I breathed "Heel," and "Stay," which he did immediately, and I said a little prayer of thanks for the week's training we had spent together and for his previous training. He didn't make a sound. I had no intention of allowing him to go tearing off around the corner, possibly into an ambush. Smart old dogs like that were worth a lot to the service, and apart from that, he was my friend.

I crouched down and slowly eased around the corner, gun in hand. Somewhere along the corridor in front of me, a gun went off with a bang and the slug smacked into the tent pile above me. I dodged back around the corner, out of sight of my attacker, and several shots followed, all ending up in the tents. As soon as I had recovered from the surprise, I poked my gun hand round the corner and emptied it in the general direction of the other gun. Rex was quivering with excitement and eager to get in on the act, but I reinforced, "Stay," and he did. After the short burst of gunfire, the silence was complete, and I needed to reload. I was struggling with the flap on my service-issue ammunition pouch, on my belt, when I dropped a couple of rounds into the sand at my feet.

"Oh, shit!" I cursed, out loud.

A call came from around the corner, "Who's there?"

"Who do you think it is, you crazy bastard? It's the dog patrol; and who the hell are you?" I yelled.

"Okay, Corporal, don't shoot anymore. I'm walking towards you, and we can talk about this." I waited a few seconds before peering round the corner and I saw a figure in R.A.F. uniform approaching. I had noticed that Rex had relaxed at the sound of the other voice, and when the owner turned the corner, Rex greeted him as a friend.

"Hello, old son," our "intruder" said to Rex, and he put out his hand to me to shake hands. "My name is Sergeant Smolt, and you must be Rex's new handler."

He had three stripes on his arm, a shotgun slung over his shoulder, a revolver on each hip, and he was carrying a rifle. I couldn't believe what I was seeing.

I must have looked shocked, and he said, "How about a cup of tea, to settle us down, Corp? I run the camp laundry, just beyond the tent area, and I've got a fresh pot brewing. I've got a little goody there for Rex, too; I haven't seen the old fellow for a couple of weeks now."

As we were walking in single file, the sergeant leading, I finally got my powers of speech back. "So, Sergeant," I called, "what were you doing in the tent storage area at night? I thought that was part of my responsibility."

"It is, son," he said, "but sometimes I like to go in there just to see if I can catch one of those thieving wogs. I've nabbed a few in the time I've been here, and the C.O. turns a blind eye to my unofficial patrols."

"Well, that's all well and good, Sergeant, but I wish someone had warned me. Somebody could have been hurt."

We reached the laundry, and he led the way into his living quarters. Rex lay down beside my legs when I sat on a kitchen chair, as the sergeant poured out two mugs of tea for us and gave Rex a biscuit. He grinned as he gave me one of the mugs and asked, "No hard feelings?"

"I suppose not," I replied, "But Billy will get hell for not telling me about you."

Ron, Mick and Billy all had a good laugh when I told them about the incident over Stella beers and watermelon the next evening. Apparently, the laundry sergeant was considered to be a bit "desert happy." "Nuts," I called it. Everyone knew he did these solo nighttime patrols, and he fancied himself as some kind of one-man army. So there I was—my first armed conflict, with a crazy man who was on my side! And I wasn't even nineteen years old yet. I couldn't help thinking of the poor souls who would one day be issued those tents with bullet holes in them. I just hoped it wouldn't be raining where they were going!

One morning we were advised by our C.O. that dog patrols that evening would be suspended. We were to let the dogs have a night off and we would join members of the provost and station police in a stakeout around the bomb dump. Information had filtered in, through channels unknown to us, that the munitions in the bomb dump might be the subject of a raid by the local bad boys, that evening. Everyone involved was to stock up on ammunition for their side-arms and stens and meet up with Sergeant Smolt outside the camp laundry building at 11 p.m. Although he was thought to be crazy by the rank and file, the authorities had confidence in him. Personally, I intended to keep one eye on the bombs and the other on the sergeant.

The bomb dump was a storage area for various types of bombs and other munitions, built up on four sides with sand rock and concrete. The main path ran through the center, a gated break in the blast walls at each end.

The plan was to disperse, quietly, from the meeting place by the laundry and to make our separate ways, as unobtrusively as possible to the dump. Once there we were to silently climb to the top of the blast walls at pre-arranged locations and, keeping a very low profile, we should be able to pick up any activity amongst the munitions below, which were covered with mounds of sand. We had been told that we couldn't expect to lose an entire bomb, but the wogs had become adept at dismantling them and stealing the contents. These weapons were not fused, so that was relatively safe for them. This took me back to my childhood, when my friends and I found German incendiary bombs and opened them up for the black powder to make fireworks! This was a little more serious, though, as the contents of these bombs would be used in the terrorist war against us.

No one was to make a move or sound until a prearranged whistle was heard from the sergeant. The silence was as heavy as the hot desert air, as we lay near the top of the rim, about twenty yards apart, straining our eyes to see what, if anything, was going on in the area below. I was aware of the adrenaline rushing through me and the blood pounding in my ears, with excitement. Of course there was no night-vision equipment in those days, and several times I could have sworn that I saw one of the bombs moving. But still no signal from the sergeant.

With the reputation that the wogs had for being invisible at night, even if there were security lights around, we didn't really expect to see full human figures. We were looking for unexplained shadows and indentations in the sand which may not have been there a second or so before.

Suddenly the silence was pierced by a shrill whistle and immediately a rain of bullets poured into the sand below. Nothing could have survived that initial onslaught which stopped as soon as we heard the second whistle from the sergeant. For a few seconds the only sound was of someone on the rim, to the left of me, cursing and swearing between heart-felt moans. There was no point in keeping quiet anymore, and everyone wanted to know who had been hurt and how. Scrambling along the top of the wall, we converged on one of the Station policemen, rolling around, clutching his groin area, with blood seeping out between his fingers. One of those closest to him had already gone to fetch medical assistance, the sickbay was less than a half mile away, and he was soon on a stretcher, in an ambulance, on the way to hospital.

We later learned that he was an Irishman, named Kelsey, and as soon as he heard the first whistle, he leapt to his feet with excitement, and caught a ricochet right in the "privates." He had just earned a trip home and an early discharge, but any children he might have in the future would be adopted. He might also have been the subject of the saying, which was in common use around that time, "As dead as Kelsey's nuts!"

The Lido was a favorite place for night-shift workers, like dog handlers, to spend some of their off-duty hours. It was a beach area on the canal, for military personnel, and was within easy walking distance of R.A.F. Station, Kasfarit. After my burnt knees episode I was careful not to stay in the sun too long and by doing this gradually, I had a really good tan with no more ill effects. Neither Billy nor I were particularly interested in playing billiards or darts in the N.A.A.F.I. so we spent a lot of our time at the beach and swimming. It was really good exercise after walking a patrol for six hours at night!

Souvenirs were big business in Egypt and vendors were everywhere. The road to the beach was no different with several hand drawn carts containing displays of leather goods, parked on the sides. As we walked to the beach, the various vendors would call out offering to show us what they had for sale. Most of the items were made of leather, many of which were beautifully carved, and they made quite unusual souvenirs or gifts. That was fine for those expecting to go home soon, but we had only just started our tours of duty, so we weren't ready to start stocking up on gifts for the folks back home. This fact didn't sit well with the owners of the carts and they thought that the Infidels, us, should be buying everything they had to offer.

One day, returning to camp from the beach, we had almost got through the line of vendors, without buying anything, when I decided to teach the last one a lesson. He was particularly loud in his demands for attention and I said to Billy, "We've got a little time to spare; let's go and have some fun. Follow me and copy what I do. We should get a laugh out of this."

I should add that I was wearing my service-issue shorts over my bathing trunks, carrying a towel, and had sandals on my feet. Billy was similarly dressed.

"Okay, Mohammed," I said as we stopped at the last cart on the road, about two hundred yards from the camp gate, "let's have a 'shufti,'" and I pointed at a large leather wallet.

I had noticed before, that, when a potential customer asked to look at an item, and it was rejected, the vendor would place it carefully on the sand behind the cart. This saved it from being confused with the other things he was trying to sell. Billy understood what I was doing immediately and asked to see one of the leather-bound jewelry boxes. After a few seconds of study, he handed it back, shaking his head. This item was also placed on the sand behind the cart. Then it was my turn and I picked on another wallet. Once again I declined, and once again it was placed on the sand. All the time the salesman was cajoling us in broken English to buy something, anything, just to make him happy. Every minute he was getting more and more frustrated with us as he kept placing items on the sand.

Eventually, the cart was completely empty and the display was laid out neatly on the sand. We had one very irate wog on our hands, and he reached under the cart and whipped out a very large knife. That's when we decided to leave. I bent down to pick up my sandals, which I had kicked off, ready to run barefoot, and the top button on my shorts broke off, no zippers in those days. Trying to hold up my shorts, carrying sandals and a towel, when I was running from a crazy, armed, camel jockey, just wasn't going to work. I kicked off the shorts, and took off up the road after Billy, both of us laughing our heads off! By the stream of loud arabic curses which followed me, I didn't have a second to lose and almost dived through the side gate, which Billy slammed shut behind me. By then two of our station police friends had come out of the guardroom to see what all the shouting was about, and they stood at the gate, in uniform, with their hands on their revolvers. Ahmed, or whatever his name was, gradually eased off with the cursing, turned, and shuffled off back to his cart.

Meanwhile, Billy and I sat on the guardroom steps, still laughing and gasping for breath, all at the same time. The Station Policemen walked over to us, and, grinning, one of them said, "You know, Don, that really looked peculiar, you with no pants on being chased by a wog with his skirt up in a bunch; I wish I'd had my camera with me!"

After that, when we went to the Lido, Billy and I always made a point of walking on the other side of the road, and Mohammed, or whatever his name was, would always snarl something unpleasant in Arabic and wave his fist.

By this time, Britain and Egypt had just about resolved their dispute over the Suez Canal and trouble was brewing in East Africa, with Jomo Kenyatta leading the terrorist faction known as the Mau-mau. With our services no longer needed in Egypt, it wasn't long before postings were issued. Billy, Mick and I were going to Kenya, with our dogs, to join an established Police contingent at R.A.F. Eastleigh, Ron would return to dog school in England, as an instructor.

5.

The aircraft which took us out of Egypt, on the way to Africa, was a lot less comfortable than the plane on which we had arrived. It was much smaller, for one thing, and there were no seats in the back section of the fuselage, behind the cockpit. We were the only passengers, along with our three dogs that were in open slat wooden crates. The flight crew had introduced themselves before we took off, a Flight Lieutenant was the pilot and the copilot was a pilot officer. It was a twin-engine Dakota, and I can remember praying silently, that at least one of the engines should keep going as we crossed the desert wastes below

Our seats were folding camp stools and we had to hold onto anything we could find when turbulence hit and to comfort the dogs, we stayed as close as we could to the cages which were strapped in. They were really scared and every one of them let us know it by frequent vomiting and diarrhea. This, combined with a lack of true air conditioning, made for a somewhat unpleasant trip and the three of us tried to keep our spirits up by telling corny and sometimes dirty, jokes. At one point the pilot officer came through the partition to see what all the laughter was about, just as I released a large and noisy gas cloud of my own!

"Stop that, Corporal!" he snapped.

"Yes, sir, " I replied smartly. "Which way did it go?"

He smirked, pinched his nose, and returned to the cockpit.

Eventually we arrived at Khartoum, the capital of the Sudan, where we were to spend the night. We were very glad to get out in the open air again, as were the dogs, even though it felt like walking into a blast furnace. Just to be able to stretch our legs again, even if only for a short while, felt wonderful. Rex, being the oldest of the three dogs, was a little slower than the others in regaining his demeanor, but after we had walked for half an hour or so, around the perimeter of the airfield, he started to show signs of his old self. When we arrived back at the plane, airmen had unloaded the kennel crates and were in the process of giving them a good clean. Rex showed his appreciation by snarling and baring his teeth at them and I had to call him to heel with a quick tug on the lead.

After the kennels were cleaned and the dogs fed and secured for the night, we took it in turns to go to the mess hall for a quick meal. Billy and Mick went first while I stayed with the dogs and then it was my turn, when they came back. We stayed all night with the dogs, taking turns at being on watch. The dogs were too important to us personally and too valuable to the R.A.F. to allow anything untoward to happen to them. Apart from any other consideration, it would have been a court martial offense.

We took off early the following morning, just as the sun was rising while the air was relatively cool, heading for Ethiopia and more desert. That's another part of the world that will never run out of sand and by late morning we were crossing the range of sand hills known as "The Northern Frontier," the boundary between Ethiopia and Kenya. This was a wild area with which I would become very familiar one day.

The primary airport in Kenya lay just outside the capital city of Nairobi and was divided between civilian and service activities. At one end of the main runway, was the civilian terminal, and towards the other end and off to one side, was the service establishment. The R.A.F. aircraft based there included a half dozen Liberators, four engine bombers, and a flight of Harvards, or AT6s, as they are named in the States. In England the single-engine Harvards were used as trainers for fighter pilots, but the men who flew these needed no extra training. They had survived the dog fights over England during the Battle of Britain in Spitfires and Hurricanes. Flying missions in Harvards, against Kikuyu terrorist strongholds in the Aberdare mountains was nothing but a picnic for them.

Our plane touched down on the runway around mid-afternoon and the air was crisp and clean. At approximately four-thousand-feet in altitude it felt very pleasant compared with the heat and humidity to which we had become accustomed in Egypt. But, everything has a down side, and it would take a couple of weeks to become accustomed to the thinner air at that altitude.

While the plane was being unloaded, we took the dogs to the dog compound where they could finally relax and rest before going back to work. The senior corporal of the Dog Handler contingent, met us at the plane and showed us the way. Corporal Ellis was a rather small man for a policeman, but he was very experienced in the ways of dogs—and men. He explained that our C.O. was a young flight lieutenant, named Baker, who was not too interested in "spit and polish and B.S.," and he did not require any fancy parades or even polished boots. He was a practical man and our patrol uniform would be khaki overalls and dark-blue plimsols, or tennis shoes. Any metal wear, such as badge, buttons and belt buckle should be blackened, not polished and we could use our own hand-made leather holsters, which we had to pay for, made by an Indian leather worker in Nairobi. Off duty, on camp, we would wear regular uniform and off duty, off camp, we could wear civilian clothes, if we chose. He was all for keeping his men and dogs happy and safe. And his support for his men, in sometimes questionable circumstances, was outstanding, as I would learn, later.

The Police barracks was one of several large rooms, on two floors, in a huge, brick-built building. On the ground floor, closest to the main door, it housed twenty four men; a mixture of Provost, Station and Dog Handlers. Everyone in the room was on shift work, so at any time there were people getting up, going to bed, at work or off duty. It was just as well the C.O. didn't require constant kit inspections. At the end of our shifts we were too tired to be disturbed by anything short of an all out raid! It didn't take us too long to fit in with the others and there wasn't a rotten apple in the whole barrel! They were a fine group of men, all loyal to the Police Section and each other.

About the only time that the whole barracks functioned in total unison, was when Cpl. Pat Morris got out of bed in the morning, after spending the previous evening in the NAAFI, drinking Tusker beer. Pat was a very large man, with a huge capacity for beer. I have known him to consume a dozen liters of beer between mid-day and four in the afternoon, and then go on duty in the Guard Room, smart and efficient and stone-cold sober. After an average evening's drinking, during the night his enormous frame turned into a great gas generator. When he arose the following morning, he would stand stark naked at the foot of his bed and shout, "Attention!"

At that signal, everyone in the room was also expected to stand at attention. Then he proceeded to play the first verse of "God Save the Queen" on the "poor man's piano," and nobody laughed!

Pat had a very finely tuned, musical rear end, a talent which could have taken him far, but naked flames were forbidden during the performance!

Two other characters were the Cardigan twins. These lads were also on the robust side and were as strong as young bulls. In civilian life they had been dockyard workers before being called up to serve their National Service. I have never known two tougher men, at work or in play. They were the top players in the Station rugby team and, when they found out that was my game, they soon had me on their side. Our favorite opposition was the Army Police team from their station on the other side of Nairobi. Traditionally, the army and air force police never got along and it was a constant state of undeclared war between them. During our first game, a week after I arrived, I was having a hard time breathing the thin air, a condition which one of the army players used to knock the stuffing out of me. A cheap shot but it was to be expected, and I would probably have done the same if the positions had been reversed. Cliff and Dave, the Cardigan boys, however, took exception to the attack, and Dave told me to move out and leave a space when the next scrum-down took place. My position was second row forward, as was my opposition's. The rest of our team had received the message and when the next scrum-down was called, we pushed so hard, suddenly, that the other side collapsed with my antagonist on the bottom. As they were picking themselves up, Cliff and Dave came charging up from behind the pack, jumping and planting all four feet on the last man to try to get up. He left the field on a stretcher with three broken ribs and a broken arm.

When the game was over and we returned to Eastleigh, Cliff, Dave and I were called into Flight Lieutenant Baker's office. He unofficially reprimanded us for excessive roughness and told the twins to ease up on the poor army lads and we heard no more about it. I believe he was secretly proud of his two dynamos! On the other hand, when I got a chance to play in a field hockey game against the army on their turf, I put one of their men, who had been constantly tripping me, in hospital for a week. I was kicked off the team and only allowed to play rugby. I suppose that's where the C.O. wanted me.

On duty, the Cardigan twins were Provost Police. They conducted mobile patrols in the areas, Sections as they were known, outside the perimeter fence. The Sections were numbered, one through three, Section one being closest to the Main Gate. On my off-duty nights, I would sometimes go with them, even though it meant dressing up in full uniform with all brasses shining, polished boots, white belt and webbing and white gaiters. It was something to do for a change and the twins enjoyed the extra company. Most of the native huts in the Sections were brothels, which were strictly out of bounds, but that didn't stop some of our troops, dodging the dog patrols and going over the fence for some "fun," which included the possibility of a whole range of venereal diseases in addition to physical violence.

One evening the three of us were in the Land Rover, cruising along the main road out of camp, keeping a look out for any white faces amongst the huts on either side. Suddenly, Dave who was driving, swung the wheel over and we skidded to a stop in front of one of the mud and wattle huts.

"Okay, boys, we've got one in here. I saw him go in, and there's only one door, so I know he's in there. Let's get him."

I brought up the rear as we followed Dave, who kicked in the door, which had suddenly been bolted. The door flew inwards as the twisted bark hinges gave way and we found ourselves standing on the opposite side of a table from a tall, muscular looking African woman. She had knocked her chair over backwards, when she stood up as we burst inside. On the table was a floor length cloth topped with various sewing instruments and some brightly colored material.

Before we could say anything she started screaming obscenities in Swahili, until, finally she settled down a little.

"What you doing here, white man?" she shouted, as she leaned forward with both hands on the table.

"We know you've got a white boy in here somewhere. We saw him come in, and we've come to take him home," replied Dave.

"That not so. No white boy in here. I no like white boy." she said, in a more normal tone of voice.

Dave looked at me and grinned, and for a split second my attention was not on the woman. Out of the corner of my eye, I sensed more than saw the woman's right hand make a grab for the sewing gear, coming up with a pair of scissors. By the time I reacted, her hand, holding the scissors up high, was on its way down in my direction. Fortunately, I was able to grasp her right wrist with my left hand and jerk her across the table towards me. While she was still off balance, I rammed the heel of my right hand into her chin as she dropped the weapon. She staggered backwards, eyes rolling, hands stretched out sideways, and fell straight through the mud wall of the hut. The hole she made was a comic book outline of her body. She was laid out cold on the ground outside the hut, where we left her while we looked for the "customer." It didn't take long to find him. There was only one place he could be, and when Cliff lifted the edge of the table cover, he peered out, pale and shaking.

"I...I.... I'm sorry, Corporal; I didn't mean to cause any trouble," the airman stammered.

"You know this area is out of bounds, don't you, lad?" demanded Cliff. "And that it's dangerous? Apart from the things you can get from going with a dirty piece of trash like that, you could also get killed.

"I know that now, Corporal," he replied, still shaking, and still on his knees, "And believe me, I'll never take that chance again."

"Okay, stand up now, lad, and take your punishment."

Thinking that he was going to be "put on a charge," the airman stood up and pulled himself to attention. Cliff studied him for a few seconds before suddenly lashing out with an open hand to the side of the boy's face, followed immediately by a backhand to the other side. The airman collapsed in a heap on the floor, the tears streaming down his face, mixing with the blood from his nose and split lip. Dave said nothing, so I also held my tongue, for once.

We helped the lad climb up into the back of the Land Rover and noticed that the woman had crawled to the side of her hut and was sitting, leaning against the wall. I gave the airman my handkerchief to use to clean up, and we set off back to camp. He was still sniveling quietly in the back when Dave pulled the Land Rover round the back of the NAAFI, where there were no lights and lots of shadows.

Turning towards the rear of the vehicle Cliff said, "Okay, son, this is where you get off. If you know what's good for you, you'll forget this evening ever happened. You're not on a charge; I think you've been punished enough. If anybody asks, and they will, say you tripped and fell down one of the concrete storm drains on the side of the road. And don't ever let me catch you again in the Sections. Next time there will be a charge involved as well as a good hiding. Now, what do you say?"

"Thanks, Corporal, you'll never see me over there again, believe me. And thanks for not putting me on a 252. I won't forget that." And he stumbled off into the darkness.

When he had gone, Cliff drove the Land Rover back round the front of the NAAFI building and met Dave and I as we had walked round. Going inside, we made our way to a table in the corner of the room and ordered three I.P.A.s, that's India Pale Ales. We were entitled to a break during our shift and we could take it at our discretion.

After the beers came, I said to Cliff, "That seemed a bit brutal, what you did to that kid, wasn't it?"

"Look at it this way, Don," he replied. "What I did to him, he will remember, probably for the rest of his life. I taught him a lesson that breaking the law just doesn't pay, and it can hurt. If I'd put him on a charge, we would've taken him to the guardroom, put him in a cell for the night, and tomorrow he would've been 'on the carpet' in the C.O.'s office. The Old Man then would've read him the riot act for a few minutes and then 'sentenced' him to a week's jankers. A week of off-duty time spent cleaning potatoes in the kitchen or cleaning greasy pots won't teach him much, and a couple of weeks down the road we'll find him back over in the "Sections." As it is, I may have just saved his life."

"You're probably right, Cliff; it just seemed a bit rough at the time."

"Maybe so, but it works. He isn't the first one I've dealt with that way, and none of the others have ever been caught over there since. So I think it's worth it, and, just between you and me, so does the Old Man, but he'd never admit it!"

A perfect example of "corporal punishment"!

Another character I came to know and respect was Randy. He was Pat's "running mate," but he was always there to help if you needed someone. One day I asked him about driving the section's 15 cwt truck and, of course, he asked if I had a licence. I told him I would have to know how to drive first, and he immediately volunteered to teach me. We would have to do it at night, when only our police friends were on duty. After that conversation, almost every night that we were both off duty, found us out on the airfield with the truck, practicing driving. Randy had a lot of patience; it wasn't easy teaching someone to drive in an old truck with a "crash" gear box, and some of the language used by both of us would have embarrassed the devil himself, I'm sure. In those days, most military vehicles had the same system of gears. When changing from one gear to another, you had to double de-clutch, rev the engine, and as the revs decreased and you felt like you had found the "sweet spot," you put it in gear. If you found it, the gear went in with a gentle "click" but if you missed it, there was a terrible rattling, elongated "crash!"

One evening we were out on the runway, there was only one, practicing changing gear and, by chance we were heading into the wind. Randy was keeping an eye on the surrounding terrain while I tried and retried to change gears. Suddenly he remarked, "You know, Don, I think it's getting lighter, but that doesn't make sense; we don't have our lights on." I looked up and sure enough, the runway was much more visible and getting more so every second.

It was then I glanced at the rear-view mirror and saw the landing lights of one of the four-engine Liberators, which had just touched down on the far end of the runway.

"Good grief!" I yelled, or words to that effect, and swung the wheel over. I stomped on the accelerator, regardless of what gear the truck was in, and we just made it to the edge of the runway as that huge aircraft passed by.

That ended our lessons for that session; we needed sustenance to calm our nerves, so we headed for the NAAFI and a couple of cold beers. The incident eventually reached our C.O.'s ears, and Randy and I were called to his office. He asked what we were doing out on the runway with the truck, and when we explained his only comment was, "Well, done, lads; everyone should know how to drive. But in future, just to be on the safe side, check with Flight Operations first just to make sure you won't be interrupted again."

"That man is a prince," I said to Randy when we were outside again. "We couldn't ask for a better boss."

Eventually I got the hang of the double de-clutch gear shift and read the "Rules of the Road" handbook issued by the local civilian police. I felt I was ready to take the test and get my first civilian driving licence. That's all I needed to be able to officially drive a service vehicle on and off camp. I needed a car to take the test, of course, and one of the cooks in the mess hall that I knew slightly, offered to lend me his car for the road test. His car was not exactly a late model. It was an ancient Morris Ten, which burned almost as much oil as it did petrol and had no guts at all. On a practice run into town, with the owner driving and Randy and Billy in the back seat, we stopped at the bottom of a short rise, and the three passengers had to get out and push, in a cloud of smoke from the exhaust, to get the car up the hill.

This will never work, I thought, but it was the only offer of a vehicle I had, so there was no option but to give it a try. On the test day, Randy drove me into the Nairobi Police H.Q. parking lot and sat on a bench seat to smoke a cigarette and wait for me to return.

I went into the headquarters building and signed in for the test. A young, white officer not much older than I, holding a clipboard, introduced himself as my examiner. I led the way to the car and when he saw it, he half sneered, "They don't pay you chaps much in the Air Force, do they?"

"Oh, this isn't mine. I borrowed it. My Rolls Royce is being serviced today. I hope you don't mind." *I can be just as sarcastic as you,* I thought.

Not a good start but it was the best I could do. We sat in the car while I answered his Highway Code questions, and then he directed me to his favorite streets for the road test. This consisted of three-point turns, parallel parking, and parking on a hill. The poor old car just managed to perform the required maneuvers, and I thought I was home clear until he said, "Now let's see you pull away uphill from a standing start." This was going to be tough and was not something I had anticipated.

"Okay," I said, "Let's give it a go!" I knew I would have to "slip the clutch," rev the engine, and hang onto the emergency brake at the same time. But it was something I hadn't practiced, and the hill we were to use backed down into a main street filled with traffic. We made it up the slope to the point where he called a halt, and I jerked on the handbrake situated between the two front seats. I think I may have applied a little too much force. When I put the car in bottom gear, revved the engine, and slipped the clutch, I was struggling so hard to pull on the brake to release it that the front seat came loose and almost tipped me over into the back. I knocked the gear into neutral again and eased off revving the engine. By this time it looked like the car was on fire, with the huge cloud of smoke we had produced.

I turned to look at the examiner, and he was as white as a sheet.

"Okay, Corporal. Let's forget I asked for that. Why don't I get out and walk back to H.Q., and I'll see you there when you arrive."

"Not a chance, sir," I said. "I need you to help me get out of this. Like you said, you asked for it. Now, I'm going to put the car in bottom gear, slip the clutch, and rev the engine. When I say, "Now," you gently release the handbrake. Maybe we can get out of this with a little team work."

It worked out as I had hoped. With smoke pouring out of the tailpipe, me balancing on the broken front seat, and the examiner easing his full weight off the brake handle, we inched up the hill without rolling back.

At the top I had a satisfied grin on my face as I turned to the examiner and said, "There, I knew we could do it!"

He still hadn't recovered his color. He just mumbled, "Fine, now take me back to the office, please!" The silence on the way to H.Q. was almost palpable; I just knew he wasn't going to give me a licence. We arrived back at the H.Q. parking lot, and I dropped him off by the main entrance. He told me to wait. He would call for me soon. I parked the car and joined Randy on the bench for a well-earned cigarette.

"How did it go?" he asked.

"You don't want to know, pal. I've been told to wait, but it's probably for a summons for reckless driving or something."

Randy laughed. "It surely can't be that bad." When he heard the story, he agreed. I would probably be spending the night in jail.

I had just finished my cigarette when an Askari came out of the building and beckoned me over.

"The examiner is ready for you now, sir, please follow me," he said as he turned and led the way to the examiner's office. I knocked on the door and was told to enter.

Inside, the examiner sat behind the desk with his fingers interlocked in front of him on the blotter. The color had returned to his face, and he was smiling as he said, "You know, Corporal, you did a fine job out there with a very difficult piece of equipment. I just want you to know that I'm sorry we got off on a sour note. After all, we're both on the same side, right?" and he passed over the slip of paper, which he had been hiding on the blotter, with the word PASS stamped on it!

Totally surprised I stuttered my thanks and left the office. The Askari waiting outside directed me to the licence office, where I handed over the photograph that a friend on camp had taken for me. In minutes I had my first driving licence in my hand. Randy was also excited about the outcome, and we couldn't wait to get back to camp to share the news with the rest of the group. The beers were on me that night.

One major disadvantage of working dog patrol, were the so-called security lights round the civilian side of the airport, which separated the Sections from the airfield. The lights shone inwards, lighting up the perimeter path and anything on it. This made the dog patrol look like a target at one of those shoot-the-duck booths at the county fair. Of course, being a cartoon duck's namesake, that might have seemed appropriate for me! But it was disconcerting to be shot at on occasion, without being able to see the shooter, who was behind the light in the pitch darkness. There were some near misses some nights but a few rounds back from my service revolver in the general direction of the shots, discouraged whoever it was. It was just one of those common events that wasn't worth writing a report about. After this happened a few times, Rex and I made our own path through the long grass, between the security light poles. It was worth risking walking into a snake or two to avoid being some terrorist's target and by keeping low, we were unseen for the most part.

We were on late shift, one night, at about three in the morning, and had managed to get through the security light area without incident and had passed the Civilian Terminal buildings. In front of us, the path led to an impenetrable thicket of thorn bushes, on the other side of which was Section three, one of the worst places to be, around the camp. The inhabitants of the shacks were all thought to be Mau-mau sympathizers if not active members of Kenyatta's band of merry men and we always had to be especially on the alert around there.

In the starlight I could just make out the silhouette of the thorn bushes, about two hundred yards ahead, when Rex suddenly stopped dead in his tracks, ears back and his tail held low. This indicated to me that he had picked up the scent of a human, rather than a hedgehog, snake or some other wild thing. I also stopped and listened carefully but all I could hear were the night sounds of Africa. I whispered Rex to "heel," and we eased towards the bushes, my gun in my hand. When we were within a few yards of the thicket, Rex started to veer off to the side and we headed around the back to a track which passed between the bushes and the perimeter fence. There were no security lights around this side of the airfield and without the night vision which all dog handlers developed, I would have been blind.

Once again Rex stopped and I sensed we were close to the target. I crouched down, trying to see something against the starlit sky and sure enough, there was an area of solid black against the silhouettes of the twigs and branches of the thorn bushes. We waited, hardly breathing, for some movement from the target and then slowly approached it. Finally, we were close enough to see that it was a human shape which appeared to be backed up against the bushes. I coughed, to see what reaction we'd get, but there was no movement. This had gone on long enough I felt, so I moved in close, ready to fire at any time.

And then I moved back again, quickly! What I had seen was the naked torso of a man, or I should say, of half a man, hanging from the thorns. The lower half of his body and legs were missing, just ragged tatters of flesh where they should have been.

It took a few minutes for me to regain my composure and then Rex and I continued our patrol around the perimeter. The body wasn't going anywhere soon and when we got back to the Guardroom I could report it and have the Askaris, the civilian police, take it away. I later learned that the man must have been anti Mau-mau and had been tortured to death. To get rid of the body, he had been hung on the thorn bushes for the hyenas to devour. Not a very nice way to go.

The path that we followed away from the body, led down into a small valley on the far side of the airfield. Here we were in almost total darkness. Looking down, I could just make out Rex's ears, and not much more than that. We were below the level of the runway and the lights of the camp buildings, on the far side of the runway. Feeling our way along the narrow footpath, Rex in the lead, it was deathly quiet. No moonlight, just stars to provide the faintest glimmer. It was almost as if we had stepped off the edge of the world and were floating in space.

I was reliving in my mind, the experience of finding the half-corpse, a short while before when suddenly the silence was shattered by an ear-splitting scream. I don't remember drawing my gun but it was in my hand ready and I could just make out Rex, who stood as still as a statue, pointing over to our right. The hair on the back of both of our necks was standing up when the extended "Eee!" of the scream ended in "Aweee, aweeee, aw!" It was a donkey, on the other side of the fence, that we must have woken up. It felt like I had been holding my breath forever, and I let it out in a loud "Damn!" as we made our way, a little quicker than before, around the rest of the valley track and back up to the airfield where we could see a lot better.

I think that was the closest I have ever been to needing an immediate change of underwear!

In addition to R.A.F. Eastleigh, our section also provided security patrols for two R.A.F. communications outposts, some twenty miles away from Nairobi, in the direction of the Aberdare mountain range, the main terrorist location. The Mau-mau gangs passing through the area on their way to or from Nairobi, would often try to interfere with the antennas surrounding these radio sites. There were only two buildings on each site; one large radio hall, which contained all the electronics and the guardroom, with three cells and a three-dog kennel compound at the back. R.A.F. Ruiru held the transmitters and three, maybe four miles away, the other site, R.A.F. Kahawa, housed the receivers. During the day a transport would bring technicians from Eastleigh to operate the equipment, returning to Eastleigh in the evening and leaving one duty operator there at night.

The dog patrol's duties were arranged so that three of us were resident at any time. We lived in the guardroom, slept in the cells and had a wood-burning stove in a kitchen area at one end of the building. One of us was on duty at all times, night and day. The compound was surrounded by an eight-foot-high chain link fence, topped with barbed wire. Inside the fence, the perimeter was no more than a quarter of a mile. Outside the fence however, the aerial fields covered several acres, holding many steel antenna towers much like today's microwave towers. Generally speaking, our tours of duty at these outposts were fairly uneventful. Occasionally we would hear activity in the aerial field and would fire off half a clip in the general direction with a sten gun and that would settle that. Our main concern at night was to guard the buildings and equipment inside the fence. Just being there with our dogs was normally deterrent enough for the terrorists.

We changed locations on a monthly rotation. One month in Ruiru, followed by one month in Kahawa and then back to base, Eastleigh, for another month. Occasionally teams were split up when accidents happened or someone went on vacation, but for the most part the same three handlers worked together. This became a bit monotonous after a few months, so we made our own entertainment.

One day, when we were stationed at Ruiru, both Billy and I had run out of cigarettes. Billy had recently bought a CZ Jawa, 125cc two-stroke motorcycle, so we climbed on board and took off down the dirt access track towards the main black top road and headed south towards Nairobi. We passed the Red Lion pub, which we knew would be closed at that time of day and carried on until we reached the Indian "duqua," or store, two miles down on the left hand side of the road. We had been in there many times before and knew the owner quite well. On this particular day, there were several other motorcycles parked outside and a group of riders inside talking to the proprietor. They were all members of the local speedway teams, "Nairobi North" and "Nairobi South." Speedway was a growing sport in Ndola, and these men were the principal riders. There really weren't any teams as such, but they made it look that way for the sake of the fans. The store's owner was also a rider and a part owner of the brick-dust track in town.

Billy and I were soon drawn into the conversation when they noticed that we had arrived on a motorbike, even though it was a toy compared with the powerful road machines parked outside, and one of them asked if we would be interested in dirt-track riding with them. Billy had no interest in racing but I said I'd like to give it a try but there was no way I could afford to buy a racing machine. The racing bikes were 350cc Japp engine, Excelsior frames with fixed gears and no brakes. The only controls were a clutch and a twist grip throttle. The track was approximately a quarter of a mile, laid out in a big oval with a ten feet high heavy chain-link fence around the outside, between the spectators and the riders. The racing surface was red brick dust which was dampened down on race nights. Speeds around sixty m.p.h. were achieved on the straights. It all sounded really interesting to me and when one of the riders volunteered to lend me his bike to try it out, I jumped at the chance. The only problem was that he was much shorter than I and didn't want to move the adjustable thigh bar from the ideal position for him. This bar could be moved so that the rider could comfortably lock his right thigh into the machine which provided a pivot point on which to balance the bike in the sliding turns at each end of the track. As I was only going to be trying it out, just for the experience, it didn't seem to be that important.

We all agreed to meet the next morning, Sunday, at the track in town. Billy and I purchased our cigarettes and got back on Billy's little bike and headed back to Ruiru. He didn't say much until we were inside our guardroom with a cigarette and a cup of tea.

"What made you say you wanted to try speedway?" he asked.

"It's something I always wanted to do since I was a kid," I replied, "and this is a good opportunity, so why not?"

"If you go and get yourself banged up out there, it's probably a court-martial offence, and the Old Man will never give you permission," he snapped back.

I let him cool down for a few seconds before I said, "Look, Billy, I won't take any chances, okay? I'm not out to win any races; I just want to cruise around the track to get a feel for it. That's all. It's not going to cost anything, and it'll be a bit of fun!" I waited a while for his answer, but nothing came. I asked, "So are we on for tomorrow morning? Will you give me a lift to the track?"

He gave me a really serious look and then said, grudgingly, "Well, okay then, but if anyone finds out about this, I had no idea what you were going to do. You'll be on your own!"

After morning coffee and a couple of cigarettes, the next day we set off for Nairobi on Billy's bike. We were the first to arrive and had to wait at the gate for a few minutes for someone to let us into the "stadium." It was the first practice of the year, and the speedway bikes had been kept locked up in the pits during the off season. The owners soon had them out in the open, brushing off the spiders and webs that had accumulated. Soon the crackle of open exhausts filled the air along with the smell of burning fuel and oil and a couple of them took to the track. Nobody was out to race it seemed, they were just getting the machines tuned. One rider found that his rear wheel was softer than the front and couldn't be bothered to take the bike back to the pits for air. To balance things up he just let some air out of the front tire. I made sure that wasn't the bike I was going to ride. Apart from the occasional spin on Billy's bike, I had never ridden a motor cycle but I felt it would be an advantage to have both wheels at the correct tire pressure.

The accepted standard for riding speedway was for the rider to tuck his right thigh behind the thigh bar, and, when coming to the corner, put his left foot forward on the ground and slide the back wheel round in a skid. The left boot was protected with a steel cap. In the early days of the sport, riders would drag the left foot behind, instead of half standing on it. This allowed the bike to get closer to the ground in the turns but also made it much more difficult to stay on the track. One such rider, rode on the Nairobi track. He was a Canadian born, engine driver for East African Railways. Instead of having a steel cap on his left boot he had a steel knee cap on his left leg. Trailing his boot behind, he would get the bike down low enough in the turns that he could ride on his knee. If he could stay on the bike he could win a race, but, more often than not, he would end up in the safety fence. It was always a spectacular pileup and all the other riders knew that it was wise to stay on the inside of him in a corner.

Billy and I mixed in with the other riders, listening in to the "track talk" and general gossip, and at last, I got my chance to ride a genuine speedway machine. The others had made it look so easy that I wasn't too nervous. I should have been! To start the engine, I had to sit on the bike with the clutch lever pulled in while someone else pushed me. When I thought we were going fast enough, I had to let go the clutch and open the throttle slightly. That would start the engine, and as it was always in gear, the bike would pull smoothly away from the start line. That was the theory; the facts were totally different! When I released the clutch, the engine caught with an ear-shattering roar, and the bike reared up on its back wheel with me hanging on for dear life, trying to force the front wheel down to hit the ground. Slithering and sliding all over the track, I finally gathered enough wits to back off the throttle and cut the engine. The owner of the bike came running over, thankful that I was still in an upright position and had not mangled his machine.

A cigarette helped calm my nerves after that first attempt, and I was ready to try again. This time when I released the clutch I was leaning forward, putting most of my weight on the front wheel. I was very gentle with the twist-grip throttle and gently eased around the track. Wisely, the other riders had decided to give me the track to myself. I think they just wanted to watch and not take a chance on missing any other antics I might try! But they were out of luck. I only had to tweak that throttle to be reminded of the raw power of the engine, and I couldn't take a chance on being hauled back to camp in an ambulance. I rode around the track for a couple of laps like a little old lady, and pulled in and gave the bike back to the owner.

Speaking to the group I said, "Thanks, chaps, that was really something, but it's not for me. You guys must either have a death wish or some enormous balls!" They all had a good laugh, but I was serious.

On the way out of the stadium I turned to Billy and said, "Well, I told you I wouldn't get hurt, and I can at least say that I have ridden a speedway bike."

"That's true, I suppose," he replied, "although that first try, I thought the bike was going to ride you!" We were still chuckling at the memory of that spectacle when we rode off on his CZ Jawa, back to Ruiru.

The turn-off from the main road to our camp was a hard gravel track with a small bump down from the black top surface of the highway. It was something Billy was always cautious about negotiating, especially with a pillion passenger. His mind must have been wandering and we were going much too fast for safety when we made the right angle turn onto the gravel track. The bump threw us completely off balance and me off the pillion seat. The bike continued along the track in a near perfect speedway-style skid with Billy still hanging onto the handlebars and riding on his left foot as he had seen that morning at the track. When it came to a stop in the long grass at the side of the track, Billy just stood up and waved back at me with a big silly grin all over his face. "Y'see, Don, " he called, "that's the way to do it!"

"You stupid bugger," I shouted back, "I got away with riding a speedway bike today without getting hurt, and look at me now!" I held my hands up, showing my new gravel rash and pointed at my legs where blood was running down my shins. He hadn't got a scratch on him, and I couldn't help teasing him, making him feel guilty, saying that he had dumped me off the bike deliberately.

Once we were back home and had cleaned up we couldn't help laughing at ourselves and at the irony of the situation.

My injuries had just about healed up when we paid a visit to the Red Lion pub down the road. At that time I could still play piano, in a very amateur fashion, but it was good enough to amuse the patrons of the pub. These were coffee farmers, pineapple growers, and the like from the surrounding countryside. This was their only entertainment for many miles around and they made the most of it. They always made a fuss of us, being servicemen and we enjoyed their company and the free drinks that they pressed on us! They had to be tough and rough to exist in that environment and we had a lot in common. There were quite a few evenings that I barely remembered going back to camp.

On this particular evening, one of the patrons asked if Billy and I knew how to ride horses. Neither of us did so he invited us to visit him at his "ranch," where he would teach us. It would be a new experience. He wasn't actually going to teach us himself, he said, but he had two teenage daughters who would. This was getting to be even more interesting by the minute!

But our expectations went down a couple of notches when he added, "I don't advise you to try anything funny with the girls, though. I've taught them to be as tough and as mean as me, if needed, and I ride wild rhinos for a living!"

"You do what?" I asked.

He laughed at my expression and explained, "I don't really ride rhinos for a living. I just do that for fun. My business is catching wild game for zoos all over the world. My 'ranch' property is divided up into paddocks with tall hedges and fences around each one. When I bring the animals home, they stay in the paddocks until shipment is arranged. My hunting team consists of half a dozen Africans on horseback and another six who work on foot. We take two five-ton trucks with us to carry the cages and other equipment. I lead the team of African riders, and we have our own method of catching wild game. One of my favorites is the rhino. We know a specific area way out in the bush where we can pretty much guarantee that we will find one when we need to.

The boys on foot take a long, heavy net and string it up between trees at the end of the open area that we know. It stretches out over twenty feet, and that is my target. Once the net is in position, I lead the hunting team back around the side of the open area to the end opposite the net. This is about a mile and a half away. Spaced out across the grassy area, we then start walking the horses towards the net. Being up high on the horses' backs, we can see any animals that might be ahead of us. As long as the wind is in our faces, we can get quite close to a rhino without him knowing we are there. Rhinos have very poor eyesight but make up for it with their sense of smell and hearing. Anyway, to cut a long story short, when we spot one that looks like a keeper, we start the chase. By the time he gets within a couple of hundred yards of the net with a gang of horsemen chasing him, he is normally pretty tired but angry. It is then that he might decide to turn and fight, so to distract him and keep him on course, I ride alongside him and jump on his back. That totally pisses him off, and in a blind rage he heads straight for the net, while I throw myself off sideways before he gets there. As soon as he is tangled up safely in the net and sedated, we man-handle him onto a slide and winch him up into the cage on the truck. I pick myself up, and we all go home, and a good day's work is done!"

I still had a hard time believing the story, but when I looked around, enquiringly, at the other listeners, they nodded confirmation, and I wasn't about to call anyone there a liar.

Billy and I decided to take up the offer of horse riding lessons the following Saturday. Greg, the rhino rider, was out on a hunt, but the two girls, Maisie and Dot, had been told we were coming and were waiting for us. Remembering their father's warning, we were both on our best behavior. After introductions had been made, we walked to the stables where the girls saddled up their horses and one each for us. Mine was called Dancer; he had a silly habit of taking a sideways step every so often which was a bit unsettling. Once we were all mounted, the girls led the way out of the property and onto the gravel road which ended at our Kahawa radio site, about two miles away. Both sides of the road were fenced with wire strung between posts every ten feet or so. The girls told us how to walk the horses and how to move with them. I couldn't help feeling I was a mile high, on the back of that horse, but it didn't seem to bother Billy.

We turned round at the entrance to the Kahawa site and waved to our colleagues on duty there. We didn't stop because I was on first shift, from four until midnight, and it was already past lunchtime. On the way back to the ranch the girls decided we should learn how to trot. This should speed up the trip home, so I wouldn't be late for duty. I found the trotting maneuver to be a lot harder than it looked, when done properly, and Dancer's occasional sideways step didn't make it any easier. By the time we arrived at the stables I was truly feeling "all shook up." We thanked the girls, politely shook hands with them, and left on Billy's motorbike.

After a quiet first shift, that night, I handed over to Billy for the second shift, at midnight. He was on duty then until eight in the morning, so we would have breakfast together before he slept for a few hours. I was sitting at the table in the dining/sitting/living room, reading a book and enjoying a cigarette and a mug of coffee when he woke up and joined me. Right away he started talking about the horse-riding "date." He was much more excited about it than I was, but I went along with his enthusiasm. He said that he would like to go again after we had lunch, and as I had nothing better to offer, I agreed.

We propped the bike up by the front door of the ranch and rang the bell. Greg's wife answered and invited us to go in. She told us that the girls had gone out to visit a friend but had left instructions, should we want to go for a ride, for the stable hands to saddle the same horses we had ridden the day before. They were sure we could handle them on our own without their help. That was when I should have listened to that voice in my head, saying, *Are you kidding me?* We thanked the lady and went round to the stables where the boys had already saddled the horses. They were fidgeting as they waited for us, eager for some exercise.

With the stable boys holding the horses we climbed on board and then gently persuaded them to start walking towards the road and headed towards Kahawa. The horses knew where we were heading; it was their usual exercise route, apparently. The only difference this time was that their riders were completely inexperienced and were not ready for anything more than a quiet stroll in the country. This wasn't what the horses had in their tiny, little minds, however, and after a few yards, with Billy's horse in the lead, we were off and running flat out.

Yelling, "Whoa! Whoa! You f****** thing, Whoa!" I was thrown forward onto Dancer's neck, which I gripped as hard as I could. I had a fleeting glimpse of Billy up ahead, sitting up in the saddle and looking to be almost in control of the situation before I turned my head and buried it in the horse's mane and held onto his neck for dear life. All I could remember of that ride to Kahawa was seeing fence posts flashing by, like ticking off the seconds of the remainder of my life. That and a strong desire never to have to sit down again. Just when I thought I couldn't possibly hang on any longer, we came to a stop outside the Kahawa camp gate. The on-duty dog handler there opened the gate and let us in. After making sure that the gate was closed properly, Billy and I dismounted. At least, Billy dismounted. I, on the other hand, half slid, half fell off the panting beast, ending up on my knees in the dirt.

"Hey, Don," called Billy, "That was pretty wild wasn't it? What were you trying to do, beat me in a race? I'd have given you a head start if I'd known."

"You silly sod," I gasped. "I wasn't trying to race; I was trying to hold on while that f****** animal did its best to kill me. If that's horse riding for you, I'd rather walk."

He laughed and helped me to my feet, and we both went inside the guardroom for tea and cigarettes. The horses we left to look after themselves; they couldn't go anywhere with the gate closed. My behind was so painful that I drank the mug of tea standing up. It felt good to be back on "terra firma," especially after I had never expected to enjoy that pleasure again.

We stayed there for almost an hour, giving both ourselves and the horses time to cool off and ease aching muscles and bones. I really didn't relish the idea of riding back to the ranch but Billy assured me that the horses would be tired out by then and he was sure that they would behave themselves on the way home. I was too tired and sore to protest too strongly and with our colleagues' help, I once more found myself sitting on top of that pea-brained lump of horseflesh. It seemed to be quiet now that it had stopped gasping for air and I was beginning to think that Billy was right; maybe it was as tired as I was. I should have known better.

As soon as the gate was opened, off we raced again with Billy leading the way, obviously having too much fun, while I dropped into my previous position, hanging onto Dancer's neck, yelling obscenities at the top of my voice. This time I had the opportunity to watch the fence posts on the other side of the road, flashing by. I had no idea that a horse could run so fast, so far and for so long.

Dancer was beginning to slow down when we reached the ranch and he stopped when one of the stable boys put up his hands to hold his head. At last I was able to hit the ground again and I almost kissed it to celebrate the fact that, as far as I was concerned, this and any other horse-riding session was over. Gradually I became aware that Billy and his horse were not present and I looked up from my kneeling position to see the stable boys laughing and pointing over towards the paddocks. I staggered to my feet, just in time to see Billy's horse jump over a stream which ran through the property and then over a final fence, clearing it by inches, before trotting back to the stables with Billy still in a riding position with a big grin on his face.

"That was great!" he exclaimed, as he stepped down from the saddle, "I really didn't think they had it in them, to run all the way home. But I suppose that's what they do with the girls."

Some people have an affinity for horse-riding I suppose; I just wasn't one of them! "Can you honestly say that your behind isn't painful after that arse-pounding I just took?" I asked.

"Well, yes, it does hurt a bit," he said, "but nothing to write home about!"

Meanwhile, blood had soaked through the seat of my pants, where my rear end had been skinned!

We must have looked like some kind of circus act, riding back to Ruiru on Billy's little motorbike. Two hefty, well-over-six-foot men taking it in turns to stand up on the foot rests to take the weight off our backsides, as we wobbled our way home along the gravel road. It was two weeks before I could enjoy a meal sitting at the table and, even today, I still can't sleep on my back.

As far as I'm concerned, horses are beautiful creatures and their pictures look great on calenders. But that's as close as I want to get!

Shooting practice was a favorite pastime of mine. The sergeant in the armory at Eastleigh was very understanding and helpful and before we left for a month's tour at Ruiru, we always paid him a visit and loaded up with ammunition for both the sten guns and the revolvers. We also found that in a pinch, a sten gun round, 9 mm, when wrapped with a thin piece of paper, would fit in a .38 revolver. This practice was frowned upon by the sergeant, as it could, and did, on several occasions, severely damage the weapon. To prevent us doing this, he would always supply us with extra rounds for the pistols.

My co-handlers on one particular tour were Billy and another corporal named Doug. Doug was a Londoner and a bit of a blowhard. He had always done everything anyone else had done, only better, and when it came to shooting, to hear him you would think he taught Annie Oakley how to shoot!

One day around noon, we decided to fire a few rounds at our usual target, a house brick at fifteen paces. We all had custom-built leather holsters, and of course we had to emulate the cowboys with a quick-draw action.

With the guardroom situated close to the property entrance, the target was placed in the area across the main path with the aerial field in the background. Outside the gate, about one hundred yards away next to the road, was a small native hut used by the houseboy who we employed to sweep up, do laundry, and cook for us. After a few shots, Doug decided he was going to visit the hut, as he hadn't seen inside it before, and the houseboy was working inside the guardroom. Already Billy and I were tired of listening to his bragging about how good a shot he was, and I couldn't resist an opportunity to shut him up.

When he entered the hut, I stood in the center of the road, by the gate, and fired a shot from my revolver well over the top of the hut. Doug flew out of the hut entrance almost falling over himself, yelling, "What the f*** is going on?"

"Come on, Doug," I called out, "Let's see how good a shot you are now. I'll give you one minute to put one between my legs."

"And if I don't?" he asked.

"Then I'm going to put one between yours, and I'm not as good a shot as you, so you keep saying."

"You crazy bastard!" he cried and started running towards me.

As he got closer, I fired off a couple of shots on either side of him well off to the side of the road. By the time he made it to the gate he was a nervous wreck, and it took a couple of cigarettes, one for him and one for me, and a strong cup of tea to calm him down again.

Eventually he stopped shaking, and Billy said to him, "Now maybe we won't hear any more bragging from you, because if we do, the story of what happened here today will be all over Eastleigh when we get back there."

It worked, because we hardly heard a word from Doug the rest of that tour, and after we returned to base, he was assigned to another team.

But that wasn't entirely the end of the incident. We were finishing off destroying the house brick, and a thought struck me about shooting over the top of the hut, when Billy said, "I wonder where that first slug ended up. At that angle it could have gone a long way. What do you think?"

"I have no idea, probably just dropped in a field somewhere," I replied but I was thinking to myself—Ruiru village is in that direction, surely it couldn't have gone that far, could it? It might have killed some innocent local there, and I began to panic, quietly. A couple of minutes later we saw a Land Rover approaching from the right side of the ariel field. *Maybe this is someone coming to arrest me,* I thought, and suddenly a plan took form in my mind. I loaded a fresh clip in my sten gun and made sure my pistol was fully loaded. I propped the sten up behind the guardroom door with the idea that, rather than go to a civilian jail, I would make a run for it in the oncoming Land Rover. I would drive as far and as fast as I could up the main road going north.

This would take me to the Northern Frontier and the Ethiopian wastelands where I could surely hide out until the dust settled.

When the vehicle arrived, the driver introduced himself and his dog, a beautiful white German Shepherd, who sat next to him on the passenger seat.

"Good afternoon, men," he said, "My name is Vince Grady, and this is my pal, Flash. We have a small pineapple plantation a mile or so away, and we thought we heard some gunfire coming from this direction. With Kenyatta's boys getting to be a bit bolder, lately, I thought we should come and have a look, in case we could help." There were several rifles and a shotgun in the back of his Land Rover, and he was wearing a pistol on his belt.

Billy introduced us in return and replied, "We were just getting in a little practice shooting, Vince. Sorry to have disturbed you, but we do appreciate you taking the trouble to check us out. Would you like a cup of tea?"

"No thanks, Billy, I think we had better get back to work, but, say, do you fellows like pineapples? I'll drop a few off for you the next time my driver takes the truck into the village, okay?"

"That sounds great, Vince, and thanks again."

I breathed a big sigh of relief as he turned the vehicle round and waved goodbye. I really hadn't wanted to get lost in the Ethiopian desert; from the plane it didn't appear to hold a lot of charm for me. I would be visiting there sooner or later but not this time, and in future I would try to be more careful with which way the gun was pointing when I pulled the trigger.

The following week we had all but forgotten the shooting incident when an old pickup truck pulled up outside the gate and the native driver told us that he had brought pineapples from "Bwana Vince." We had all been out back, cleaning the kennels when he arrived, so Billy told him to just leave them in the kitchen and we went back to work. It seemed to take the driver a little longer than we expected but guessed he was socializing with the houseboy. When he finally drove away, the houseboy came outside and asked us what to do with the fruit.

Expecting maybe a couple, we couldn't believe our eyes when we saw the huge stack of pineapples in the kitchen.

It didn't seem right to throw away good pineapples so we were all giving the problem a lot of thought.

"We could give some away to any passing natives," said Doug, "Put a sign outside the gate—Free Pineapples!"

"And how many do you think that will get rid of?" I asked. "They can pick all they want from the fields they walk by. And half of the locals probably work for Vince, and their brothers work for the coffee plantation next door. D'you want to give them free coffee, too?"

"Well, I tried. Now you come up with something, genius!"

"How about…. now I don't know much about this, but maybe we can use them to make some kind of booze. One thing I learned in chemistry class at school was that yeast works on sugar to produce alcohol, and fruit contains sugar, and wild yeast grows on the skin. All we need are some containers of some kind so we can let it ferment. Any suggestions?" I asked.

I didn't know it then but this was probably the beginning of my lengthy association with making and distributing illegal alcohol.

Billy spoke up after a couple of minutes' thought, "You know, Don, that could be a good idea, if it really makes booze. I'll get one of the cooks I know in the mess hall at Eastleigh to save the empty tomato sauce bottles for us, and then we could siphon the stuff out and sell it for a shilling a bottle. That could make us some extra pocket money!"

"That's fine, Billy," I replied, "but we still need to have something for the fermenting. We either need about twenty buckets or a couple of clean oil drums. Wait a minute, I think I've got it. How about a couple of those old water drums at the back of the radio building? They shouldn't be too rusty. We'll find the cleanest ones and give them a good wash out. They've even got taps fitted for the water, so we won't need to siphon."

The drums were left over from when the site was built, before they drilled the well. All the water had to be trucked in during the early stages of the site construction and the drums were used for emergency storage. So they were reasonably clean and just to make sure, we rinsed them out again before we started chopping up the pineapples and loading them into the drums. We had selected two of the cleanest looking drums and moved them from the radio building to the back of the guardroom. The drums had lids with retaining clips on them, which made for easy loading, and we set them up on leftover bricks so there would be enough clearance to get a sauce bottle under the tap at the bottom of each drum.

Each drum was loaded up to an imaginary two thirds full line with the chopped up fruit and as much of the juice as we could save. Then they were topped up with water and the lids fitted. Although they were for the most part in the shade, behind the guardroom, there was enough heat during the day for the fermentation process to begin within a couple of days. We soon knew that it was working when froth started oozing out around the lids, and the smell of fermenting pineapples filled the air. It wasn't too unpleasant, though, and we learned to ignore it. We had agreed that we wouldn't disturb the drums for at least two weeks; this would give us a week to get rid of the stuff before the end of that particular tour.

Finally the smell started to ease up and the froth stopped escaping from the lids and we were able to draw some of the liquid off into a clean bottle. Nobody wanted to try drinking the stuff so I took a sip of it just to try. It tasted just like pineapple juice and not the least bit alcoholic. Disappointed, we left the drums where they were and told the team relieving us at the end of our month, just to ignore them—it was an experiment that hadn't worked. We would clean it up and get rid of the drums when we came back in two month's time.

After a month at Kahawa and another back at Eastliegh, we had just about forgotten the "experiment" when we were due to return. Billy had gone over to the mess hall to see his cook friend, to see what he could scrounge in the way of extra rations and the cook asked him if he still wanted empty sauce bottles. Billy didn't want to seem ungrateful, so he said he would take all that was available and loaded up two large cartons full, into the transport. On the trip to Ruiru, Billy reminded us about the pineapple juice and the sauce bottles, and we were all keen to see if the stuff would be any better with the extra time.

After we had off loaded our gear and put the dogs in the kennels, the other team loaded up their stuff and set off for Kahawa. We waited until they were well out of sight and then dashed around the building to find the drums exactly as we had left them. With quite a bit of anticipation, I drew off a tin mug full of really thick, cloudy liquid from the tap. It looked terrible and smelled even worse.

"So much for our big money-making scheme," said Billy.

Jerry, who had taken Doug's place on this tour, stated, "Nobody's going to buy that shit!"

"Now, wait a minute, chaps. Maybe we're doing this wrong. All the sediment from the fruit must have settled to the bottom, so perhaps we should be taking a sample from the top."

With that I loosened off the clamps on one of the lids and removed it. Sure enough, the liquid at the top was only slightly cloudy and didn't smell nearly as bad. Gingerly, I took a small drink from the mug and was pleasantly surprised to find that aside from the slight smell, it really wasn't too bad. And it definitely contained some alcohol.

Actually, the smell was nowhere near as bad as that of the local beer. Anyone who has driven behind a ful "pombi" tanker headed for the local beer hall, would know what I mean. Now that's a smell that would gag a buzzard!

"Looks like we're in business, boys," I said. "Let's get busy with filling some bottles. We'll send Joseph off into Ruiru village tomorrow with a sample, to see if he can drum up any business for us." Joseph was the name we had given to our houseboy.

The next morning, Joseph set off for the village on his rusty old bike, a bottle of pineapple booze stuffed in his shirt. And we set to, filling sauce bottles as fast as we could go. We had only got half way through our supply of bottles, before an old truck made its way up to the main gate. Billy was on duty and went to see the visitors. Joseph had found a native shopkeeper who was interested in buying some of our stock and wanted to see our operation. Billy told him he was not allowed on the premises, but we let him have four dozen bottles of our booze, at

D.J. SWEETENHAM

one and a half Kenya shillings per bottle. He was grateful for that and asked when he could come back for more. I told him not to come back for at least two days.

Over the next two days we took it in turns to work on filling the rest of the bottles and Billy had to make arrangements with his cook friend, to get another shipment of empties sent up on the weekly ration wagon. This continued until we had bottled almost 70 gallons of pineapple booze. The rest was waste and we took it out into the ariel field and buried it deep enough to kill the smell. The drums were washed clean and replaced behind the radio building.

The native shop keeper took all that we could sell him but we kept a few bottles back for Joseph as his commission.

None of this, of course, was legal, and it wasn't too long after the last bottle was sold, that we had a visit from a Kenyan police officer. He was a white colonial and a very "understanding" kind of person. Over a cup of tea, in the guardroom he told us that there had been some kind of fight over a bottle of unknown liquor in the local beer hall, and one of his native policemen, Askaris, had been a witness. When the Askari made enquiries, he was told that the bottle came from the R.A.F. radio site, a couple of miles away.

"From here?" I asked. "I don't remember seeing anything like that around here. Surely making booze would have to be quite an operation, wouldn't it, and there's just nowhere around here that sort of thing could be hidden."

"You're absolutely right, Corporal, but that's how it was reported to me, so I'm afraid I have to ask to have a look around so that I can complete my report for the captain."

"Of course, Officer, I'll be happy to give you the grand tour of the entire facility. It'll only take a few minutes. There's not much of it."

As we walked around the small compound, we talked about the dogs and our patrols. He had more contact with the locals than we did and saw a lot more of the terrorists's actions. Some of his stories of how the Kikuyu tribe members were indoctrinated into the Mau-mau were stomach churning, to say the least. It was hard to believe that so-called human beings could behave that way. I showed him the rest of the guardroom and the cells, which we used for sleeping quarters. He didn't get too close to the kennels out back, where the dogs greeted him with snarls, and we made our way to the radio transmitter building. Inside I asked the duty technician to show us the transmitters and explain the function of the operation. There wasn't much to see, and we left to return to the guardroom.

When we had walked a few yards, he turned to look back at the radio building, and said, "I just had a thought, Corporal, There seems to be a space between the fence and the back of the building, and we didn't look there. Would you mind?"

I had a bit of a sinking feeling as I answered, "Not at all, sir; let's go," and we went back to have a look round the back of the building. There wasn't much to see round there. A gravel path led past several transformer boxes, a set of steps leading up to a rear entrance and lined up along the far wall, several water drums. Most of the drums appeared to be rather dusty, but the last two were relatively clean. He turned his head to look at the drums but made no comment as we walked to the end of the building and rounded the corner.

"Well, everything looks okay to me here," he said with a half smile on his face. "I can fill in my report with an easy conscience, knowing that the stuff probably didn't come from here." He emphasized the word "probably" a little, and I knew that he knew!

He went on to explain, "You see, the trouble with this sort of deal is, we really don't have time to spare sorting out bar fights amongst the locals, and Lord knows, we handle enough calls when they've been on the pombi, never mind this unknown brew. But I would really appreciate it if you would keep a lookout for me, in case you come across anything I've missed. I'll stop by in a day or two, to see if you've found out anything." With that parting remark, we said our "Goodbyes," and he got back in his Land Rover and left.

I went back into the guard room where the other two were waiting.

"Well," Jerry asked, "did we get away with it?"

"Not exactly," I replied, breathing a sigh of relief. "He knows, all right. But he's giving us a chance to clean up our act, I think."

"What're you talking about?" said Billy. I then explained how he had seen the two clean drums standing beside the others and that I was sure he had made the connection. I also told him that the police officer would be back in a day or two for another look around and by then all the drums must be dirty. It didn't take too long to correct our mistake. With a few handfuls of dirt thrown over the drums and then rolled around in the dust for a few minutes, they looked just like the others.

When the officer returned two days later, he went straight round the back of the radio building and glanced at the drums. He said nothing until we reached his vehicle and then he said, "Good job, chaps; everything is fine now. But let's just keep this between us, okay?" and off he went. So much for my initial entry into the brewing business. It didn't last long, and split three ways, it didn't make a fortune. But I did save enough to help pay for a week's vacation in Mombasa after we finished that tour and returned to Eastleigh.

I hadn't had a vacation since I joined the R.A.F., except for a couple of 72-hour passes, when I was in England, and I spent those at home with my parents. I'm not saying they weren't enjoyable, but by this time I was almost 20 years old and just a little wild. I was in a great country, and I wanted to see some more of it. I couldn't go away for a week with Billy, as this would have put too much of a strain on the dog patrol schedule, so another chap named Randy, the musical Pat's sidekick, got leave at the same time, and we headed to Mombasa. We actually had two weeks' vacation allowed but it worked out that we didn't have quite enough money for that long.

On the day that our leave started, we took a taxi from Eastleigh into Nairobi to catch the four p.m. train to Mombasa, the port city on the east coast. As we were already on vacation, we left Eastleigh, soon after breakfast and by ten a.m. we were sitting in the New Stanley hotel bar, sinking a few Tuskers. We were both in civilian clothes and didn't look much different from the young farmers sons who called in for a quick drink during the day. Except for the fact that we weren't carrying weapons, whereas just about everyone else had at least one revolver in a holster. We couldn't afford to buy our own guns and our service weapons had to be turned into the armory before we left camp. This alerted the locals as to who we were so, except for the black bar-steward who was taking our orders, we were somewhat ignored. Most of these people were either British or of recent British descent, so they were masters of the art of keeping to themselves. I won't go on too much about that, after all, I was born in England. I just found it hard to accept the upper-crust accent that most of them affected and not for the first time, I developed a strong feeling that I didn't belong there.

For lunch we left the New Stanley and went to a small Indian restaurant where we each had a dish of curry, and a few more beers. Finally it was time to make our way to the railway station. We had plenty of time which was just as well. By now we were both just a little unsteady on our feet and it was a relief to arrive at the station to find the train waiting at the platform. We bought our tickets, climbed aboard and found our sleeping compartment where we crashed for a couple of hours.

At seven p.m. the dinner gong sounded and we woke up, starving. Lunch was long gone and the effects of the beer had worn off. We were ready to party. Having cleaned up and put on clean shirts, we made our way to the dining car and were stunned to find we had walked in on a movie set, or so it appeared. The maitre d' wore a white outfit with a black bow tie, and the passengers were all in their finest. We were accorded many frosty glares as we were shown to our seats. Our dining companions on the other side of the small table, were much older than us and met us with a rather strained politeness. It soon became known that we were dining with a colonel in the Army and his lady, and two R.A.F. police corporals would not have been their first choice for dining companions. Randy and I did our best to exchange small talk with them, but it was obvious they were uncomfortable with us, and except for a few greetings of "How do you do?" and "How are you?" silence pretty much prevailed until the meal was served.

The train had left the station in a cloud of steam and smoke as it made its way from the four-thousand-foot altitude of Nairobi to the sea-level city of Mombasa, when dinner was served.

Before the meal, Randy and I had already had a couple of beers to whet our appetites and we were feeling good, until the waiter brought an empty plate for each person and started bringing in separate bowls of vegetables, a gravy boat and a platter of meat. The colonel and his wife served themselves first of course, passing the various dishes to Randy who helped himself. To make matters worse, the vegetables consisted of fresh green peas and new potatoes. Little, round white potatoes with a touch of mint. I couldn't help laughing as Randy struggled to keep the food on his plate with the swaying of the dining car, but he managed somehow and then it was my turn. I was cramped into the corner and didn't have much room.

I whispered to Randy, "Give us some space, mate. I'll never get this lot on my plate without some elbow room!"

He slid over a little on the bench seat to give me some more room, and I picked up the bowl of peas. Just as I had a large spoonful of peas on its way to my plate, the train driver hit the brakes for some unknown reason and the peas shot off the spoon, across the table, into the colonel's lady's lap.

She threw up her hands and screeched, "You fool!" while the colonel spluttered and turned a brighter shade of pink.

"Oh, f*** it!" I said and picked up the bowl of potatoes and emptied them into the colonel's lap.

Randy was laughing so hard he nearly fell out of the seat, and I joined in. With the other diners looking on in absolute horror, we staggered out of the dining car, holding our sides, gasping with laughter. The first and eventually the last thing we did, when we reached our sleeping compartment, was to order another beer.

The next morning we awoke when the train stopped at a country station. There had been several such stops during the night, but we had missed them. I wasn't feeling too "chipper," as the colonel would have said, when I opened my eyes. Daylight was filtering in around the edges of the window blind as I rolled over and the temperature in the compartment was much higher than the night before. I thought it might be a good idea to open the window to let some fresh air in and groped for the pull cord on the bottom of the blind. I gave it a tug and the string slipped out of my fingers as the blind rolled itself up with a loud rattle, ending in a "bang." Randy and I both were now wide awake. Peering out the window, which was still closed, I couldn't believe my eyes! Right in front of my face was a pair of the biggest brown breasts I had ever seen or dreamed about. My eyes and mouth were wide open as I stared at this sight.

Randy said "What's going on, Don? You look like you've seen a ghost!"

"Take a look at this," I gasped, and moved out of the way.

At that moment the owner of the enormous boobs, stepped back from the edge of the platform where she had been standing, and the entire figure was revealed. She must have been nine and a half months pregnant, about four hundred pounds, and six feet tall. And all she was wearing was a grass skirt which disappeared under her huge belly. Her hair was plastered to her skull with mud, and her snaggle-toothed grin did nothing to improve her looks, when she noticed us looking at her. With one eye on us and the other looking off to the side somewhere, she wasn't a sight that two queasy, beer-filled stomachs could handle, and while I opened the window and emptied out onto the platform, Randy made a dash for the toilet in the corridor. Fortunately, the train started to pull away from the station just then, and we left behind a very upset local lady!

The train pulled into Mombasa station at nine a.m., and we took a taxi to the Y.M.C.A. that had been recommended to us by several of our colleagues back at Eastleigh. It was a compound surrounded by a high brick wall with a large, native guard on duty at the gate. Inside, at an office, we checked in and were shown to one of the rooms which were all at ground level and in a row along one side of the compound. A rose garden occupied the rest of the walled area, on which hung a rose-covered trellis. The rooms were all very clean and the bathroom facilities were adequate. Each room had its own houseboy who, for a few shillings extra would take care of any laundry and would bring a wake-up mug of hot, strong coffee each morning. The climate here was very different from that in the Nairobi area; much hotter and a lot more humid and we soon changed out of long pants, shirts and shoes, into sleeveless shirts, shorts and the local flip-flop leather sandals that were for sale at roadside vendors.

Apart from the many bars, there wasn't much to interest us in Mombasa. Shopping wasn't high on our list of things to do and we spent most of our time just strolling from one bar to the next, enjoying meeting new people, mostly merchant seamen from the docks and trading stories with them. Most of our days, which didn't start much before noon and didn't end until early the following morning, were spent that way. We did manage to fit one excursion into our crowded schedule when we joined in a tour with four other tourists we met in one of the bars. We were going to a place called Malindi, the home of the Giriama tribe, about eighty miles north of Mombasa.

We arose early that morning with the usual mug of coffee. After a quick egg and bacon breakfast, we met up with our new friends at their hotel to catch the bus. It was a ramshackle, old truck with wooden bench seats in the back, with a canopy for protection from the sun. Painted all the colors of the rainbow, in typical native style, it looked more like a carnival float than a tour bus.

After finally agreeing on a price with the driver, we set off on what was to be a truly uncomfortable ride along eighty plus miles of a winding, bump-filled sandy track. There were no such things as seatbelts in those days and we spent as much time off the seats as we did on them, all the while trying to hold onto anything we could find that appeared to be solid and attached to the vehicle. Several times we had to get out and push, when the bus bogged down in loose sand. The whole trip took almost six hours and the scenery didn't change much the whole way. An occasional glimpse of the Indian ocean and mile after mile of dense tropical foliage. One break in the trip was when we came upon the remains of an ancient ruined city, which was supposed to have been built by Phoenician explorers, centuries before.

Finally we arrived at the Malindi Beach Hotel, the most civilized thing we had seen all day. This was a truly first class place and Randy and I both felt a little uncomfortable. Once we located the bar however, it didn't take long for us to feel a lot better. Dinner that evening, was also a new experience. There was a set menu so the only option was to take it or leave it! Naturally, wanting to get our money's worth, we took it, whatever it was. The first dish was artichoke with some kind of fancy sauce, and Randy and I were completely lost when it was served. It was definitely not something that we would have encountered in the mess hall at R.A.F. Eastleigh, and we had no idea what to do with it. It looked like some kind of alien cactus that had been in an accident.

Randy and I were sharing a table with two of our traveling companions and, not wishing to seem too ignorant, I whispered to Randy, "What the hell do we do with this?"

"I suppose we just chop it up and eat it," he whispered back and picked up his knife and fork to attack it. Seeing this, one of the other members of our party, sitting at a nearby table, got up and came over to ours.

"How's it going, chaps? Everything okay?"

"Well, not exactly," I replied. "Just how do we eat this?"

He bent down, smiled, and said quietly, "Don't see much of this stuff in the R.A.F. mess, right? Well, don't worry, just follow the rest of us. All you do is to pull off the leaves and dip the thick end in the sauce. Then you suck that end to get the soft stuff out and put the empty leaf on the side of the plate."

We finally got the hang of it, but it did seem to be a lot of trouble to get something to eat. The huge steak which followed more than made up for it, though!

After dinner we were scheduled to visit a Mosque in the jungle a couple of miles north of the hotel. The Muslim faith was very strong in this region and two of our companions were keen to witness a prayer ceremony. We piled into our bus and once more suffered the torment for another couple of miles. We had each taken a beach chair from the hotel, as we didn't know what kind of seating arrangements there might be. The bus stopped several hundred yards away from the mosque, and we had to walk the rest of the way, carrying our chairs. The Imam's call to prayer was still blasting out from the tower as we approached a large open area, surrounding the mosque, almost filled with the faithful. They were all dressed in the traditional Arab style, long, white "night shirts" and various forms of turban-style head coverings. None of them looked particularly happy to see us, but one of them directed us to a vacant area, on the edge of the congregation, and we set up our seats and sat quietly, waiting for the service to begin. As infidels, of course we were not allowed to go inside the building. Randy and I sat closest to the edge of the clearing. Suddenly there was a brief silence from the tower, and then the praying began. Everybody in the clearing got down on their hands and knees, except us tourists, and began bowing their heads, in unison, to the sand.

Sitting up on our chairs, unable to understand a word of what was going on and looking out over a sea of Muslim rear ends pointed skywards, we soon began to feel uncomfortable. The occasional poisonous glances directed our way when the faithful raised their heads, didn't help to ease that feeling.

At last Randy couldn't take any more, and he whispered to me, "The next time they go down on the sand I'm out of here, back to the bus. They wouldn't break off their prayers to chase us, but if we stay to the end, we may be in trouble. And there's too damn many of them for us to put up much of a fight, Okay?"

"I was about to suggest the same thing," I said and passed the message along. We didn't have long to wait. After a short "sermon" or whatever, the praying started again.

While the faithful were busy with their heads in the sand, the infidels picked up their chairs and quietly slid off into the night. Once clear of the prayer ground we ran the rest of the way back to the bus, which the driver had turned round in anticipation of this happening. He had taken tourists here before.

Closing time had not been called when we arrived back at the hotel bar and we all sat around discussing the evening's entertainment as several rounds of cold beer disappeared down parched throats. No one was feeling much pain when one of the others said he had been told by the maitre d' in the dining room earlier, that the Giriama tribe were holding their fertility dances in a nearby village tomorrow. It was within walking distance of the hotel and was a sight not often witnessed by white people. Was anyone interested?

It would mean spending a second night at the hotel and there was a limit to what we could afford. But we felt the experience would be worth it and if we were very careful we might just make it. So we all agreed to meet up the next day at lunch for our walk to the Giriama village and then made our way to the front desk to extend our stay, before heading off to bed.

The following morning after breakfast, Randy and I were at a loose end and with nothing better to do we decided to go for a walk along the beach. There were several other hotel guests enjoying the fresh morning air and golden sand and we started off heading south, facing into the wind. A quarter of a mile or so, along the beach, we noticed an underwater shelf of coral which appeared to stretch from the beach straight out to sea. It was only about a foot or so underwater with many deeper pools. It looked pretty inviting to me, but not to Randy.

"I'm going to take a walk out there, Randy. Want to come along?" I asked.

"No thanks, pal. I'll stay here with my feet dry," he replied.

"Okay, then," I said, "I just want to see how far it goes out."

"Just don't fall in the deep end and drown your stupid self; you know I can't swim, so you're on your own," he called.

The tide was going out as we were speaking and as I carefully picked my way over the coral, getting further and further from the beach, the reef beneath my flip-flops was becoming more visible. By the time I reached a distance of fifty yards most of the water had receded from the reef and I had just decided to return to the beach. As I turned to head back, my foot slipped down into one of the deeper pools. Looking down, I could see a wriggling mass of tiny tentacles covering my bare foot, which immediately made me think and shout, "Spiders!"

I jerked my foot out of the pool and took off, flip-flops flapping, spray flying, arms waving wildly and yelling, "Oh, shit, oh, shit, spiders!" at the top of my voice. I could hardly see where I was going, I was in a flat panic, but I headed for the sound of Randy's laughter. I hit the beach, literally in a heap, by which time several of the other hotel guests had come running to see what all the fuss was about.

I finally got my breath back and told them of all the spiders hiding in the deeper pools on the reef. They had never heard of sea spiders before. Neither had I and when one of them went to have a look on the reef he found that the creatures were in fact, baby squid or octopi. They were perfectly harmless, and he carried back a couple to show us all.

I had always had a dread of spiders and my imagination was playing tricks on me.

Randy was practically choking, he was laughing so hard. "I've never seen anything like it!" he burst out. "When you were on the way out, from here it looked like you were walking on water, but on the way back, it was more like low flying!"

After a big sigh of relief on my part, and a lot of laughter and teasing on the part of the spectators, we all walked back up the beach to the hotel. A few beers later, my nerves had settled down enough to be able to deal with lunch and then it was time for those who wanted to go to the village to assemble by the front entrance where we were met by our native guide.

Shortly after leaving the hotel, we followed the guide down a narrow sandy path in pairs, which led into ever thickening jungle. It was steaming hot under the canopy of trees, which were thick enough to preclude any movement of air. We were all soon perspiring freely and the guide slowed the pace a little after frequent requests.

Eventually the path opened onto a large clearing surrounded by thatched huts and we stepped clear of the trees to the sound of beating drums and high-pitched shrieks and yells. The background chanting was almost hypnotic and the smell was devastating! Dancers whirled and stomped, rushing together and apart, black shiny bodies glistening in the sunlight filtering through the branches above. And all of them dressed in their finest short grass skirts and nothing else! This tribe had yet to accept western ways in their dress code.

It soon became evident, as we approached the dance area that there was something peculiar about the female participants. Each had one, beautiful perfectly shaped up-tilted breast and one which hung down like a leather belt, almost to the waist. The contrast was shocking, and when I asked the guide to explain he said that what I found shocking was what they found attractive. The women spent many hours massaging the perfect breast with coconut oil and animal fat while the other had weights tied to it to achieve the long, empty look. That also explained another mystery—the terrible smell. The guide said that the main reason their bodies glistened was not the sweat but because they rubbed raw animal fat over themselves to make their bodies shine for the dance. This made them more attractive to a potential suitor, which was the object of the dance.

As we walked around the dancing, the smell seemed to be getting worse and we noticed that some of the dancers were starting to get closer to us. I was a little wary at first, but they were just curious. Many had never seen a white person before, particularly the younger ones and they were just as interested in us as we were in them. But that stink of rancid animal grease was finally too much for the ladies in our group, and we had to leave. And not too soon, as far as I was concerned. I was almost ready to part company with my lunch and the last half dozen beers, when we left. We didn't get to see any of the more intimate details of the dance, but that was just fine with me.

We returned to the hotel, along the narrow path and it was a big relief to get out of the overhanging vegetation, into the open air. Sea breezes never felt or tasted so good. Like a long drink from a mountain stream after nothing but swamp water. It would take a long time to get that smell out of our systems.

After settling up with the guide, we headed for the showers and a change of clothes, by which time a cold beer was calling. We beat the rest of the "dance party" to the bar, but not by much. Of course the main topic of the conversation was the smell we had experienced that afternoon until we all agreed that just talking about it was bringing back vivid memories, which, if we weren't careful, would ruin dinner.

Changing the subject, Randy, our four traveling companions and myself, started planning our trip back to Mombasa. We had previously told the bus driver to pick us up no later than 9 a.m. as some of the others wanted to take a closer look at the Phoenician ruins on the way. It made no difference to me, in fact I was looking forward to taking a last swim in the Indian ocean, while they practiced archeology.

9 a.m. came and went the following morning, and still no bus. Sitting around complaining, at the front of the hotel was doing no good

so we left our luggage in charge of the front desk clerk and told him to call us from the bar when the driver arrived. Lunch time came, but the bus still hadn't, and when it finally arrived around two p.m. the driver received a really frosty welcome.

Nobody was looking forward to another six hours in that old bone-shaker, but we had no other option. Apart from the usual hair-raising near misses and being stuck in sand several times, the ride to the ruins was largely uneventful. I couldn't be bothered to go for a swim, so I settled for a short nap while Randy and the others examined old rocks. They didn't stay too long, as they were also anxious to get back to Mombasa and to start repairing fractured backsides. The rest of the journey was little different from the first part, and by the time the light started to fade, when things could have been really interesting, we were almost home.

Arriving at the hotel our friends insisted that we stay and have dinner with them. Being as "broke" as we were by this time, we couldn't afford to turn down a free meal, so we gladly accepted the invitation.

Everyone was having a great time, and the drinks were flowing freely. We apologized for not being able to buy a round and were told that the evening was all on them, and they would hear no more about it. They were interested in hearing about our experiences in the Air Force and the evening was full of memories and soon over. Randy finally noticed the time and said we would have to get going. We said our farewells, thanked our hosts, picked up our bags at the desk and started the walk back to the Y.M.C.A. We didn't even have taxi fare.

Expecting to find the guard at the gate, we were a little surprised to find no one there. A small framed notice on the wall by the gate, informed us that curfew was 11 p.m. and the gate was locked after that. As it was closer to midnight by this time, there seemed to be no chance of getting in.

Sitting on the sidewalk with our backs literally, against the wall, we finally came up with the obvious answer to the problem. We would climb over. It was only about eight feet high, and in our slightly inebriated state, that didn't seem to be much of an obstacle. Selecting a spot on the wall farthest from the street light and as far away from the rooms inside the compound as possible, we made our move. Fortunately there was no barbed wire or broken glass on top of the wall and Randy had no problem reaching the top with a boost from me. I passed up the bags which he dropped in the yard on the other side and then reached down a hand to help pull me up beside him. We were actually quite enjoying this until I felt something prick me on the leg I had hanging down the inside.

"What was that? Something just stung my leg!" I reached my hand down to feel my leg and lost my balance on the wall. Randy made a grab for me as I started to fall, and we both ended up in a pile of rose bushes, trellis included, at the bottom of the wall, but inside the compound. With all the noise we must have made and the laughter, it was a wonder that no one heard us, but we were able to pick ourselves up, collect our belongings and slink into our room, without disturbing anybody. Once inside with the light on, I removed the rose thorn from my leg, which had been the cause of the incident.

The next morning, when he brought the coffee, the room boy asked us if we had heard anything the previous night. I asked why and he said that someone had broken into the compound during the night and destroyed the rose garden, but nothing seemed to be missing. He said the police would be round later but didn't expect them to catch the culprits. Once he left, we hurried to get ready to catch the train back to Nairobi. Looking at my face in the mirror while I shaved, I couldn't believe that the room boy hadn't known who the culprits were. We were both covered in scratches, and it looked like we'd been in a cat fight.

We made it to the station, just before the train left, having run the last half mile. About all we had left was our round trip tickets and a few shillings for bus fare to Eastleigh. The long day's train ride was spent catching up on lost sleep and by the time we arrived at Nairobi, we both felt human again.

The first thing I did, when we reached home, was to go and see my pal, Rex, in the dog compound, and when I saw the poor old fellow, I cried. He was in a shocking state, and when I sounded off at the senior corporal in charge, I was told that Rex had refused to eat or exercise while I was away. He had lost so much weight and he was so weak that he could hardly stand. And at more than thirteen years old there wasn't much we could do with him. It was time to say goodbye to one of the most faithful and bravest friends I ever had. Billy drove us, in the section's truck, to the vet's office in Nairobi, Rex laying with his head in my lap. He was so far gone, I don't think he even knew who I was, and tears streamed down my face the whole way. I carried him into the examination room, laid him on the table, kissed his muzzle, and said a last goodbye.

We were silent all the way back to Eastleigh; all I could think of was Rex and all the good times we had enjoyed together and of the many times he had saved me from getting into trouble. If I had only not gone on that trip to Mombasa, I kept telling myself, perhaps he would still be alive now. But I also knew that time had caught up with him and the long patrols at night were starting to wear on him, even before I went away. I still felt very guilty about leaving him, while I was away enjoying myself and even to this day, I still regret going.

The week after Rex was put to sleep, another tragedy happened. Jerry Skillert, one of the other dog handlers, accidently killed himself playing Russian Roulette at the Kahawa site. It was a stupid game but we had all played it at some time or other when we were bored, at the radio sites. It almost seemed that if there was not some kind of action or excitement going on we had to make some. Looking back now it's hard to imagine that normal, intelligent well-trained young men could act so irresponsibly. But Jerry was the one who paid the ultimate price for it.

It so happened that Jerry's dog was also named Rex, and after the funeral at which I was a pallbearer, the corporal in charge of the dog section asked me if I thought I could work with Jerry's Rex. He was a much younger and more active dog than I was used to, but he was smart and could be trained to my ways fairly quickly. It wouldn't be for too long; I had just extended my National Service commitment for an extra year.

Not long after we settled back into our daily routines, a rash of arson broke out in Nairobi. A new ordinance was passed that any native carrying inflammable material was subject to arrest and questioning. This seemed a bit absurd as most of the natives in town, used kerosene for cooking but the authorities thought something had to be done to ease the fears of the colonists.

On dog patrol one night, I had just checked in at the guardroom by the Main Gate. It was getting close to midnight, the end of my shift and I was making my way towards the dog compound to put Rex to bed for the rest of the night. It had been an uneventful patrol for a change, when I noticed a small, native man walking a little unsteadily on the side of the road. He appeared to be clutching something in his arms. I called out to him, "Simama!" telling him to halt. He turned and looked my way but continued walking away from me. Again I shouted "Simama!" and drew my pistol. This time he stopped, and as I approached, I recognized him as one of the helpers in the mess.

"So what are you doing out after curfew, and what are you carrying?" I demanded.

"Just walking, and I got some paraffin," he replied.

"You'd better give that to me before someone else catches you. You know the new law, you're not allowed to have that, particularly at night." Thinking that I knew the man and that as a mess worker he should be okay, I relaxed a little and holstered my gun.

I reached out my hand for the bottle, and without warning he dropped to the ground at the side of the concrete-lined storm ditch which bordered the road. The bottle shattered, and he leapt up clutching the bottle neck and crouched in an attack posture. Rex was straining at the lead to get at him, but I couldn't risk having Rex injured, so I drew my gun and aimed at his head. He quickly dropped the bottle neck and raised his hands. Now he was under arrest, and I started to march him to the Askari post, on camp.

I told him where we were going and immediately he turned to attack me with his fists raised. This time I let Rex have his way. He clamped down on the man's arm and had him on the ground in a flash. A few seconds of snarling, flashing teeth and the man was crying out to stop. I called Rex to heel, although I knew he was enjoying himself, and the man staggered to his feet. Once again we continued our walk to the

Askari post, the man staggering along in front, Rex a close second, and me bringing up the rear, holding tight to Rex's lead. Rex was looking to finish what he had started and came close to doing just that when the man tried to get at me for a third time.

This time I let up on the lead and Rex charged the man so hard that he knocked him off his feet and into the six-foot-deep storm ditch. It had rained earlier that day and there was still some six inches of muddy water in the bottom. Rex wanted to follow, but I stopped him, and the man finally scrambled up over the edge, covered in mud, soaking wet and bleeding from his torn right arm.

"Okay, kaffir," I said, "that's enough. The next time you try that I will just shoot you and be done with it. This is getting to be too much trouble, and we're off duty in a few minutes."

He said nothing but glared pure hatred at me as he turned and resumed the walk to the Askari post.

We were met at the door of the Askari guard hut by a corporal. He was a very tall, muscular man, probably a member of the Masai tribe who were the natural enemies of the Kikuyu. Traditionally, the Masai produced very few female children and stole women from the Kikuyu for wives. The Kikuyu, in return, stole cattle from the Masai herds. At the beginning of the conflict with the Mau-mau terrorists, it was said that the Masai had made an offer to the British Government to clear up the whole Mau-mau problem for them. All they wanted was a free hand to get the job done. Of course the offer was refused. Civilized people couldn't behave that way! Given half a chance, the Masai would have cleared the entire Kikuyu tribe out of Kenya.

The Masai soon found a way to help, however, when recruiting began for the Kenya Police. Many of them became policemen and they did a great job.

I explained to the Askari corporal, the reason for the arrest and he grabbed the man by his shirt front and practically threw him into the cell at the rear of the building. I asked if it would be okay if I left the official report writing until the following day as it was time for Rex to get to bed and for me to sign off duty. "That will be fine, Corporal. Any time tomorrow will do."

I wished him a good night and told him I would see him the next afternoon.

I wasn't on duty the next afternoon, so Rex wasn't with me. I walked up to the Askari guardroom and asked to see the big corporal. The duty officer asked if my visit concerned the man who was arrested the night before. When I confirmed this, he told me that there was no need for any paperwork. The prisoner had been killed trying to escape. Now that was some serious corporal punishment.

Christmas Eve, 24 December, 1955, Billy and I were both off duty for the night and decided to visit a bar in Nairobi, owned by an acquaintance of Billy's. It was my turn to wear the one civilian suit we had between us, Billy was in uniform. Whoever wore the suit, carried his service revolver in a shoulder holster under the jacket.

Someone had already called for a taxi and it was waiting for them at the gate. Whoever it was had to call for another, as Billy and I pretended it was ours and we drove off into town. When we entered the bar it was packed, and the air was thick with smoke. We forced our way up to the bar and ordered our usual party drinks, brandy and coke. Most of the brandy sold in places like this was the cheap, rough, South African brandy, which had a kick like a mule.

We stayed at the bar, trading drinks with some of the other barflies, swapping stories both clean and dirty. Much later in the evening, I got off the barstool to go to the men's room and found I had trouble keeping upright. Once inside, I did what I had to do and started for the door but before I could open it I turned around, went into the nearest stall and threw up. It dawned on me that I hadn't had dinner or anything else to eat before leaving Eastleigh, which was probably why I was feeling so bad. It couldn't possibly be all the booze I had consumed!

When I got back to my seat at the bar, Billy asked me what was wrong.

"You look like you just saw a ghost. Why are you so white?"

"I feel like shit," I said. "I just brought up lunch and breakfast too; we didn't eat dinner, remember? Man, I'm ready to call it a night; I've had enough for one day."

"Aw, come on, Don; the party's just starting. We'll be good 'til daylight," he said.

"Not me," I replied, "Get me a taxi, will you? You can stay as long as you like; I don't care."

By the time the taxi arrived, I had already been sick again, and Billy helped push me into the back seat and told the driver to take me to R.A.F. Eastleigh. I promptly passed out or fell asleep, when the taxi pulled away from the curb.

We hadn't gone very far when I woke up and called for the driver to stop. I needed to vomit again. He pulled to the side of the road and I unloaded. Once we were moving again, I became aware that the road was a lot rougher than I remembered. Peering blearily from the back seat through the windshield, I could just make out in the headlight's beam, that we were on a dirt road lined by thick trees. Gradually the thought penetrated my alcohol-soaked brain, that this was not the way to Eastleigh; that road was tarmac all the way. Slowly it dawned on me that the driver saw a man in uniform helping me get in the taxi and he suspected that I was also a service man. He would have scored big points if he could deliver a comatose white serviceman to the terrorists, if he wasn't one himself.

Trying to keep my wits about me I reached for my pistol, pulled it out of the shoulder holster, and stuck the barrel in the back of the driver's neck. Thinking that I was still crashed out in the back seat, he hadn't expected that, and he jammed on the brakes. I barely held off squeezing the trigger as we came to a sudden stop with him crying, "Don't shoot, Bwana, don't shoot!"

In a mixture of Swahili and English, I told him exactly what I thought of him, and I'm pretty sure he understood. At last I calmed down enough for the driver to turn the car around and we set off back towards Nairobi. We had been on the road to the Ngong Hills, in the opposite direction to Eastleigh. I kept the revolver stuck in his neck the whole way, despite his pleading. Struggling to maintain consciousness, I was feeling worse and worse as the journey progressed and he was lucky that I was in no shape to drive or I would have perforated his neck right there.

We finally reached the Main Gate and I saw one of the station policemen approaching. I had been riding in the back seat with one hand on the door handle and when the car jerked to a stop, the door opened and I fell out, complete with gun in hand. Not waiting to get paid, or arrested, the driver rapidly backed up, turned around and took off. I was out cold, on the road.

Pat, the musician, was one of the men on duty in the Guardroom that night and he arranged for a truck to pick me up and take me to the barracks. My pals in the barracks took the suit off and laid me on my bed. They thoughtfully acquired a zinc bathtub and placed it beside the bed so I had something to throw up in and then left me to either die or recover. It was the day after Boxing Day, 27 December, when I finally surfaced and found enough strength to pull myself into an upright position. I had missed Christmas completely. I only had to get a whiff of brandy after that incident, to make me start retching, and I still can't stand the smell of the stuff.

There was a lesson to be learned there somewhere, but it was many years later before it took effect with me.

A notice appeared one day, in the NAAFI to the effect that Flight Operations would be offering rides in the Harvards for a small fee, to benefit the local Red Cross. The only condition was that if a passenger was airsick, he would have to clean the plane on landing. Cost of the flight was five Kenya shillings. These flights would be attack runs on terrorist positions in the Aberdare mountains. The coordinates for these attacks were supplied by Army ground patrols. The mountains were a tangled mass of bamboo and trees and there was very little return fire. In fact the target was rarely visible, and only the ground patrols could determine if the air attacks had been effective.

This I had to see and, after talking Billy into it, we signed up for a flight the next day. We checked into Flight Ops ten minutes before the scheduled takeoff time and met our respective pilots. These men were considerably older than we were and, of course, were officers. They didn't act that way, though, and they made us really feel at ease.

There were to be five aircraft on this sortie, as the mission was called, already armed and waiting on the tarmac. I had brought with me a small camera, hoping to get some pictures of the countryside from the air. The planes were two-seaters, the passenger in front, the pilot in the rear. The ground crew showed Billy and I how to climb into the seats and closed the canopies over us. Strapped in tight, I felt a little bit claustrophobic until we started to move. Billy's plane led the way out to the end of the runway and the rest of us packed in close behind in two rows of two. This was the formation in which we took off and flew the entire trip.

I think I mentioned before that these pilots had seen service in the Battle of Britain and were flying wizards! As we were blasting over farm lands and coffee fields at maybe a hundred feet altitude in wing-tip-to-wing-tip formation, I twisted my head round to get a glimpse of my pilot. He had one hand on the control column and the other was supporting his head as he leaned against the canopy frame, totally relaxed! When he saw me looking at him he grinned, mouthed, "okay?" and gave me the thumbs-up sign. I returned the thumbs-up and tried to relax and enjoy the ride.

Leaving the flat land we started to climb up into the mountainous regions of the Aberdares and continued to climb until we were high over the target zone. And that's when the fun really started. The flight broke formation and suddenly we were in a mock dogfight. The sky above the target point seemed to be filled with gyrating aircraft pulling all kinds of crazy aerial stunts. I didn't know, at any one instant, which way was up, and if I was coming or going! All this wild activity was intermittently interrupted with the crackle of the wing guns, when the plane was in a dive towards the target, which looked no different from the rest of the bamboo thickets which covered the ground below. The small, twenty pound bombs which were held under the wings on each side of the plane, disappeared into the bush below with, apparently no effect. I found out later that they were anti-personnel weapons, which scattered large amounts of shrapnel, making clean-up operations much easier for our ground forces after the raid. The bush was so thick that the explosions couldn't be seen from above.

During all this twisting and turning, I tried to take some photographs through the side of the canopy, but finally gave up. I just could not hold the camera up high and steady enough to get a good shot. The G-forces were much too strong, and the camera felt like it weighed ten pounds.

At last the melee was over and the planes returned to their formation for the flight back to Eastleigh. I let out a large sigh of relief and pent up breath which I seemed to have been holding for ever.

Heading down over the foothills we were much closer to the ground, and we even had to rise a little to get over the coffee trees on a plantation below. We were flying over a different part of the country and I didn't understand why, when I saw in the far distance, two extremely tall blue-gum trees. They stood close together and towered over the surrounding scrub. Soon it became obvious that we were heading towards them.

Blasting over the countryside at almost ground level, the formation stretched out into a line with Billy's aircraft leading the way. As we got nearer, I started thinking, *We can't possible fly between those trees. They're too close together. We'll take the wings off!*

Closer and closer and still we aimed straight for the trees, like a line of lemmings headed for the cliff edge and disaster.

At the very last second, the lead aircraft flipped over into a quarter roll to the right, his wing vertical as he passed through the narrow gap between the trees. The others followed close behind, alternating roll direction, and in a flash we were all safely on the other side of the trees, climbing and reforming into our original formation.

That was yet another time in my life when I came close to needing a change of underwear! The rest of the trip was uneventful with the pilots settling back into their normal, seemingly relaxed attitude, with the wingtips of their aircraft only a couple of feet away from each other.

When we arrived at Eastleigh and landed, still in close formation, the planes taxied up to the parking area outside Flight Ops. Only one passenger had been sick, it wasn't Billy or I and he stayed behind to clean the plane. Billy and I were both too excited still, to really be coherent and it was only after we had been in the NAAFI for a while sinking a couple of cold beers, that we calmed down enough to talk sensibly about our experience. One thing we both agreed on—those R.A.F. pilots had to be a special breed of people, and we had just been flying with the best of the best!

Towards the end of my three-year commitment to the R.A.F. I began to make enquiries about getting a local release. I really didn't want to have to go back to a boring existence in cold, wet, dreary old England. There had to be more to life than that. I was told that I had to fulfil three requirements. As I was still not 21 years of age, I would need my parent's permission. Secondly I must prove that I could support myself by showing proof of employment, and finally, I must have a place to live. Kenya was still a British Colony at that time, so citizenship and getting a passport was not an issue.

My parents decided to let me go my own way without objection; in fact, I think my Dad was a little envious of me. He would've liked to have done something similar when he was my age, he told me much later on. The accommodation requirement was soon settled when I answered an advertisement in the Nairobi newspaper for a room in a boarding house on the outskirts of town. Getting the job was a little more difficult, but with the help of a couple of civilian contacts, I ended up with a position as manager of a Customs Bonded Warehouse for a company known as Express Transport Co. By then I spoke and understood quite a bit of Swahili, the common language of East Africa, and was able to manage the all-African staff.

With only a week to go, I decided to take a couple of my colleagues for a trip to the National Park, outside Nairobi. By then I had retread, mud-grip tires on the car, which could dig out of almost anywhere. They were ideal for the rough going in the park but they howled at speed on the tarmac main road. We started off early on Saturday morning and were in the park area by nine. Most of the park was covered in long grass with thorn and acacia trees widely scattered across the plain. Tracks ran through the park and visitors were told to keep to them; only the game wardens were allowed to go cross-country. I had been in the park many times to observe the animals and I had a good idea of where to find lions, zebra and giraffe. There was one place where the tracks led very close to a twenty feet deep ravine and the car had got stuck one day, hanging over the edge. It took the game ranger's Land Rover to pull me out if it. That was the reason for the extra deep tread on the mud-grip tires and I felt confident that at least we wouldn't get stuck.

There wasn't much to see that particular morning: a few Thompson's gazelles and an occasional giraffe, chewing the leaves off the top branches of a tree, in the distance. Following the tracks round a curve and up a short rise, we saw that the path in front of us was blocked by a line of cars. In the front of the line was an old Morris Minor. I drove up close to the Morris and rolled my window all the way down. I always kept the windows almost closed, while in the park. Baboons were notorious thieves, and like lightning, they could jump on a car and steal sunglasses off a person's face before he could move!

The driver of the other car looked to be a bit worried. I shouted out, "What's the problem?"

He called back, "I don't know. We stopped to look at the family of lions over there, and the car wouldn't start again."

I looked over on the left side of my car, where he had indicated, and sure enough there was a lioness and three cubs lying down and playing together, and a male lion sitting off to the side, licking his paws. They showed no interest in the cars and had obviously had a successful night's hunting and a good breakfast. They were about ten yards away from the track and were in plain sight. The owner of the Morris appeared to be quite agitated, he had been there for some time, holding up traffic and I guessed that the people behind him not only wanted to see what he could see, but they wanted to get on with their tour.

"Okay, sir," I called, "open the bonnet catch, and I'll get out and take a look."

"You're crazy!" I heard coming from the back seat of my car, but I ignored it. I got out of the car and walked over to the front of the Morris. I glanced at the lions as I went. The female and cubs completely ignored me, busy with their games, and the big male stopped what he was doing for a couple of seconds and then, he too, ignored me and went back to cleaning his paws. I had the bonnet up, or "hood" as I now know it to be, and was knocking on the battery terminal with a small rock to make sure that there was a connection, when I heard the sound of a Land Rover approaching across the plain. I told the driver of the Morris to try starting again, and the engine cranked right away.

"You might want to clean up that terminal when you get home; that's all it needs," I said as I closed the bonnet, waved "Goodbye," and turned to go back to my car.

I hadn't taken a step when a game warden's Land Rover stopped in the grass beside me, and the driver piled out of his seat, waving his revolver, obviously very angry.

"What the hell do you think you are doing?" he shouted at me.

"I was just fixing that car. He was stuck and holding everyone up. He had a bad battery connection, but he's okay now. If you will just move your vehicle, everything will be just fine." I replied.

Still very irate he demanded "Don't you know there are lions over there, you fool? They could have had you for breakfast at any time!"

Now I was getting annoyed, but he was the one with the gun. "Officer, when I looked at the lions they had obviously had breakfast and were not the least interested in what I was doing, but with all the fuss you've created, that might be a different story now."

We both looked over the hood of my car towards the lions. The lioness was staring our way and the cubs had stopped playing. The big male was standing up, glaring, as if daring us to make a move towards his family.

"Now do you believe me? And if you think you are going to do any good with that little pop-gun against those cats, you're crazier than I am!" and with that I promptly got back in my car.

The game-warden followed my example and jumped into his vehicle and drove off, still red in the face and glaring angrily. As he left the scene there was a round of laughter and jeers from the occupants of the other cars, and as they went past us, they cheered and gave the thumbs-up sign.

After getting all the signatures on my check-out documents, handing in all my service kit, weapons, etc., and collecting my final payoff, including savings, I said goodbye to young Rex. The lads in the barracks cheered me off as I left camp for the last time in my 1941 model Ford Pilot and, with a little sadness at leaving my friends and Rex, but with a lot of excitement too, I started up the road to an entirely new and different chapter of my life.

6.

The job at the Customs Bonded warehouse was quite interesting in some ways. At the time I took over, after a brief training period, a movie was being made in the desert of Ethiopia, just across the Northern Frontier. All the equipment and film props were imported into Nairobi and trucked North to the site. I was fascinated with all the "rubber rifles" and other paraphernalia that was required to make a film and of course, all the paperwork that had to be completed and signed by everybody and his brother, just to make it a legal entry into the country. This was a British colony, so we had to go through all the British red tape and B.S. I had never met any famous people like that, and I wondered if they might have to come and clear any of their stuff themselves. Of course, that didn't happen. I didn't even get to see them; not in Nairobi, anyway.

A few weeks later, when shooting the film was well under way, I was called to a meeting at the Express Transport Co's office across town. It seemed that the film crews were having trouble moving their camera trolleys and other heavy equipment across the desert sands and their schedule was beginning to slip. Someone had decided that what was required was a temporary, movable road, in the form of large sheets of concrete reinforcing steel mesh which could be laid down on the desert floor in front of the moving equipment. As the camera equipment moved across the road, the panels over which they had already traveled could be picked up and moved to the front to extend the path. The steel mesh had already been purchased, three tons of it, and loaded on a five-ton open ghari, or truck, and was required to be on site no later than the following day. Our company's problem was that nobody in the transportation dept. wanted to go. None of the white employees wanted to go and none of the black drivers or loaders would go without a white man in charge. Strictly speaking, it wasn't an area frequented by the Mau-mau, but no one wanted to take a chance.

This sounded like an interesting challenge to me, an over-night ride over the Northern Frontier. I wouldn't have to drive, just be there for moral support! I explained that I hadn't yet bought a gun, but as long as the boys didn't know that, and respected me as the boss, we should be okay. If everything went as planned and we left after work, we should be on site in the very early hours of the morning.

After the warehouse closed for the day, I made a quick trip to my room to pick up a jacket as I was told that it could get cold in the hills at night and then I drove to the transport yard to meet my gang. The driver was the head man, who spoke a little English as well as Swahili. We checked the tie-downs of the load and made sure that the fuel tanks were full. The engine oil and radiator were topped up, and by the time everything had been checked, we were on our way, just after seven p.m. I rode as passenger in the cab beside the driver. The six African loaders rode in the back sitting on old mattresses on top of the steel.

With only a relatively light load on board, the truck steadily ate up the miles and by midnight we were on the packed sand road heading through the mountains. The night was pitch black except for the headlight beams which shot off into black space when we navigated around the tight bends, following the mountain sides. The "boys" in the back were asleep on their mattresses, and I was trying to keep both myself and the driver awake by practicing my Swahili on him.

Rounding a tight corner in the darkness, the truck suddenly lurched, stopping in a very nose-down position. Fortunately, we were only just creeping along. The road/track wasn't built for speed. I heard scrambling sounds from the gang as they woke up with a start, and I screamed at them to stay where they were. They froze in silence, and when I found the flashlight under the seat and shone it through the window, I could see that it was a good thing they had listened to me. The truck was teetering on the edge of the mountain, and any sudden movement could have sent it over.

Very carefully, the driver eased out of the door and climbed over into the bed of the truck, getting as close to the tailgate as possible, and he directed the rest of the gang to join him as far back as possible to put all the weight on the back wheels. Then I joined them. Naturally we carried two shovels on the truck, as we were going across desert terrain, and I told two of the smaller natives to gently climb down and start digging under the rear wheels to secure the truck. Gradually the truck leveled off and was safe enough for the rest of us to "abandon ship." With the truck's rear wheels now in a hole, we weren't going anywhere soon. And it could be several days before anyone came along this way to help us.

It was getting cold, and I was glad I had my jacket. The only way I could see to get out of this mess was to dig a path back up to the track. Once we had removed enough sand, we could lay one of our pieces of steel mesh which we carried, under the rear wheels, and hopefully get the truck back on the road. It took three sheets of mesh and a great deal of digging to finally get the truck into a driving position, but we managed it just before daylight. By now everyone in the party was worn out and I told them all to take a nap. I let them sleep for an hour, then we loaded up the shovels and the three sheets of mesh and started off again. In daylight we could see that if the truck had gone over the edge, it would have landed about three hundred feet down the sheer hillside.

Once again, someone was looking out for me!

Now that we could see where we were going, we made much better time and we were soon down on the desert floor. All we had to do now was find the turning off the road, which I had been told would be clearly marked. This would lead us to the movie site. The road was still just a gravel and sand path, wide enough for only one vehicle but as we were the only ones using it that day, it didn't matter. For several miles, a barbed wire fence ran parallel to one side, about fifty feet from the road. Out of the corner of my eye, I glimpsed something moving far out

141

amongst the thorn bushes in the desert on the right side, as we drove along. A cloud of dust was keeping pace with us and closing in and it began to look as though we might have trouble on our hands. We hadn't gone too far before we could see that it was a herd of zebra and something had been chasing them, probably a lion. They rapidly closed the gap and for a short while, we were surrounded by panicking animals.

Whatever had been chasing them had given up but now they were scared of us! I told the driver to slow down and stop, while the zebra collected themselves and headed up the road. The panic lessened and they slowed down, breathing heavily after their run. As soon as we started up, the panic returned and they took off again. For some reason they wouldn't go back onto the open desert, but stayed close to the fence on the left side of the road. This stop, start progress continued for a couple of miles, until the fence abruptly ended and they went racing off into the desert. Half a mile further, we found the turnoff on the left side of the road with a sign reading "Express Transport" on a stick stuck in the sand.

It was almost noon when, after following the track for a mile or so, we arrived at the camp site. The crew boss welcomed us warmly. His film crew had been stuck for two days, and everyone was getting restless. The actor had almost demolished a beautiful, new Chevy Biscayne, just "cowboying" around in the desert, out of boredom. It was a rental car from Nairobi and didn't look the least bit new when I saw it.

We were all hungry and thirsty, and while we consumed lunch, which consisted of chicken salad and a few beers, we explained our late arrival with a description of the night's happenings. The Boss, I'll call him that as I can't remember his name now, understood and didn't seem to mind having part of his temporary roadway used to get us there. He did insist, though, that we should stay and rest for a few hours at least before we headed back. I crashed out on a lounger in the shade of an awning stretched between two thorn bushes, and didn't wake up until I heard a bell ring. It was the cook's call to dinner. My gang was off somewhere with the natives who worked with the film crew, and I guessed they were being taken care of there.

The dining tent contained several long, folding tables placed end to end, with enough chairs to seat the entire crew, myself and the two main stars of the movie. The third main actor, an Englishman, was too drunk to attend dinner. I believe he remained in that condition for much of the movie.

Janet Leigh sat at the far end of the table from me, and I didn't even recognize her at first. Without all the screen makeup she looked totally different. She was complaining loudly about the effect that the camp food, which I thought was excellent, was having on her stomach. I heard later, that the next day she had to be taken to Nairobi to see a doctor. All she needed was a dose of "Pepto." Victor Mature practically carried the entire dinner-table conversation. I suppose a person as large as he was entitled to an equally large ego. He really was a "big man on campus" in every sense.

After dinner, I sent a message to my gang to load up their gear on the truck, ready for another overnight trip back through the mountains to Nairobi. It seems strange now, that there wasn't some form of border post to mark the boundary between Kenya and Ethiopia, but that was over half a century ago, and things were a lot different in those days.

Having said our farewells, we climbed aboard the truck and started back along the track to the road, about an hour before sunset. Except for a few scattered zebra amongst the thorn bushes, we didn't see any animals on the way. We had the entire road to ourselves, all the way back to the foothills, in fact we were well into Kenya territory on the other side of the mountains before we saw any more vehicles. Definitely a "road less traveled." Not the kind of place to have a serious breakdown. When we reached the spot where we had been stuck the previous night, we slowed to a crawl as we eased around the curve. By the absence of any other tire tracks it was obvious that there had been no other vehicles on the road since our event. Once we had cleared the area, it was plain sailing the rest of the way home. Traffic was more evident as we got closer to Nairobi and we arrived back at the yard at close to three a.m. I signed off on the time cards for the gang and drove back to my room for a couple of hours' sleep before going on duty at the warehouse.

I never did get to see the film, *Safari*. Maybe I will some day, if it's on DVD. I like to think that I had a part, a very small part, in the making of it.

As I mentioned before, I had a room at a local boarding house. This establishment was operated by a lady, whose husband was a white hunter. He didn't actually hunt wild game for shooting purposes; he conducted photographic safaris for wealthy, snap-happy Americans. My room was located in an outbuilding at the end of his extensive property, which was perfect for me. I was never very good at interacting with strangers, and even today I am happier with my own and my dogs' company. Bruce, the husband, knew of my love for animals and that the house rule, "No pets," was particularly hard on me.

One afternoon, after a day at the warehouse, I returned to my room and found a note on the door. It was from Bruce who had just returned from a safari, asking me to see him at the house. I immediately thought I was getting my notice to vacate the room but for the life of me, I couldn't think what I could have done wrong. I had made a serious effort to cut back on the drinking; I just couldn't afford it any more at civilian prices and I spent most evenings in my room, quietly reading westerns and science fiction novels. The love for Sci Fi remains with me to this day. Unfortunately, TV was in its infancy and wasn't common in Africa at that time.

When I knocked at the back door of the house, Bruce invited me in and we sat in the living room. I was on the edge of my seat and Bruce, noticing my discomfort, said, "Relax, Don. I may have some good news for you."

"Really?" I asked, "I could use some; I've been worried in case you want me to leave."

"Quite the opposite," he continued. "I know how much you miss your dogs, and I don't want to relax the wife's 'No Pets' rule, but I have a proposition for you."

Now I was intrigued, and I said, "Let's hear it, Bruce; as long as it doesn't involve me leaving, I'm interested."

Right out of the blue he asked, "What do you know about cheetahs?"

Cautiously, I said, "Not very much, except they need exercise and raw meat; why?"

"As you know, I've just returned from safari, and while we were tracking, looking for wild cats to photograph, my trackers discovered two baby cheetahs. Initially we thought they had been abandoned by their mother, until we found the mother's body, killed by poachers for the skin. The babies were too young to fend for themselves, so we put them in the cage that we carry on one of the trucks for such occasions and brought them home. This wouldn't be the first or last time that we've rescued orphans from the bush."

I was getting excited and said, "I'm not sure where you are going with this, Bruce, but I can't deny I'm interested. Go on, please."

"Well," he said, "I reckon they're about two months old now, and it will be at least another six months before they stand a chance of surviving alone in the bush again. And by then they'll be a real handful. But I thought that with your experience with police dogs, you might want to take care of them for me. We can keep them in a pen in the yard near your room, and you could exercise them and feed them. I'll buy the meat for them and anything else they may need so they won't cost you anything. What do you say?"

I was so excited, words wouldn't come out right away until finally I gasped out, "Yes, sir!" and I jumped up, just like a child, and said, "Can we go see them now?"

He led the way to the truck which held the cage, and there I saw the most beautiful, cuddlesome little cubs I had ever seen. Cuddlesome that is, until I put my hand near them, crouched as far back in the cage as they could get. They snarled and showed me their teeth.

"That's okay, babies," I whispered, "We are going to be real good friends before long, and you'll be eating out of my hand before the week's up."

"It may take a little longer than that," said Bruce, "Depending on how much time you can spare them. I'll get my boys to build the pen for them tomorrow, and that will be their new home."

The light was beginning to fade when I said, "And how about tonight? I'm not leaving them out here alone. I'll bring my mattress and a pillow from my bed, and I'll sleep with them."

I didn't have to do that; Bruce had the houseboy fetch me a cot mattress, blanket and pillow from the house and I settled down with my new charges. As I lay down next to the cage, I heard Bruce say to his wife, through the open kitchen door, "I knew I had found the right person for the job!"

The cubs, "Him" and "Her," soon became used to me, and they did, in fact, eat out of my hand by the end of our first week together. I spent a lot of time talking to them as if they were my best pals, which they were. Animals may not understand every word, but I firmly believe that they can sense when a human cares for them by the sound of that person's voice.

It wasn't long before I could put their collars and leads on them and take them for walks around the property. I tried letting them loose in my room one evening and wished I hadn't. They had so much pent-up energy to lose that it was like sharing a room with two spotted tornadoes! As a result of that experiment, I asked for and got permission to exercise them on the huge lawn, in front of the house. A thick hedge hid a chicken wire fence down the road side of the lawn and Bruce had a temporary fence built on the other sides, with a gate in one of them.

Now that we had somewhere to exercise, Him and Her could stretch their legs more and my fear of them getting rickets eased a bit. They were also able to enjoy running in the sunlight and their diet of raw, ground up horsemeat, also helped prevent that disease. These were two healthy, very active little chaps who were enjoying their taste of civilization.

Eventually, I felt confident enough to let them off the leads inside the fence. They responded to my call of, "Come," when it suited them, but I couldn't totally rely on them to obey. This was a good thing, as I still needed them to be independent of me if they were to make it in the wild. Really, they only had one similarity with my police dogs and that was they could not retract their claws/toenails like a cat. Obedience training was out of the question, if I wanted them to follow their wild instincts later on, when they were bigger. And they were getting bigger by the day, it seemed.

Whenever I was not at work they were with me. They loved to ride on the back seat of the old Ford Pilot and all three of us enjoyed the reaction of the gas-pump attendants when I pulled into a service station to fill the tank. At the pump they would sit, rock still, looking straight ahead, like a couple of statues, while the attendant held the nozzle in the tank. Curious, he would put his face against the rear window to see inside and suddenly the cheetah nearest the window would jerk its head around and snarl right in the man's face. Dropping the hose, he would run screaming and shouting in Swahili and waving his arms over his head, into the office. For some reason, natives had a hard time differentiating between leopards and cheetahs. It always made me laugh and I could swear I saw a smirk on the faces of Him and Her. The word soon circulated amongst the pump-boy fraternity in Nairobi, however and the joke was then on me. From then on it was self service for me, even without the cheetahs!

Playtime on the lawn was a lot of fun and exercise, for all of us. A chicken leg on a string, whirled round and round faster and faster, was a favorite for a while. It didn't take them long to figure out that it was quicker to take a short cut across the circle. Rough-housing was more strenuous for me than them, I believe. I would let them off their leads, inside the fenced lawn and start to run away, as if I was scared of them. They would chase after me for a while, just keeping up with me. Suddenly I would be buried under a mess of paws, legs, tails and teeth, as they knocked me down and pretended to eat me. Although they often had my flesh in their mouths, they never broke the skin and were much more gentle to play with than my first police dog, Valdi. It truly was a unique experience for me and it served to enhance my respect and love for God's creatures, other than mankind.

When it came time for them to be returned to the wild, I was both sad and apprehensive for them. They were my good friends and I couldn't bear to think that something bad would happen to them, as it did to their mother. There really was no way of knowing how they managed, but Bruce said he never saw one sign of them after he released them from the cage, on their return to the plains where he had found them. As much as I loved them, I know Bruce wouldn't have told me, even if he knew.

Almost as soon as they were free once more, something came up which gave me something else to think about and helped to ease the sudden loneliness.

One of my colleagues at Express Transport Co. was the lady to whom I delivered my daily reports and records. She was located in the Head Office in the heart of Nairobi. She was a very sweet, motherly kind of person and always seemed to be interested in my welfare. She had no children of her own and I felt a little as though I had been adopted. She wasn't too happy when she heard of my little adventure crossing the Northern Frontier and one day, a couple of weeks later, she invited me to lunch. Intrigued, I accepted and at midday I met her in a local coffee shop which was a tasting site for many of the locally grown coffees. Frequented by international coffee buyers as well as local experts, a huge assortment of Kenya-grown coffee beans was displayed in tall glass jars lining the shelves behind the service counter. Customers could choose the beans they wished to taste, which were ground while they waited and brewed especially for them. It was then served in a large cup, which resembled a deep soup bowl with a handle. At the far end of the counter, a doorway led into the tasting room, where patrons could sit and relish their brew. It was a favorite place to meet and I'm sure many deals, some of them shady no doubt, took place there.

To save time, both Anne and I selected the same beans, and we were soon seated and enjoying the coffee. A cup of coffee as large as this and a couple of cookies was enough for lunch. Without wishing to seem too eager, I asked her the reason for the date.

She laughed and said, "Don't be disappointed, Don. It's not what you might be thinking." She continued, "What I had in mind is a change of job for you. You know you will never get anywhere, working in the warehouse for Express. That really is a dead-end job, if ever there was one. In fact, the previous manager did die on the job, as you know, of a heart attack. I know he was much older than you, but I wouldn't want to see you go the same way."

I knew she was right, but I thought I was getting settled in and was starting to feel comfortable after Service life. "So what did you have in mind?" I asked.

"Well, my husband, Jim, works for H.G. Barton, Ltd, an earth-moving company, as their accountant, and he is in need of a bookkeeping clerk. The pay won't be any less than what you are getting now, maybe a bit more, but he will be training you, and it's a good opportunity to learn something that could be useful to you later on down the road."

Somehow the thought of being a bookkeeper didn't seem to be that appealing. It certainly wasn't my idea of an exciting career, but then neither was warehouse management.

Anne sensed my apparent lack of interest in the proposition and said, "I know it doesn't sound like much, Don, but why don't you just go and speak to Jim about it. He'll explain everything about the job and the company and, who knows, you might get on well together. Their office is just round the corner from ours, and I'll tell him to expect you. How about after work today?"

The warehouse closed at 4.30 p.m., and I had nothing particular planned for the evening, so I agreed, to please Anne as much as anything. If I didn't like what I heard, I could always say, "No." Anne reminded me that we should not discuss this at all in the Express office, as she might get fired for attempting to recruit one of their employees for her husband's company, and she really liked her job.

After I closed up the warehouse, I drove back into town and around to the offices of H.G.Barton, Ltd. There were three offices, one for the company secretary, a large, military-officer type, another for the chief accountant, Jim, and the third was a long narrow office, with just enough room for a couple of desks and chairs, which was the bookkeeper's place.

Jim's office was the middle one and the entrance door from the landing opened into it. Jim was sitting behind his desk, back to the window, at the opposite end of the room when I entered in reply to his "Come in." He was a middle-aged man of average build with a neat, dark, graying-at-the-edges head of hair, and he smiled as he invited me to sit.

After the introductions, he said, "So, my wife tells me that you might be interested in leaving Express Transport and coming to work with us. Is that correct?"

"Well, not exactly, sir," I replied. "It was really her idea. I hadn't even thought about changing jobs until she mentioned it, and I suppose she's right. The job I have now is pretty much a dead-end deal, and I'd like to have a little more excitement in my life. I just can't see that happening, though, being a bookkeeper. That's got to be boring!"

He laughed and said, "I understand, Don, and please call me Jim; we're not in the services now. But look at it this way. I hear that you don't know anything about accountancy and record keeping, and I'm willing to teach you everything you need to know so that you could get a great job anywhere. Company accountants are in great demand anywhere in Africa and generally speaking, the pay is good. Until you learn enough to be useful of course, I can't offer you much, but that will soon change if you show any aptitude for the job."

"I just don't know, Jim. I appreciate the opportunity to learn something new," I replied, "But sitting crunching numbers all day doesn't sound very exciting to me. I don't know if I could sit still long enough. In any case, why me?"

Again he smiled and said, "Well, this is the situation, and I'll lay it all out for you. According to Anne, you've had some experience of living rough in the Air Force, and that experience could be very useful to us. Our company has been awarded a very large earth-moving contract down in Northern Rhodesia, and we will be moving down there in a couple of months. But we have a little problem. If we can't clean up our records here for tax purposes, we will have to keep an office open here, and we don't want to do that. Right now, I have all the documents concerning two earth-moving contracts we completed for the Kenya government for which we have to compile two sets of books. Having done that we have to combine them for the record. All the ledgers, journals, etc., will have to be written up, and a lot of sorting of relevant documents will be needed to get this job done. Now I could do this if I had the time, but I don't, so I need help. If you take on the position, I can promise you that you will learn bookkeeping in a hurry. and if you are interested, we'll take you to Northern Rhodesia with us. Our contract there is to build the north access road, through the Zambezi valley, to the new Kariba dam site on the river. We will be connecting the main north/south road between Northern and Southern Rhodesia to the new dam. A similar access road will be built on the south side of the river. When I mentioned living rough, I was thinking about this. It won't be too bad, after we get established, but it will mean living in the bush many miles from civilization, and that's not for everybody. So what do you think, so far?"

By this time, my eyes were wide open, and I was definitely sitting up straight and paying attention. What a great opportunity! Living in the bush, close to the animals that I loved—it was almost too good to be true. There was that boring bookkeeping chore to be tackled first, but that wouldn't last for ever. And it certainly seemed to be a much more interesting life than working in the warehouse, so what did I have to lose?

"Sounds great, Jim, but I do have some doubts about the bookkeeping part. I know nothing about that and wouldn't know where to start."

"Don't worry about that; as I said before I'll show you everything. If you can follow simple instructions we'll get through it together in short order. I just want your word that, after we get finished with our work here you will transfer to Northern Rhodesia with us when we go."

I just couldn't let this opportunity slide. Jim might get someone else if I didn't make a decision right away, and I might lose the chance to cross another border and to experience life in the bush. That wasn't going to happen if I could help it!

"Okay, Jim, sign me up. I wouldn't miss this for the world! I'll have to give Express two week's notice, but I'll start right after that, if that's okay with you. Already I can't wait to get the bookkeeping work behind me!"

He grinned and put out his hand. We shook hands to seal the agreement, and he said, "Well, that's a relief. Anne was right, I think I'm going to like working with you, and I think you are going to enjoy what we'll have in Kariba."

Express Transport Co. wasn't too pleased with me when I handed in my resignation, but I think they understood when I told them I had an opportunity to learn bookkeeping and accountancy with a different company. I think they already had someone in mind for my position anyway, and I later learned that a relative of the Managing Director had taken the job.

On my first day at H.G. Barton Ltd, Jim showed me into the long room with two desks, which was to be my space until we moved to Northern Rhodesia. There was an adjoining door between Jim's office and mine. Apart from the two desks and chairs, the only other items in the room were two, three feet square, plywood boxes called tea-chests. These were stuffed full of invoices, receipts, progress reports, notebooks, scribbled journals and time cards. This was all that remained of two contracts which had been completed but for which no books had been kept nor proper accounts compiled. Jim left me alone with the boxes for a few minutes while he answered the phone in his office and the more I looked at the contents, the more I felt overwhelmed. How in blue blazes was I ever going to even get started on this job, never mind finish it? Jim finished the call and came back into, what was to be my office.

He saw the expression on my face and said, "Don't look so worried, Don. It really isn't as bad as it seems. We'll just take it step by step. First of all we need to separate everything into two piles, so we have that which belongs to contract #1, let's call it, in one pile and that which belongs to contract #2, in the other. Everything is marked, so that won't be difficult. While you are doing that, and it will probably take the rest of today, I'll write down an action plan for what happens next, and so on."

He was right; it did take all day to separate the records, such as they were. The following day, I sorted each pile by document type, invoices, receipts, etc., and then by date order. I then filed everything in a four-drawer filing cabinet. Jim showed me how to write a set of books, and I learned the principals of double-entry bookkeeping. A couple of weeks later I had the ledgers and journals complete for both contracts, and I checked out the trial balance on each with my hand-cranked adding machine, with the paper-strip printout. There were of course, no computers in those days, so everything had to be hand written, and the Kenya monetary system consisted of shillings and cents. With a hundred cents to a shilling and twenty shillings to a pound, everything was still expressed in shillings and cents, not pounds. A shilling was worth approximately ten U.S. cents. You can imagine the size of some of these entries. A fuel invoice alone, for a piece of heavy earth-moving equipment, could be as much as thousands of shillings and a few cents.

Jim completed the balance sheets and complied with all the tax requirements, and we were finally cleared to leave the country. The heavy equipment on transporters, and several low-loaders formed a convoy for the long trip south, all on dirt roads. One of the low-loaders carried the personal effects of the staff who were relocating to Northern Rhodesia. I always traveled light and all my belongings fitted in one small cabin trunk I had sold my car and all I had left was hand luggage when we boarded the plane at Nairobi airport for the flight to Lusaka, the capital of Northern Rhodesia.

I had enjoyed my stay in Kenya, except for some of the atrocities committed by the Mau-mau, not only against the white settlers but also against any of their own people who were non-sympathizers. At least we wouldn't have that kind of terrorism to deal with, where we were going.

7.

We were met at Lusaka airport by a local guide with a Land Rover. There were only four of us in this advance party, the Company Secretary, Jim, Jock, who was another clerk who had been hired just before we left and me. We were all anxious to see what we had let ourselves in for and no one wanted to waste time looking around town. We did stop at a small restaurant to grab a quick snack before leaving Lusaka and then we headed off along the wide, black top road heading to the great Zambezi River and across the border into Southern Rhodesia. Northern and Southern Rhodesia, since independence was granted by Britain, are known today as Zambia and Zimbabwe.

The trip was uneventful, boring even, until we reached the point where we turned off into the thick bush on the right-hand side of the road. A two-wheel track led between mpani trees and thick scrub and it became a really rough ride. Along the way we encountered several family groups of baboons who immediately disappeared, screaming and chattering and one large, black mamba which was crossing our path. The guide stopped the vehicle to let him go and explained why we should never try to run over a snake with a vehicle. It often happened that when someone had done this, the snake had hung onto something on the underside of the car. When the vehicle stopped, the snake had let go and bitten the driver as he stepped out. That was a good lesson to be remembered. There was no shortage of snakes in the Zambezi Valley.

Finally we arrived at an open space, cleared by a gang of natives. Another gang was in the process of erecting wooden frame buildings which would serve as our living accommodations when they were finished. A small stream ran around one edge of the clearing, known as the Lusito river, and it was on the bank of the stream that we set up camp for the night. This consisted of wrapping up in a blanket on the ground, with our hand-luggage for pillows, and an African watchman to keep the fire going. The fire wasn't for heat but to deter crocodiles and other predators. I slept with one eye open, trying to keep watch on the watchman.

As the sky started to brighten we got up and had breakfast in the mess tent. It was a cold meal of cereal and milk but lots of hot coffee. So far everything was going as expected, even the mosquitoes were no surprise.

After breakfast, with the sun just beginning to rise over the trees, we walked around the area designated for our permanent camp. Building sites were marked with stakes in the ground and these were indicated on a rough, hand-drawn plan. Most of the living quarters were located on the top of a twenty foot bluff overlooking the Lusito, along with a mess hall and kitchen. On top of the slope of the opposite side of a small valley, the larger areas marked indicated the living quarters for the Company executives, including the owner, H.G. Barton himself. Between these two housing areas, in the bottom of the valley, would be the heavy equipment workshops and maintenance area, the main stores and offices. All the structures were of a temporary nature, two-by-fours and corrugated iron, or "wrinkle tin." The African workers, when they were hired, would build their own houses in an area set aside for the"compound.

By nightfall, we had temporary sleeping arrangements made in makeshift huts. Dirt floors but at least a roof over our heads and a door which could be bolted. So progress had been made. The following mid-morning, the first of the low-loaders pulled in from Nairobi and we started to unload the smaller items. Most of it was left on board until the respective storage areas were ready. The crews from the transports joined in to help the construction gangs and things began to take shape much faster. Over the next week or so, buildings went up, the mess hall and kitchen were functioning, showers were built and toilets dug and we had the beginnings of a jungle community.

Speaking with some of the original gang of builders, I found out that our base camp on the Lusito was approximately half way between the main north/south highway and the Kariba dam. We had a total of almost forty miles of bush bashing and road building to look forward to. This was not going to be an overnight job. In fact it was the largest contract undertaken by the Company to date. So far all we had was a survey track through the bush. We had to build a high grade, gravel road with proper drains and storm ditches, culverts and bridges to accommodate all kinds of heavy transport carrying supplies and equipment to the Kariba dam site on the Zambezi river. At first I couldn't see how our little earthmoving company could do it, but our little company didn't stay that little for very long. Recruitment started within days, with mechanics, equipment operators, shuttering carpenters, masons, electricians, etc arriving on site daily, attracted by the prospect of good money paid for hard work. These were men of all nationalities, mostly South Africans but there were also British, Italian, Greek and of course, some local whites.

Initially the work consisted of bush clearing and we had Caterpillar tractors, from D-6s to D-8s working on either side of the camp, clearing trees and grading the future road bed. As the work progressed, the local people started to show interest and it wasn't long before we had over nine hundred Africans on the payroll, spread over forty miles of bush, working on various projects, preparing for the road builders.

Working from dawn to dusk, six days a week, the job was coming along nicely. But we were missing something. We needed a place where we could meet socially. The nearest pub was the Chirundu Hotel, on the main north/south highway, on the north side of the Zambezi river. Twenty miles of driving through the bush and another twenty on the highway was a bit far to go for a beer and a game of darts so we decided to build our own bar on camp. There was an expression going around camp at the time that referred to unqualified men applying for artisan-type jobs. It was said that they were "chancing their arms." It was a "natural;" our bar was to be known as "The Chancer's Arms!" A couple of Sundays and several evenings later, we had a working bar with a bartop, stools, and a room with four small tables with chairs. The toilets were two separate "wrinkle tin" outhouses between the building and the twenty-foot bluff to the Lusito river below. The company supplied the fridge, and the shuttle bus from Lusaka brought the supplies.

Opening night went very smoothly; no one got drunk or rowdy. Everybody was on their best behaviour, and the bar was considered to be a great success. It definitely improved the quality of life in camp and brought people together. We came to know each other much quicker over a glass of beer in our own pub.

One of our diesel mechanics was a white South African, named Van. He was an excellent mechanic but before he joined H.G. Barton, Ltd, he had been doing a little crocodile hunting on the Zambezi, for a living. He told me his hunting methods one night at the bar. He had a small, sixteen feet, wooden boat in which he carried his rifle and little else. He would go out onto the river at night, strip off all his clothes and with a head mounted light he would spot a croc's eyes. Curiosity can kill, as the croc found out when he approached the boat and Van fired his rifle. Van would then drop his light and rifle in the bottom of the boat and dive overboard to man-handle the body back into the boat. With blood from the croc in the water and no defenses, this seemed a bit extreme to me, but he had been getting away with it for some time. His luck ran out however, when one night he thought he had killed a large croc. He dived into the river and started to wrestle the body into the boat and discovered that the croc still had some life left in him. In the ensuing struggle Van lost his boat, rifle and headlight and barely (no pun intended!) made it back to the bank in one piece. That night, driving back to his camp, he decided to find a safer job. He had two sons living in South Africa with their Aunt to consider. He was the sole source of support for all three of them. I asked him why he didn't just stay in the boat and gaff the croc and he explained that the valuable part of the croc's skin was the softer underside. And that was the only area a gaff would penetrate. A croc's skin without a gaff hole in it fetched a better price and he figured it was worth the extra risk involved.

Van was a small man, maybe five feet six or seven, but as hard as nails. His hands were oversized for the rest of his body and they were like a couple of vice-grips, covered in calluses. I once saw him with a five inch long, black scorpion, teasing it to sting his finger. The stinger just bent; it couldn't penetrate the skin. He then held the scorpion in his fist and nonchalantly strolled into the bar. Several of the equipment operators were sitting on the stools, elbows on the bar, enjoying an after-dinner drink. Van opened his hand under the level of the bar, pulled off the scorpion's stinger and dropped the very irate and dying, insect on the bar. It dashed along the full length of the bar, zig-zagging all over the place. Arms, hands and beer glasses all flew up into the air as the drinkers pushed back out of the way. Most of them went flying backwards as their stools toppled over. They hadn't moved that fast in weeks. Van and the rest of us held our sides, gasping with laughter.

It didn't take long for the operators to gather their wits and then the chase was on! Van took off like a bolt of lightning with four very irate and large, men after him. Cussing him out as they ran, they chased him into the virgin bush surrounding the camp. Once inside the jungle, in the dark, there was no way they were going to find Van so they gave up and returned to the bar. They knew when they were beat. Wisely, Van waited until the following day before he showed his face again.

On one other occasion Van led a small party of patrons of the Chancer's Arms into the bush. We had been talking about "bush babies," or "night apes," as they were known in South Africa. This is a small, furry marsupial with a very cute face and huge eyes. Some people had them as pets. They made delightful pets but had one obnoxious habit. Their feet, or hands, had suckers on the fingers which enabled them to climb anywhere. To moisten the suckers the animal would urinate on them, and this left tracks over walls, furniture, etc. Van had been explaining how to catch a bush baby by spotting the reflection from their eyes when a flashlight was shone on them. Having had several beers already that evening, Van offered to demonstrate the technique right then, and five of us followed him out of the bar and into the bush on the other side of the maintenance area. As usual I had my little .22 rifle with me, although what good that would do I couldn't imagine.

With Van leading the way we entered the bush in single file, trying to be quiet. That was almost impossible as all of us had been drinking fairly heavily that evening. Van was shining the flashlight into the branches of likely trees ahead of us, looking for the eye reflections which would indicate a bush baby when we suddenly found ourselves on the edge of a small clearing. Van started to lead the way around the clearing but stopped dead when we heard a muffled grunt and the sound of undergrowth being flattened, coming from the opposite side.

Everyone froze, hardly daring to breathe. The effects of the alcohol were starting to wear off. The noise stopped almost as soon as it had begun and we were beginning to think that it might have been imagination, when Van shone the flashlight directly at the place from which the sound had emanated. Facing us across the clearing about thirty yards away, was a small herd of elephants. The leader, an old bull, was front and center with his huge ears erect, glaring back at us. We instinctively moved from a line to a huddle. There was nowhere to go. The few surrounding trees were too small to climb and in any case, they couldn't possibly stand up to an elephant's charge. One of the members of the party expressed everyone's feelings when he let out a loud, "Oh, shit!"

Van turned off the light but it was too late. The old bull expressed his rage with an ear-splitting trumpet and he charged across the clearing towards us, the rest of the herd following behind. I was convinced that this was my last day on earth. I knew that a shot from my rifle wouldn't even penetrate the hide of that old bull so, out of pure fear, I pointed the rifle skywards and squeezed the trigger. The resulting noise of the shot must have made the lead elephant think twice about running us over, and he swerved off to one side, taking the rest of his herd with him.

When the ground stopped shaking and we regained our wits, we decided that the bush babies would be safe from us for the rest of the evening and made tracks back to the bar. But I'm sure I wasn't alone in wondering if I needed a change of underwear that evening!

By the time that the camp was fully constructed and all the functions of the Company were working, one of my responsibilities was to pay the work-force every month. This meant calculating the individual wages from the time cards, entering the time-sheet records, drawing the checks and getting the cash from the bank in Salisbury, Southern Rhodesia. All wages were paid in cash each month.

In order to get the cash from the bank, a bush pilot named Barry would land his small plane at a sugar plantation air strip, just over the Zambezi river in Southern Rhodesia. I would drive my company-issued Land Rover to the strip, with the checks, and Barry would fly me to Salisbury to get the cash. On my first trip to Salisbury, I had bought a single shot, .22 rifle and I always carried it with me on these trips. It wasn't much but I felt I needed some kind of security when I was carrying over twenty thousand pounds in cash. I was a terrible shot with a rifle and I suppose I would have been better off with a hand gun after all the R.A.F. experience, but I wanted to learn. It was said that I couldn't hit a barn door from the inside of the barn!

The second time I went to Salisbury with Barry, we had to pick up some documents from an attorney's office for our Company Secretary. This took a lot longer than we expected; the documents were not ready when we first called for them. By the time we got back to the sugar plantation, it was too late for Barry to safely fly back to Salisbury so he decided to stay the night with us back at base camp. I had long ago removed the doors and rag-top from my vehicle, and it was a pleasant ride with a cooling evening breeze blowing over us. As we approached the turn-off from the main road, we were talking about what might be available for dinner in the mess hall when we arrived. Barry was just telling me that he hadn't had any "wild" meat for ages when, up ahead I saw a flock of guinea fowl crossing the path.

"How about one of those, Barry?" I asked. "Would you like a guinea for dinner?"

"I sure would if you know someone who can cook it!" he replied.

"That won't be a problem," I said. "We recently hired a great cook. He's Cordon Bleu trained, I'm told, and he really knows what he's doing, especially with game. The real problem will be catching one of those birds."

While we were talking, I reached down for my little rifle which was between my leg and the vehicle body. Approaching the place where we had seen the birds cross the road, I slowed down and, holding the gun over the window frame with one hand, I fired a shot into the weeds and grass where I thought they had disappeared. I was shocked into silence when there was a squawk, and a puff of feathers arose from the grass.

I slammed on the brakes and Barry shouted, "What a shot! That was incredible!" I still couldn't believe I had hit something, but sure enough, when we ran over to the spot, there in the grass was a nice, fat, dead, guinea. I tossed the body in the back of the Land Rover, and we drove off.

"No one's going to believe this back at camp, you know. It might be better to say we just ran over it. Everyone knows my targets are perfectly safe; that was just a total fluke," I said as I passed Barry a cigarette. Lighting up, we drove quietly for a while and then I turned the conversation to the local fishing opportunities on the Zambezi and the Kafue rivers. Fishing in this part of Africa was a great sport. One of my favorite pastimes. By the time we arrived at camp, I had just finished telling Barry the story of one of my fishing adventures on the Kafue river.

Three of us from Lusito camp had planned an overnight trip to the Kafue game reserve, to go fishing in an area where the Kafue ran into the Zambezi. There was a small station in the bush not too far from the river, where we could rent a hut for the night. Al, my particular friend at that time, Tommy and I set off in Al's Opel Kadet station wagon, early one Saturday morning. We arrived at our destination by mid-day and were soon looking for fishing areas on the overgrown banks of the river. Thick grass and reeds made it difficult to cast and few other fishermen had been there before us to clear the way. The other two had wandered off up-stream, looking for a clear space and I decided to go the other way, downstream. Pushing my way through the bush, rod and tackle box in hand, sweat running down my neck from the heat, I finally found what appeared to be the perfect spot. There was a wide break in the reeds, with a clear view of the water. I couldn't believe my luck! Without thinking about why this place was cleared, seemingly just for me, I baited my hook and cast out into the river. I was using very heavy-weight line, as I was hoping for a "vundu," which is a very large catfish. These could often top a hundred pounds in weight. It wasn't long before I felt a tug on the line and I jerked back to set the hook. The pull on the line increased and started to strip off the reel against the drag. Gradually, whatever it was and it felt like a submarine at this point, made its way upstream. I kept increasing the drag, hoping to slow it down, but it made no difference. Suddenly my catch reversed its direction and started to come back towards me and I was able to reel back in most of my line. Until it stopped, no more than fifteen feet in front of me.

With an explosion of water and noise, a huge gaping jaw filled with enormous teeth that resembled iron spikes, burst open and showered me with river water. This was one very irate hippo and he wasn't taking very kindly to the fact that I had caught him with a fishing pole. After his dental display, he came charging out of the water and up the slope to dry land. By then I had recovered enough from the shock of meeting him up close and I had taken to my heels ahead of him. He still had my fishing gear attached to him as raged up the path but I had dived into the thick brush on one side of his run-way and thankfully, he passed by.

I crawled back out of my cover, scratched and still in shock and as quietly as I could, I made my way back to where I had left the others. They had heard all the commotion and had made their way back towards me, to see what was going on. When I told them what had happened, they had a good laugh at my expense. We all did. How could I be so stupid as to not think about why that cleared piece of bank was there before I cast my line. If I had been paying more attention I would have seen signs of the hippo and realized that this was his normal way in and out of the river.

Hippos are supposed to be vegetarians, but I was glad I didn't have to prove that point.

We made our way back to the place where I had dived into the bushes, and I found my tackle box. The fishing rod and reel were long gone, along with my "catch," and we went back to the camp where we had rented the hut. We had left the car and the rest of our gear there, and I had a spare boat rod in the car. There was a small bar in the main building so we decided to have a beer with lunch while we decided our next move. We were telling the African barman about the morning's events when he suggested that we try fishing from a boat. His brother made his living taking fishermen out on the river in his boat, and he would be pleased to take us.

By the time lunch was over, the boat owner appeared. Carrying our fishing gear and boat rods, we also managed to fit in a hessian sandbag, containing half a dozen beers. These were suspended from the stern of the boat, into the water, to keep them cool. The boat was tied to a tree on the bank and was hidden amongst the reeds. It was an old, native made, flat bottom craft, just big enough to fit all of us. A small and smelly outboard propelled us along at a walking pace; there were very few currents to worry about in this part of the river. We kept fairly close to the banks as we headed towards the confluence of the two rivers, keeping well away from the occasional pack of hippos we could see playing out in mid-stream. There was a distinct change in the coloration of the water as we turned into the Kafue, and the skipper explained that it was caused by silt being washed downstream from native farming operations. We were now in a much narrower stretch of water, and we dropped anchor, which was a large rock on the end of a rope.

After beers all round, we rigged our fishing poles and settled down to some quiet contemplation of the natural beauty surrounding us. That afternoon we caught several good sized barbel, another type of catfish and a couple of small tiger fish, so-called because of their fearsome array of teeth. After the beers had all gone we finally agreed that it was time to return to the bar. I had pulled my line in and Al and Tommy were doing the same when Tommy gave a shout. He had hooked onto something that was giving him a good struggle. His rod was bent over, almost touching the water and he was so excited that I had to remind him, loudly, not to stand up or we would all be in the water. Al passed the gaff to me as I was closer to the action and I waited to see what we had. Tommy said it felt like a log and I was beginning to think that perhaps he had caught a croc when this huge catfish mouth broke the surface. It was the vundu we had all been hoping for. It really was a monster, the skipper estimated ninety pounds. I reached over the side of the boat with the gaff which had a screw-on hook, positioned the hook under the fish's huge, flat head and jerked backwards, expecting to feel the weight of the fish on the gaff. Instead of which there was an almighty splash alongside the boat, as the fish kicked, broke the line and swam off. When I examined the gaff, I found that the hook had not been screwed into the handle tight enough, and it had turned and slid off the fish when I tried to gaff it.

It wasn't totally my fault, but I couldn't help blaming myself for not checking the hook first. No one else seemed to be concerned that we had lost the fish. Just getting a look at it was enough. It would have been a trip getting it back to camp anyway. So we settled for the fish that we had caught and gave them all away to the skipper and his brother who ran the bar, when we got back to the camp.

Back to Lusito and Barry's dinner of guinea fowl. The chef had done a wonderful job of preparing the bird and with the large selection of vegetables, it was a meal fit for a king. Not all visitors were treated that way. Of course, Barry had to tell everyone who would listen how we came by the bird. Nobody really believed him I'm sure, when he said I had shot it, one handed, from a moving vehicle that I was driving. My ability, or lack of, with a rifle was well known. Nicknames like "Dead-eye Dick" and "Jesse James" were bandied about for a couple of days, but none of them stuck.

The trip to take Barry back to the sugar plantation and the air strip, the following morning, was uneventful, except for my stopping off for a beer at the Chirundu hotel bar, on the return leg. It was a really hot morning and the road had been dry and dusty. I was sitting at the bar enjoying my beer when a white man sat down on the stool next to me. He looked a bit scruffy and didn't smell that good and I wasn't sure I really wanted to know him, up close. He had a canvas pouch on a strap over the shoulder of his bush jacket, with his hand holding the flap down as though he might lose something.

He didn't order anything from the bar and after a minute or so, I turned to look at him.

He said, "Let me ask you a question," as he took his free hand out of his pocket and placed it on the bar and opened it. "That's a full box of matches, there. You look like a tough young fella. D' you think you could squash that box, end on?"

"I've heard this one before, so I know I can't, and neither can you," I replied.

"How about buying me a beer if I can show you how it's done, right here, without using any tools." He smiled.

"Sounds good. No tools. Okay."

With that he opened the flap on his pouch and pulled out a baby croc, its snout taped up with some black electrical tape. It was only about eight inches long but the man held him firmly on the bar. Taking the tape off its snout, he gingerly held the match box by the sides, in front of the croc and, in the blink of an eye, the croc had smashed the box and its contents into splinters. The man hurriedly re-taped the croc's snout and returned him to the pouch.

As I ordered a round of beers for both of us, the man introduced himself as Bobby and said, "That was just a little demonstration of the power of a croc. They can be really mean with it too. And I should know; I hunt the big ones for the skin."

"Funny you should say that," I answered. "I have a friend on the construction camp at Lusito where I work, named Van. He used to be a croc hunter before he came to work for us."

Bobby laughed out loud and said, "Well, I'm damned. This really is a small world. I've worked with him on the river before, some time ago, but I reckoned he was crazy, some of the stunts he pulled. Does he still dive in after them?"

"Not any more, he doesn't." I said, "He works as a diesel mechanic now on heavy, earth-moving equipment. And a bloody good one he is, too."

Suddenly serious Bobby said, "You know, I wouldn't mind settling down a bit myself, if I could get a regular job like that. I'm no mechanic, though. I don't know what I could do. Before I started croc hunting, I served two years in a Nyasaland prison for poaching elephant tusks for ivory, and I'm just getting too old for that kind of thing now."

"You know, I just might be able to help you out here," I said, "The company I work for at Lusito, H.G. Barton, Ltd. has just finished building a warehouse to store supplies for the native workers. You know, mealie meal, peanuts, and so on, and they are looking for a white man to be responsible for the stock and the two African workers who handle the stuff. It's not much of a job and won't pay much, but a room, bedding, and three meals a day are thrown in. What d'ya say?"

"But what about my prison record?" he replied.

"I won't tell them if you don't'" I said. "But there's one condition."

"What's that?" he asked.

"Just make sure you let that little croc loose in the river before we leave here."

He shook hands with me and went outside right then and dropped the croc into the river from the bridge. He followed me back to Lusito in his rusty old truck, and it was quite a reunion when he met up again with Van. I introduced him to my boss, Jim, after telling Jim how we had met. I told Jim I couldn't vouch for him, but he seemed good enough to run the ration store, and nobody else seemed to want the job.

Bobby worked well in the native supplies warehouse and re-established his friendship with Van.

Al was still my best friend at Lusito. He was the company blacksmith and worked on anything metal which needed making, mending, adjusting or modifying. He was a wizard with gas or electric welding equipment and was always in great demand, keeping the heavy equipment running. He was also a natural good shot. He just couldn't miss a target whether he was shooting a gun, throwing darts, shooting a bow or even throwing a stone. He could have made a lot of money with that talent if he chose to but he always felt sorry for his opponent. He tried to teach me with my rifle, but I was hopeless. Once I lay on the ground under a big baobab tree, with a big fat pigeon sitting on a bare branch no more than 20 feet above me. I fired the rifle ten times at that bird, finally hitting the branch. The pigeon looked down at me in disgust, I thought, and quite lazily flew away. I was convinced there was something wrong with the weapon, and I asked Al to check it out for me. He took an empty cigarette packet, set it up against a bank of dirt about 75-yards away and promptly put a hole through the center of it. "It checks out fine," he told me, as he tossed me the gun.

Now that we had such a great chef (we couldn't call him "the cook" anymore!), Al and I would go bird shooting once a week and bring back enough wild fowl for the mess, and the chef would prepare a special dinner with all the trimmings. Many of us received our education in fine dining in that outpost of civilization in the Zambezi valley.

As the work progressed, and the road took shape, travel became a lot easier. We started to see a lot of features that had previously been hidden by the vegetation. Tracks and animal trails into the bush were uncovered, and Al and I would follow them for a mile or so, just to see where they led. One such track led us to a large basin-like clearing in the bush, filled with stagnant water, reeds and water lilies. The center of the small lake was clear of growth but almost covered with wild geese and ducks. This was to be our favorite hunting ground on our weekly trips to supply the mess hall. We would leave Al's station wagon on the road-side, walk in to the water's edge, and I would take a sitting shot at the birds on the lake. It was hard to miss, even for me, with so many targets packed in there together.

At the sound of the rifle, all the birds would take off in a cloud of beating wings overhead as they circled the lake. Then Al would point his trusty old pump shotgun up in the air and almost without aiming would bring down at least a couple of birds with each shot. The birds kept circling the water; it was the only water for miles and they had no place else to go. Once we reckoned we had enough to feed the crew, it was my turn to work. I had to wade out and collect the bodies. It wasn't a very pleasant job, pushing through the reeds and waterlily pads, not knowing what else was in there, with the mud squishing and sucking underfoot. But it was the only way and having shot the birds, we were not just going to leave them. After we had them all on dry ground we loaded them into large sacks and hauled them to the car. Most times we had to walk the track twice to get all the birds back to the car.

One evening, we had just finished loading the car and were standing at the back of the car enjoying a cigarette. We were on the side of the road which disappeared in the distance into a setting sun. Enjoying the moment, I was aware of a distant, "Quack, quack," and high in the sky over the center of the road, a lone duck was heading towards us.

As he got closer I said to Al, "Just one more for the pot, what d'ya say?" and I tilted my gun towards the sky, one handed.

Al laughed out loud, "In your dreams, Don," and I pulled the trigger.

That poor little duck didn't know what hit him, and he came tumbling to the ground, almost at out feet. He had been shot clean through the head. Al and I looked at each other in amazement. I couldn't believe it. With Barry's guinea fowl before and now the duck, that was the second time this sort of thing had happened. And once again, I had to put up with the good-natured teasing about my shooting ability when the story got out, back at camp. There was no way that Al could keep that story to himself.

On several of our bird-hunting trips we encountered a small group of elephants, grazing on the vegetation at the side of the road. The herd generally consisted of three females, a larger male and a couple of babies. They appeared to be a very peaceful, happy little family. One day, as we approached them, I asked Al to stop the car.

"What for?" he asked.

"I want to see how close I can get to them." I replied.

"Are you nuts? Those things will stomp you into the ground as soon as look at you."

"I don't believe they will, I've just got a feeling they might tolerate me if I don't pose a threat to the babies. I won't take the gun with me, not that a .22 would be any help, anyway."

He stopped the car, and I got out and crossed over the road to the place where the elephants were feeding.

I walked at a normal pace so as not to give the impression I was stalking them, and when I was within about 25yards, the bull elephant stopped eating and turned his head to stare at me. I stopped where I was and returned his stare, while he checked me out. Satisfied that I meant them no harm, he turned his head away and resumed his meal. The herd was moving slowly along the side of the road eating as they went and I went with them, still keeping my distance of 25 yards or so. I tried moving in a little closer, but each time I did, I got a dirty look from the big guy. The fact that he tolerated me as close as he did was a huge honor, so I didn't push it. I kept pace with the family for about a hundred yards and then I stopped and just watched them. As they slowly moved away from me, the bull turned his massive head to look at me. With a final flick of his tail, he resumed the walk with his wives and children following.

I was totally elated when Al drove up. "Weren't you scared?" he asked.

"A little, at first," I answered, "But after the bull checked me out and didn't charge, I just felt at peace."

"And what would you have done if he did charge?" he continued.

I grinned, "I would have bent down and picked up a lump of dung and thrown it at him."

"So what if there hadn't been any dung on the ground?"

"Oh, I would have known where to find some!" I said.

Al smiled. "I fell for that one, didn't I?"

One evening, in the Chancer's Arms, the discussion was about hunting with a bow and arrow. Apparently, some American hunter had recently killed an elephant with a bow in a different part of Africa. There was a sporting goods store in Lusaka and Al wanted to find out about archery. It was a target type of sport which he had never tried and we were all interested to see if he would be as good with that as he was with a rifle. The following Saturday, Al and I drove into Lusaka in Al's old station wagon. It was a drive of eighty miles, the first twenty on our gravel road from Lusito to the main road. Arriving in Lusaka we visited the sports store and ended up with a plain fibreglass bow for me and a compound bow for Al. My bow was an 80-pound pull, and Al's was 90. We also purchased ten aluminum practice arrows each and a packet of paper targets. We then stopped by the Northern Breweries outlet and stocked up with supplies for the bar. No trip to town would be complete without picking up supplies for the bar! After a quick lunch and a couple of beers we headed back to camp. There was no D.U.I. in Africa in those days. Most people had enough sense to drink and drive responsibly. On the trip back we talked about our new toys.

Thinking about where we could set up a shooting range, we came up with the idea that we could use the face of the sandy bluff, between the bar at the top and the Lusito river at the back. Between the river bank and the base of the bluff was a distance of about 35 yards, which would be good enough for a start. And there was already an access path from the top of the slope to the bottom, made by people going down to fish for barbel in the river.

As soon as we arrived back at camp and offloaded the bar supplies, we took the archery gear down to the river bank. The distance from there to the base of the steep, sandy slope in front of us was just as we had thought and the rough sandy path led up to the two outhouses at the back of the bar. I set one of the paper targets up against the slope, while Al fitted an arrow to his bow. The storekeeper in Lusaka had already put the string on Al's bow when he showed him how it was done. I rejoined Al at the river bank and he let fly at the target. Dead center! Of course, I never expected anything else. He just couldn't miss. I hurried to fit an arrow to my bowstring and took a shot at the target and was pleasantly surprised when I hit it. Not in the center, naturally, but in the top right-hand corner. It was still an achievement for me, and I felt that, with practice, I might become a fair shot with a bow.

Now that we knew the bows worked okay we had to find out how far they would shoot. There was a large baobab tree situated about two hundred yards away, along the river bank, with no structures behind it so we made that the target. Alec took the first shot and with enough elevation, the arrow fell close to the base of the tree. My bow seemed to be a lot flimsier than Al's and hadn't cost half as much; I was about to see why. I pulled back on the strung arrow as hard as I could, aiming at the top of the tree for elevation. As I paused to adjust my aim there was a resounding "crack!" and the bow broke into two pieces.

To say I was ticked off would be putting it mildly! Al laughing his head off didn't help, either. Finally I settled down and picked up the broken bow pieces. "Well, these are going back to the store and I'll get my money back—or else!" I growled.

"Now wait a minute," said Al, "I don't want to be the only one with a bow; there won't be much fun in that, and I've been thinking. Suppose we get some floodlights down here, tidy up the area, maybe build a couple of bench seats, and get some of the other lads interested. We could hold shooting competitions in the evenings, instead of just sitting around in that crowded little bar. It would certainly give us something else to do, and it might cut down on the drinking."

"You know, that's not a bad idea for an old fella," I replied.

Al was twelve years older than I, which is why I got to do the retrieving on our duck hunts.

"And if we dug out some steps in that path down the slope, we might even get some spectators. So okay, I'll go back into town, if I can get a day off next week, and see what I can get that sports store owner to cough up. But I don't just want a replacement, I want something better. Can I borrow the car?"

"Of course you can as long as you remember to bring beer for the bar."

Bow shooting and our suggestion to make a shooting range down by the river out back, was soon a hot topic in the bar. Several of the machine operators wanted to join in and I promised to bring back catalogs when I went back into town to get a new bow. Everyone agreed that it could be a good way to cut down on beer consumption. Some of the men had bar tabs so big that they handed over most of their pay each month to the bar and the beer was sold at cost, so no one was making a profit out of them.

We estimated that it would take a week or so to complete all the improvements we had suggested but with so many willing hands, everything was ready by the time I arrived back on camp the following Tuesday afternoon with my new bow and a handful of catalogs and pamphlets.

"So what kind of bow did you get?" asked Al, as he finished helping me offload the beer for the bar. It was still in its brown paper wrapping, in the back of the station wagon.

"Well, I can assure you it's not a fiberglass piece of rubbish. I told the man at the store what he could do with his fiberglass junk, and he came up with this one. It was more expensive than the other, but he said he wouldn't charge me for it. I think he knew he'd be wasting his time trying!" I untied the string, removed the packing, and brought out my new bow. "This time it's tubular steel and guaranteed not to break. It might rust, if I don't look after it, but it won't break. I also bought an arm-guard. If you're not careful, when you let fly, that string can hit the inside of your arm and raise a welt. And it's pretty powerful, more so than the other one at short range, the man said."

"Looks good," said Al. "Let's see it shoot. See if it will penetrate the wrinkle tin on the outhouse over there."

While we were speaking, I had been stringing the bow, and I now notched one of the new arrows, stretched back, and let fly at the latrine wall, about five yards away.

There was a series of impact sounds and a yell as the door of the structure flew off its hinges, flat on the ground. A terrified Italian concrete worker bolted outside with his pants round his ankles, cussing up a blue streak. On the outside of the wall on the ground was a small heap of feathers from the arrow and on the inside the arrow shaft was firmly stuck in the horizontal two-by-four bracing the other wall. Both Al and I stood there with our mouths open and it wasn't until the Italian got his wits together and his pants up that he explained in broken English, how the arrow barely missed hitting him in the head as he sat on the seat of the toilet. I apologized sincerely to him and offered to buy him a beer, but he was too upset to accept the beer. I just hoped he accepted the apology; I had momentary thoughts of the Mafia tracking me down!

After he left, Al and I went into the bar to calm our nerves. It was on the second beer that the funny side of the incident hit us. The memory of the sight of that poor unfortunate man, smashing the door down and flying out of the toilet with his pants down, screaming Italian obscenities at the top of his voice was too much and we collapsed with laughter, as did everyone else there when we told them what we found funny. After that, for a while, before anyone went outside to the "Loo," I would be asked if I had my bow with me.

Everyone concerned in the incident was very fortunate that day. It could well have had a tragic ending.

The Chancer's Arms Archery Club soon became a popular evening activity. It didn't do much to cut down on the beer consumption, quite the opposite, in fact. In all the shooting matches, the losers bought a round. Two part-time mess-hall workers acted as beer fetchers and spent their evenings running up and down the steps to the bar with arms full of bottles.

It was a lot of fun, no one got hurt, and Al could score a free beer anytime he chose.

As our road continued to progress, reports started to filter in on the bush network that the coffer dams were complete in the Kariba gorge and that work was well underway on the main dam wall. The coffer dams would divert the Zambezi river away from the main dam work area. In the dry season, the mighty Zambezi was not much more than a rapidly moving shallow stream, through the gorge, with rock walls climbing hundreds of feet on either side but when the rains came it became a rushing torrent. Timing of the construction was most important and in the rush to keep up with the schedule, several workers had been lost in the millions of cubic yards of concrete, poured to form the main dam wall. When complete, the roadway over the dam would join our Northern Access Road to its counterpart on the south side.

In the Chancer's Arms one Saturday evening, I mentioned that I would like to visit the dam site and suggested a trip the following day. It would be something different to do. Al said he would like to go and Van and Bobby joined in. Around mid-morning the next day, we met at the bar, loaded our lunch and beer supplies into my Land Rover and we set off to visit Kariba Dam. Several miles of the road outside camp had been completed and the first part of the trip was a relatively smooth ride but then it deteriorated as we reached the work areas where bush clearing was underway, preparing for the road-building operations. Some gangs were scattered all along the road in various locations and some of them were working overtime, this being a Sunday, to catch up with their individual schedules. Once we left the built-up road, we traveled by the bush path which I knew quite well. I drove over it at least once a month when I made my payroll runs, but I had never taken the time to go all the way to the end as we didn't have any workers that far along, at that time.

There were several miles of rough and very bumpy track that we had to cover, under overhanging branches, in the heat of midday. The noise of the motor was the only sound for miles around and the sweat poured off us.

Bobby commented, "I sure hope this trip is going to be worth it; right now I feel like losing my breakfast!"

With that I hurriedly put on the brakes and we took a break to relax a little from the gut-wrenching ride. I really didn't want to finish the rest of the trip in a vomit-smelling vehicle! Nobody felt like a beer so we took turns at the water bottle and lit up cigarettes. While we smoked, we walked along the track a short way, to straighten out stiff and sore muscles.

Feeling refreshed, we got back in the Land Rover and resumed our journey, a little slower this time. As we bumped along we became aware of a really bad smell in the air, and I looked accusingly at Bobby.

"It isn't me, honest!" he said, and turning a tight corner in the track, we found the source. Hanging in the center of the track from an overhanging tree branch was a beautiful, ten feet long, python. It had been shot in the head and tied to the branch as some kind of warning, or a sick joke. It must have been there several days as the smell was outrageous. I would have liked to cut it down, but it would have meant standing on the hood of the Land Rover to reach it and then it would probably have fallen into the vehicle. We decided to leave it where it was and let nature take its course. When the road was finally built, it had a slight bend in it right about where we found the snake, and thereafter that bend was known as Python Corner.

After a few more miles of the torturous track, we broke out of the bush into a clearing which stretched to the edge of the Kariba Gorge. There were a couple of temporary buildings, one of which housed a winch. Cables ran from the winch, through a series of pulleys attached to a large metal pylon, set in huge concrete blocks, anchoring it to the rock. The cable stretched across the gorge, over the dam site, to a similar structure on the south bank. Attached to the main cable by smaller steel cables at each corner and lying on the ground at the edge of the gorge, was a wooden platform about fifteen feet square.

Cautiously, I drove the Land Rover towards the edge of the gorge. I never have liked heights and I wasn't interested in getting too close to the edge. I stopped just short of the wooden platform as a worker came out of one of the buildings and called to us. He was a large, black man who looked like he had been training with weights. He asked where we wanted to go and I said,

"We're looking for a path to take us down into the gorge. Is there a bridge of some sort down there so we can go up the other side?"

"No, sir," he replied. "The only way across from here is on the cable. There's room on the platform for your Land Rover, and the weight is no problem, so drive on. I'll get my man on the winch to take us over."

And with that he turned and walked back to the winch house. I suppose I must have lost a little color in my face at his words and Al said,

"What's up, Don? Not scared of a little sky riding, are you?"

"Terrified is the word that comes to mind," I answered. "I don't know if I can do this."

"Well, you'd better," chimed in Van. "You'll never hear the last of it, if you don't."

And I knew I had to go through with it. As I positioned the vehicle on the platform, I had the others guide me so that it sat dead in the middle. I turned the ignition off. There wasn't a lot of room to spare on any side and when the winch boss returned he squeezed on the corner of the platform, hanging onto one of the corner cables. He waved to the operator, and the platform rose up slightly off the ground. I re-checked for the second or third time that the emergency brake was full on and the motor was in low gear. Slowly the platform swung over the edge and we were suspended in mid-air over that enormous chasm. The huge boulders in the bottom of the gorge looked like pebbles from that distance and I had to force myself to breathe.

Our extra passenger, noticing my discomfort called out, "Relax, boss, I haven't lost anyone yet," and, holding onto the corner cable, he swung out over the gorge.

"Okay, okay," I yelled, "I'll relax; just stop doing that and don't ever do it again, at least not when I'm around!"

He just laughed, but he stayed on the platform for the rest of the ride.

Once over the south bank, the platform lowered, and I drove off. The winch boss told me that when we returned, we just had to blow the horn and wave, and he would come back over to fetch us for the return trip. He also gave us directions to the new Kariba hotel that had just been opened on the south bank, where we could get a cold beer. Never before had that suggestion sounded so good!

Four rather dirty, sweaty, scruffy looking bush hogs like us didn't really fit in at the rather up-scale Kariba hotel bar and after a quick cold beer each, we continued with our tour of the site.

There really wasn't much to see around the dam site at this stage of construction but the enormity of the task and challenges to be overcome were obvious. This dam would one day, create the largest man-made lake in the world, at that time. Thousands of wild animals had to be rescued from the rising waters in one of the biggest operations of its kind, "Operation Noah."

We found a construction road that led to the bottom of the gorge and we were able to walk across the river on rocks sticking out of the water. I went back to the Land Rover on the south bank and found my small fishing pole which I always had with me along with the rifle in the vehicle and dangled a hook in the water from a rock in the middle of the stream

"What the hell are you doing?" called Bobby.

And I replied, "One day when the dam is built, this will all be under deep water. I'll be able to say truthfully that I went fishing in the middle of the mighty Zambezi river without a boat." The expressions on their faces showed me clearly that they thought I was crazy.

After half an hour we had seen all there was to see, and we returned to our arrival point on the south side. At the sound of our horn, the platform started back over the gorge towards us, with the winch boss on board. Somehow, I had thought that the platform traveled straight across, but now I could see that it sagged down in the middle so that it appeared to be going downhill on the first half of the trip and climbing back up on the second half. Somehow that was even more nerve-wracking to me and my hands were white-knuckled on the steering wheel, all the way back. Each of us gave the winch boss a good tip, when we arrived safely on the north side and we hurried off back down the path leading to our camp, some twenty miles away.

It took us almost three hours to get back to camp, but the journey was relatively uneventful. The only thing a little out of the ordinary happened just after taking a corner on the track a little too fast and arriving right in the middle of a pack of baboons who were as surprised as we were. I jammed on the brakes and we skidded to a halt in a cloud of dust and flying baboons, some even carrying babies. When we calmed down and the dust settled, I fully expected to see baboon corpses all over the road. But they had moved so fast that we didn't hit one of them. There was a great deal of baboon chatter coming from the surrounding bush and I guessed that what they were saying amongst themselves wasn't very polite. I couldn't blame them and was a lot more careful the rest of the way.

We arrived back at camp just in time to grab a quick shower and a change of clothes before dinner. Al and I spent the evening in the Chancer's Arms, being too tired to join in the archery shoot down by the Lusito. On top of being worn out from the drive, I wasn't feeling at all well. This was most unusual for me; I couldn't remember the last time I was sick. By 8 p.m. I was feeling even worse, with an increasing pain in the belly and a powerful headache. Our only medical resource on the camp was a nurse, an old South African lady who had a very high opinion of herself and her talents. I told Al I'd see him the next day and made my way across camp to the nurse's quarters.

I knocked on the door and stood waiting. Finally the door opened and Sister Anne, as she insisted on being addressed, asked me what I wanted. I explained that I was feeling sick with stomach pains and headaches and asked for her to check me over. She glanced at her wrist watch and back at me and said, "Do you know what time it is? And it's a Sunday! I'm not even on duty on Sunday, and I'm certainly not opening the dispensary at this time of night, anyway. Come back and see me tomorrow, at work." And with that she closed the door in my face. I resisted the urge to kick the door down and strangle the old b...lady, and stumbled off to my room.

During the night, the pain in my gut worsened and I was groaning in agony. It didn't matter whether I was standing, sitting or lying down, I couldn't get any relief from it and I could hardly wait for morning. When I didn't show up for work, Jim, my boss, sent a message to Al, for him to check up on me. Al found me rolling around on the floor of my room, moaning and groaning in agony, too weak to stand. He quickly returned to his workshop, told one of his helpers to join him and came back to my room with his station wagon. They picked me up and stuffed me in the back amongst all the old duck and goose feathers left over from our last hunt and then took me up to the dispensary. When I was carried into the examination room, Sister Anne said, "That's the fool who woke me up last night. What's wrong with him?"

"Isn't that your job, Sister? You're supposed to know what to do with sick people, aren't you?" replied Al in his most diplomatic fashion. "And if you saw him last night, why didn't you treat him then?"

She really didn't know what to say to that and busied herself with taking my temperature, blood pressure and all the usual tests.

"You've got a high fever," she said, "But I can't really tell what's bothering you. Are you sure it isn't something you ate...or drank?" she sniffed disapprovingly.

"That does it," snapped Al, "I'm taking him into Lusaka where there are real doctors—this could be serious. While I get him back in the car you can be writing a letter for me to take him to the hospital. You can also get a message to the workshop manager, my boss, to explain my absence and to Jim, Don's boss."

She gave me four aspirin tablets for the pain before we left, which did nothing to alleviate it. The ride to Lusaka was excruciating and I kept dropping in and out of consciousness. It was an 80-mile journey which felt more like 800. Al drove right up to the emergency room doors, blowing the horn wildly when we arrived at the hospital. People in white coats started appearing from everywhere, it seemed, and I was soon on a stretcher and then inside on an examination table. It didn't take too long, after taking blood samples and doing other tests, to determine that I had contracted bilharzia. I was told that this was a disease caused by exposure to stagnant water. Certain snails living in stagnant water carried microscopic worms that entered the body through any opening in the skin. They then made their way to the stomach or bladder, where they proceeded to eat the lining of the inside of the organ. Most cases saw either the stomach or the bladder being infected, but, wouldn't you know it, I had both.

They started the treatment immediately, large injections daily, in the thickest part of my thigh and after a few days I felt more like my normal self again. When the doctor asked me how I thought I might have got the disease, he confirmed that wading into a stagnant pond to retrieve dead ducks was the most likely cause and recommended that I stick to guinea fowl in the future. He also told me that the swollen stomachs sometimes seen on African children were mostly caused by bilharzia and not malnutrition.

Right then I decided, that if I ever developed a paunch, the cause would be bilharzia, not beer!

The company shuttle bus collected me from the hospital at the end of a week. I carried a small package containing enough injections for another two weeks, which Sister Anne had to administer. She wasn't too happy when she found out I was really ill, and she made them as uncomfortable as possible. The injections had to be stored in a fridge, and I quickly learned that near freezing liquid, of any kind, injected into a large muscle like the thigh, was very painful. The nurse at the hospital had always warmed it up by rubbing the syringe between her hands for a few minutes before sticking me. I told Sister Anne about this, and she just brushed it aside as nonsense. After that I made it a point to arrive early for my shot and by the time she arrived, I had already warmed the stuff up. I looked forward to the day when I might get even with the old b...lady, and that wasn't long in coming.

One Saturday evening, as we sat at the bar in the Chancer's Arms, I mentioned to Al that I was getting a bit tired of the noise coming from the place during the week in the evenings. The single quarters were quite close to the bar and the noise carried, particularly when things became a little rowdy. I didn't care about Saturdays; I stayed up as late as anybody on Saturdays. That was my night to howl! But during the week I liked to get to sleep around nine and get up no later than five. That gave me plenty of time to get a shower, have a good breakfast in the mess hall and be ready for work at seven. I hated to be late for work and was always the first one in the office. Al was living in married quarters with his wife and teenage daughter, a good distance from the bar, so it didn't bother him. But he did have a suggestion that might solve my problem. He told me about a small wrinkle tin building, set back in the bush about twenty yards from the rear wall of the maintenance shop. It was located beside the trunk of a big dead tree, which could be seen above the bush and had been the living quarters for the boss man in charge of the original camp construction. If I was interested in moving into it, Al said he would help with any bush clearing and whatever was necessary to fix it up for me to occupy.

Sunday morning, after breakfast Al and I walked down to the maintenance shop and he pointed out the dead tree. If nothing else, it would be well away from the bar and the other quarters. I really would be on my own and that sounded fine to me. The path to the hut had long since overgrown and we had to cut our way in with a couple of pangas, or sugar-cane knives, which we picked up from Al's office in the maintenance area. The door was closed but not locked and I was pleasantly surprised when we entered. Inside was a small room containing a sink with two faucets on top of a small cupboard. A door on the left opened up to a sleeping area with just enough room for a single bed, a bedside cabinet and a wardrobe on the other side. The furniture was still there and intact. All I could think of, that I might need, would be a couple of chairs and a new mattress. From the foot of the bed to the rear wall of the building was a distance of six feet and directly opposite the bed, in the rear wall was a small four feet square extension which was a shower stall. The place would need a good cleaning before I could live there, and fumigating, too, to get rid of the insects that had taken up residence, but it looked perfect to me.

I would have to get approval from my boss to occupy the place and get the mattress and chairs out of the main stores but that shouldn't be difficult. After all, it would free up my room in single quarters for another employee. Al and I talked about little else the rest of the day. He said he would get a D6, which was in the shop for maintenance, and clear the bush around the house. I asked him to leave the big dead tree and to only clear a wide path around the rest of the place—I wasn't interested in gardening in those days. The plumbing attachments were still in place and a connection to the main pipe line supplying the maintenance facility would be simple.

As usual, I was the first one in the office on Monday morning. As soon as Jim came in, I cornered him.

"I need to ask a favor, Jim. I want to change my living quarters, and I think I've found the perfect place. It's the old shack that was used by the foreman of the camp building crew before we arrived here, and it's been abandoned since then. But I will need a few things to fix it up. What d'ya say?"

"Well, I'll have to have a look at the place first. Where is it? I don't know of any building that isn't occupied," he replied.

"If you've got a spare couple of minutes right now, I'll show you," I said. We took my vehicle down to the maintenance area and stopped near the back wall.

"I don't see any shack," he said.

"Just follow me, and I'll show you." I led the way along the rough path that Al and I had cut through the bush. It was only a few yards, but so thick that the shack was completely hidden. I opened the door and we went inside. Jim didn't say anything as we looked around. There wasn't a whole lot to see and it looked pretty scruffy but I knew I could get it to be livable. Finally Jim said,

"Well, okay then, if you're sure this is what you want. But it's going to need some work done on it. A good clean for a start, and maybe a coat of paint on the walls to hide the rust patches. The roof probably leaks, too, and the rains will be here in a couple of months, so that will need fixing. If you can get that all done before you move in, then it's okay with me, but I would like to see it again before you move in."

"Thanks, Jim. That's all I need, that and a new mattress and a couple of chairs. But they can come after the work is done," I said.

Jim didn't say much on the short ride back to the office building and I didn't want to pester him in case he changed his mind about my new house. When we arrived he asked me to wait for him in his partitioned office, in the corner of the building. I went in and sat in the chair facing Jim's desk. I felt a little apprehensive; this was a first for this kind of invitation. Jim soon returned carrying two mugs of coffee, one of which he gave to me, then sat on his chair on the opposite side of the desk.

He must have read the uncertainty in my expression. He said, "Don't look so concerned, Don. What I've got to tell you is good news, I think. Now what I'm about to tell you must go no further than this office. You can't tell this to anyone, not even your friend Al, and I want your solemn promise on this before I carry on. One part of it you can tell, and that's about me promoting you to site accountant. With all your responsibilities, including the primary one, the payroll, I've been wanting to do that for some time. But it would have meant moving you out of the regular single quarters into more executive-type accommodations, and we just didn't have anywhere suitable. Now it seems you have solved that problem for me. So, congratulations! Now the other part; do I have your word?"

"Of course, Jim, and thanks for the promotion!" I replied with a smile.

He continued, "Well, H.G. (The owner of the company) has been chasing other earth moving contracts here in Northern Rhodesia, so that we can carry on after this road job is finished. It won't happen for quite some time yet, but it looks like we have a really good chance of going to work on the Copperbelt with the mining company. If it happens and you are agreeable, I would want you to transfer to that job as site accountant. There will be a site engineer, who will be in charge, and you will be his deputy, as you might say. Again, it will mean living in the bush, and you seem to have become quite a 'bushman' since you arrived here. Now, I can't tell you any more than that, for right now, but how do you feel about it?"

I was really sitting up and taking notice now. "That sounds almost too good to be true," I replied. "When do we leave?"

"Not so fast, young man." He laughed. "We've still got a long way to go here, yet. It could be another year before the other job opens up, and we still have this road to finish. I just wanted you to know that we want you to stay with us when this job is completed, and that there will be other work."

"So, Jim, does the promotion mean more money?" I asked.

"Not right away, but certainly when you take over the new contract on the Copperbelt. You'll be number two in charge, and even though it won't be such a big job as this, you'll have a lot more responsibility. Anyway, for the time being, keep that all to yourself. Now, let's get you a requisition for the mattress and chairs from the main stores."

Just as I got up to return to my own office space, Jim said, "Hey, Don, I just had another thought. If you're looking for someone to help you clean your new place, I have a suggestion. My houseboy brought a local man to see me the other day who is looking for a job. It seems he just appeared out of the bush several days ago, a mile or so down the road. He was in a highly agitated state, and when he calmed down he told my boy about finding a water hole which was frequented by many kinds of animals. He had been trapped there, up a tree for two days, or so he said. Anyway, my houseboy has been looking after him, and he wants to find him a job. He's quite a bit smarter than the average laborer, and he'll soon pick up enough English to be useful. He could get your 'mansion' cleaned up for you and maybe do a bit of painting."

"That would be great, Jim; maybe your houseboy could bring him to meet me at the mansion after work today. I know Al and I would both be interested in learning where that water hole is, if nothing else."

At lunch in the mess hall, I told Al that I had been given permission to move, if the place met with Jim's approval when it had been cleaned up. I left out all mention of the promotion, it didn't amount to much if there was no extra money with it, not yet, anyway. I was really anxious to get into my new quarters, so Al made sure the D6 was gassed up and ready to work and by dinner time, he had cleared a small space around the shack, leaving the dead tree as I had asked..Just enough to let a little daylight in. Jim's houseboy brought the newcomer to meet me and he impressed me right away. There was no way I could remember his native name, so I named him "Joseph," after my dad in England. He was delighted with his new name, and after agreeing to his "terms of employment," he went to work right away scrubbing and cleaning. By my pointing and saying the name of something a couple of times, Joseph soon had a basic English vocabulary going. He was definitely smarter than the average African, and by the end of the week, we had established a good working relationship. With Joseph's efforts during the day, and mine and Al's during the evenings, the place was as neat as it was going to get by Friday. We had even tidied up the mess that the D6 had unavoidably made when it was bush clearing. The water and electricity had been re-connected, and all I needed was a mattress to replace the old one, which had been dumped, and something on which to sit besides the bed.

I asked Jim to come and make his inspection, which he did after work on Friday and we were all pleased when he gave it a passing mark. Jim's houseboy was there also, as he and Joseph were staying together in the compound and would be walking home together. He explained to Joseph in his own language, that the job was finished and that they should go, and Joseph asked me for "pay." I gave him a few shillings and his eyes lit up, but he looked a little down as he turned to leave.

"Wait a minute, Joseph," I called, "I'll meet you here at six in the morning. We've got to bring my stuff from single quarters, and then get the new mattress and chairs. Then, if you want to stay, I suppose I need a houseboy, if you're interested."

His friend rapidly translated what I had said, and Joseph hurried back to me and reached for my hand to shake it as he had seen the others do, when Jim gave us his okay. His eyes teared up a little and he stammered out, "Thank you, baas." I thought I had made a friend.

Once I had settled into my new house, a pattern soon developed. I had acquired a one-ring electric burner, and Joseph's first job in the morning was to make me coffee, while I showered and got ready for work. He then spent the rest of the day cleaning up after me, washing my clothes, and even ironing, a job that his houseboy friend taught him. I was still having my main meals in the mess, so he didn't have any cooking to do. I gave him some of my old clothes, and you would have thought that I had given him the world. All the time he was learning English, and it wasn't too long before we could communicate pretty well, and I asked him about the water hole he had found out in the bush. He started to jabber away in his native tongue, and I had to stop him.

"Wait, Joseph," I said. "Slow down. I cannot understand you."

"Sorry, baas," said Joseph. "When my friend come tonight, he tell you." Jim's houseboy arrived that evening to walk to the compound with Joseph, and before they left, Joseph asked him to translate while he told me about the water hole.

Joseph had left his village many miles away, across the Zambezi basin, and was walking towards the place where he had heard on the jungle grapevine that there might be work. He didn't want to be a farmer like the rest of the tribe. He knew there had to be something better, just around the next mpani tree. I certainly understood that feeling. Anyway, there were no roads to follow and he was navigating by instinct when he came upon a pond in a small clearing, miles away from anywhere. It was surrounded by reeds and elephant grass and there were many signs of animal tracks going into the water. Thinking this would be a good place to catch his dinner, he crouched down in the tall grass, spear at the ready, hoping for a small buck or other animal to pass by. Hearing a slight rustling sound in the bush at the edge of the clearing, he quietly and slowly raised his head over the grass and made out a family of warthogs approaching. The piglets were small and the parents were on guard. Not wishing to confront the family with just one spear, he moved slowly away from their path towards the edge of the clearing and the trees. He had almost reached the trees when a small herd of water buffalo appeared. Sniffing the air, they knew he was somewhere near but their thirst overcame their curiosity, fortunately for Joseph, and they lumbered on to the water's edge. Alone and in the close company of two of Africa's most dangerous and unpredictable animals, armed only with a spear, Joseph wasn't feeling very happy. Doing his best to keep calm and cause as little disturbance as possible, he gradually made his way towards the biggest tree he could see.

Inching his way through the grass and reeds, he was making no sound to attract attention when a sudden, mind blasting, elephant call split the silence and a huge bull appeared at the edge of the clearing.

At that stage Joseph was so frightened, he dashed towards his target tree, throwing caution to the wind and almost flew up it. As high as he could safely go, he wedged himself between branches and the trunk and settled down for the night. All night long, all kinds of animals were either arriving for a drink or leaving and he was too nervous to get more than an occasional catnap. Daylight finally came but he was still too scared to climb down and continue his journey. Although very few creatures showed themselves during the day he remained in the tree for another night. It was the following morning before hunger forced him down to the ground again. His water bottle was also close to empty although he had been drinking very sparingly, but he wouldn't take a chance on filling it at the water hole. He just wanted to get as far away from that place as possible.

Having reached the edge of the bush, he moved quietly around the clearing until he was at a point directly opposite to where he had arrived. His autopilot told him that he was again headed in the right direction and he pressed on through the bush in the sweltering heat of the day. Skirting thorn bush thickets, climbing over dead trees and weaving between mpani trees, it took him several hours before he came across a huge ridge of earth and broken trees stretching to the left and right, as far as he could see. He had found the road. One of our dump trucks was passing by returning to camp after work, as he stumbled close to exhaustion, down the road side of the ridge. The driver stopped and helped him into the cab, and he had his first ride ever, in a motorized vehicle back to camp. No one could understand him when he spoke until someone called Jim's houseboy, who came from a village adjacent to Joseph's and understood his dialect. That was how Joseph arrived at the camp and became my houseboy.

During the week that followed, I told Al the story of Joseph's water hole. Al said he would really like to see it and of course, so would I. But how to get Joseph to lead us there was another matter. Joseph had no interest in going back to the hole, with or without an armed guard. I think he was still having the occasional nightmare about the place. The best I could do was to get him to draw a rough sketch of the location, in relation to the road, sunrise and a gravel pit which I showed him.

On the following Saturday morning we packed a couple of sandwiches and our water bottles and Al and I drove to the gravel pit. We parked the station wagon there and took the rifle and Al's shotgun with us. It was late in the morning, almost noon when we left the car and set off into the bush. From Joseph's sketch it didn't appear to be very far from where we left the car, so we thought we had plenty of time. As we walked along through the straggly mpani trees and around the rhino thorn bushes, we made no attempt to hide our presence but kept a watchful eye on our surroundings. Most wild animals will get out of the way of humans, providing the humans don't pose an obvious threat. Buffalo and wild pigs are two exceptions. Leopards were also known to attack, unprovoked, but there weren't many around that area. It was a hot and thirsty trek and we had to remind ourselves that the water had to last. After the bilharzia episode, I had no desire to be drinking water from the pond, even if we found it.

Plodding onwards I felt that we were going in the right direction, following Joseph's spoken directions and his sketch but it was getting to be a lot farther than I had imagined. We had both just about decided to give up and turn back when we pushed through a patch of tall grass and there it was. At least we could see the clearing, overgrown with grass and reeds, surrounded by trees. We approached the pond carefully, not knowing where the solid ground might end. Closer to the water, the earth had been churned into mud and slime by the feet of dozens of creatures that frequented this little oasis in an otherwise dry land. Moving back to the tree line we found a place to rest, on the trunk of a fallen tree and finally ate our sandwiches. By then we were both very hungry but we still had one full water bottle left.

From all the tracks around the pond, it was obvious that Joseph hadn't been exaggerating when he told us about his experience there. Neither of us were in a hurry to get up and start walking back to the car. We were enjoying the afternoon, smoking a few cigarettes and resting our weary legs when I realized that the light was beginning to fade. It would be getting dark around six-thirty and, according to my watch, that would be in another hour.

I said to Al, "So, do you think we had better get moving before Happy Hour at the old watering hole?"

He replied, "I suppose so. I don't want to get swamped by the crowd. But I sure don't fancy the walk back. We'll be able to follow our tracks, I suppose, while there's still light, but after that it will be guess work. And for as long as it took us to get here, it could take twice as long to get back. We could be in a bit of a bind."

"Okay, then," I said. "I think we can shorten the hike if we don't go back out the same way we came in. I believe we were walking parallel to the road most of the way, and if we set off at right angles to the way we came in we'll be heading towards the road. It's a full moon tonight, so we'll have that for light and direction. What d'ya say?"

"Damn, I don't know. I don't even know which way we came in here now. Maybe we should follow Joseph's lead and climb a tree for the night," he said.

"And how will that help?" I asked. "We still have to get back to camp sometime. Look, I know what I'm doing, and I can lead us back to the road. We'll have to catch a lift back to the gravel pit to pick up the car, but that'll be easy once we hit the road. And it shouldn't be as far to walk this way."

The light was really going by the time Al agreed to let me lead the way. If we weren't back on the road by nine p.m., I would have to buy all the beer for one day, for both of us, at the Chancer's Arms. It was daylight turning to dusk when we left the clearing, but it was almost dark when we had gone only a few yards into the bush. I had taken a bearing from the position of the setting sun and I had a very positive feel that I was going in the right direction. The trees were closer together and the brush thicker, or so it seemed, walking in this direction and we had to walk in single file, me in front. There was a short period between total darkness and the moon rising when we made very little headway, but we were able to pick up the pace a little when we had the moon to guide us. I had no doubt at all that we were on the right track and I tried to convince Al, who wasn't quite so sure, that we would soon be gulping down the cold beers, in the fridge at the Pub, that were calling our names.

We had been walking for ages it seemed, pushing our way through vegetation between the trees, when we came up against a huge rhino-thorn thicket. These bushes had thorns like darning needles and were something to keep away from, even in daylight. As soon as the first thorn stuck me, I called out, "Whoa!" and we both came to a halt.

Al asked why we had stopped and I told him what had stopped us. The thicket appeared to extend, to the right and left of us, as far as we could see, in the half light. I told Al to wait where he was, while I surveyed the obstacle. From what I could make out, it was something like a hedge. It was a lot longer than it was wide, and the narrowest part seemed to be in the center. There still didn't seem to be any way we could get across it but to go all the way round. I had no idea how long that would take but there seemed to be no alternative.

Until I bent down to remove a piece of tree branch that had become stuck in the laces of one my boots. I happened to glance sideways at the thorn bush and noticed an opening through the hedge, under the lower branches. Presumably some animal had forced its way through and had left a fairly clear path, wide enough for a man to get through, if he was really careful. Probably a warthog I thought, as I made the suggestion to Al that we should crawl through.

"Are you crazy?" he said."How the hell are we going to do that in the dark?"

"Very carefully," I answered, "Unless you want to find the end of this mess and walk round. It could go on for miles. But suit yourself—I'll wait for you on the other side." I dropped to the ground and started crawling. It was slow going, and I was punctured and scratched all over by the time I got through. But it was a much shorter crawl than I had bargained for, and I was soon calling encouragement to Al as he followed. He was not enjoying himself, which was evident by the long string of obscenities, many of them leveled at me, which indicated his location under the thorn bushes. When he stood up, after clearing the thorns, a pungent odor arose on the evening air.

"What happened, Al? Were you that scared?" I laughed.

Another round of cussin' and fussin' before he informed me that a previous thornbush crawler, probably a warthog, had left his calling card, and Al had put his arm in it. It was all over the sleeve of his bush jacket. It certainly stank, and I was grateful to be in the lead.

Once I located the moon through the tree tops and checked our heading, we set off once more. By now we were both very tired but I was still sure we were on the right track. After a while, the thick bush in front of us seemed to be getting thicker and higher and we had to look up about twelve feet to see the ragged edge against the night sky. Eventually we could see that it was a huge bank of dirt, rocks and broken trees, that stretched out on both sides of us.

"Now say I don't know where I'm going," I teased Al. "This is the pile of stuff cleared before the road was built and our last obstacle. The road is on the other side. So who buys the beers now?"

We dragged ourselves over the heap of piled-up dirt and broken trees and there was our road. The headlights of a truck were coming towards us, and I stepped out into the road and waved. The truck stopped, and we had a ride to the gravel pit to collect the station wagon. By the time we finally arrived back at Lusito, we were both dead tired. Al dropped me off at the maintenance area and I walked up the path to my mansion. I stopped for a second when I saw what looked like some kind of bundle on the front door step. And then the bundle jumped up. It was Joseph. He was so pleased to see me he was shaking my hand and rattling away in his own language. Laughing, I tried to calm him down, until at last he was able to catch his breath. He had been unable to go to sleep, worried about us. He had been back to the compound to try to sleep, but it had been no good, so he returned here to wait and see if we came back. He was obviously relieved when I told him not to worry; we were fine. Just a few scratches, which were minor. A good night's sleep would make us all feel better. He gripped my hand firmly, shook it, and turned and headed out for the compound, and his bed. I knew I had made a friend.

I slept in late on Sunday morning; it was seven thirty by the time I showered and made it to the mess hall for breakfast. Al and his family were already there and, after filling a plate at the counter, I joined them.

Al was telling them the story of our little trek to find the water hole and they had a good laugh when I interrupted him with my version of the thorn thicket incident. I asked Al what had happened to the bush jacket with the pig poop on the sleeve, and he told me that he had dumped it in the maintenance area garbage can after he left me. No doubt some native mechanic's helper would soon be sporting a new look.

Now that I was living in my little house, behind the maintenance area, I was able to enjoy a good night's sleep every night, during the week. I was far enough away from the Chancer's Arms that I couldn't hear any laughter or shouting going on up there and the maintenance area wasn't functional before I got up in the mornings. This meant that I could enjoy a little social interaction and a few beers in the evening and then go home to bed without being disturbed. Saturday evenings were different. I enjoyed staying at the bar until it closed. Unless I had plans for the day, Sunday was a day of rest and I liked to lie in bed in the morning, sometimes nursing a hangover and not getting up until eight or even nine a.m.

I had only been in the house a couple of weeks when my Sunday mornings were no longer peaceful. A troop of small monkeys started making a habit of visiting the dead tree, beside my house, and throwing dead branches down onto the wrinkle-tin roof. I don't know what pleasure that gave them but it make quite a racket inside the house. There was no sleeping with that going on. The second time it happened, I staggered outside and saw the leader of the pack, the biggest one there, hanging from another tree, just above my front door, directing operations. I shouted some un-Sunday-like words at him and he just stared back at me. The rest of the monkeys hung in the dead tree, not moving but watching to see what their boss was going to do. I must admit, he won the staring contest and I bent down to pick up some of the dead sticks and branches that his gang had thrown down on the roof. All I wanted to do was to get back to bed, but I knew it would be useless, unless I got rid of them first. I selected a stick and threw it at the big monkey as hard as I could. He nimbly dodged behind the trunk of his tree with, what sounded like a chuckle. I threw more sticks and each time he dodged; there was no way I was going to hit him. This went on

191

for several minutes when he called to his gang and away they all went through the trees, swinging from branch to branch.

As I lay back down on the bed sleep wouldn't come. All I could think about were those "blankity-blank" monkeys. I didn't know if they did this every morning, after I had gone to work, though I hadn't noticed any more branches lying on the ground than usual. Surely they didn't know what day of the week it was and were punishing me for having a hangover! I asked Al to get his boys, working in the maintenance area, to watch out for them. They could see the dead tree easily from behind the building. By the end of the week, no one had seen any monkeys near my house, and I enjoyed my Saturday evening with the crew in our pub, convinced that the monkey harassment was over.

Once again, I was wrong. At daybreak the next morning, I was awakened by a huge crash, and I almost fell out of bed. *What the hell was that?* I asked myself, and before it dawned on me that the monkeys were back, the roof was bombarded with even more missiles. My head was pounding and threatening to explode at any moment, and I grabbed my little single-shot .22 rifle, which was leaning against the wall by the bed. Dashing outside, raging mad, I spotted the boss monkey in his favorite spot. I pointed the gun in his general direction and fired, expecting the noise to frighten him away. Looking down at the gun as I was reloading, I didn't notice that I had hit him in the foot. When I looked back at him, he was hanging out from behind the tree trunk, and I jerked the rifle up and fired off the other round. I was so angry and hung-over I could hardly see, and I never expected to hit him. But I did, right through the heart, and he fell out of that tree like a rock. All the chattering amongst the gang stopped immediately. A few seconds went by in total silence, and then they slowly started to make their way back through the tree tops and into the bush. After making sure that the monkey was dead, I moved the body to a box I had been keeping behind the house, just in case it might come in handy.

I showed it to Joseph the next morning and told him the story and he assured me they would never bother me again. He also asked if I wanted him to get rid of it and when he left for the day he took the monkey with him. I asked him the next day what had he done with the monkey and he said that they had a party in the compound and that the monkey had tasted really good. He wanted to know if I wanted the skin for a trophy, or something, and I thought about my archery arm guard. I asked him if he could cover it with the skin and by the end of the week, my arm guard was the envy of the Chancer's Arms.

That was the last I saw of the monkey marauders and my Sunday mornings were again peaceful.

Apart from the bilharzia, which I am sure came from the stagnant water in which I used to wade up to my neck to retrieve the bodies on our duck-hunting trips, the only other illness I suffered in Lusito was malaria which was not uncommon there. Sister Anne would dispense quinine pills for those who wished to take them as a preventative, but most of us forgot. I did, however, take advantage of the salt tablets which were available on every dining table in the mess hall, along with the other condiments.

One Friday afternoon, as I was leaving the office for the day, I noticed my head was aching and I was sweating one moment and cold the next. I thought if I went and lay down for a few minutes before dinner I would feel better. I was too restless to sleep and got up and walked up to the mess hall. While I sat with Al and his family, picking at my food, Al said, "Don, you don't look too good; are you feeling okay?"

"Not really," I replied. "I think I've got a touch of fever, maybe flu, or something."

"Let's hope that's all it is," he said. "Can I drive you up to see Sister Anne at the dispensary? I've got the station wagon outside."

"Thanks all the same, Al, but it's likely to be a cold day in hell before I go to see that old witch again. I'll just take a couple of aspirin, and I'll be as right as rain in the morning. But I don't want anything else to eat, so I'll go on home now and lie down. I'll see you sometime tomorrow, maybe shoot some arrows or something. G'bye, ladies." I left.

By the time I reached my house and went inside, I was feeling really rough. I didn't have the energy to take a shower but I did open the curtain on the front of the shower stall, in case I needed to throw up in the night, and the way I felt, that was a distinct possibility. I swallowed a few aspirin, kicked my shoes off, and crawled between the sheets. That was the last thing I remembered until I woke up the following afternoon, freezing cold. The sheet and blanket, which were strewn across the floor, the clothes I was still wearing and even the mattress was soaked with my sweat. One chair was lying on its side in a corner of the room and my rifle, which should have been leaning against the wall by the head of the bed, was lying on the floor beside the bed.

I had no idea what had been going on and I was too weak to even give it a lot of thought. Then I noticed on the shower wall, opposite the foot of the bed about halfway up, was a black blob with a hole through the center. I knew that hadn't been there before. I dragged myself off the bed to investigate and found that it was the remains of a very large hairy black spider, stuck there with a bullet hole through the center and through the wall. I never did like spiders. I had trouble believing that I had shot it, but when I checked the gun, the hammer was lying on a spent shell. Obviously I was a better shot when I was delirious than when I was lucid.

Joseph stopped by, later that afternoon, to see if I needed anything and I sent him to get Al with the wagon. Al arrived and I told him that I thought this must be the cold day in hell that I had referred to previously, and that I needed to go and see Sister Anne. She wasn't too happy when we showed up at her office, just before closing time but she did arrange for a driver to take me to the hospital again, in Lusaka. The staff there remembered me from the bilharzia incident and I was soon receiving treatment for malaria. I was told that if I had ignored it any longer, it could well have turned into black water fever, which may have been deadly. When he released me a few days later, the doctor asked, "So when can we expect to see you again, and what will it be next time? Sleeping sickness?"

"I don't think so, Doc, but who knows?" I replied.

I didn't get to see him again, but I did get other bouts of malaria after that, but none as severe as the first. About every three or four months after that it would return, decreasing in strength each time. A few quinine pills and a couple of days' rest always took care of it.

When I returned to Lusito on the company shuttle bus, all the "buzz" was about the next contract, on the Copperbelt. With only a few months to go on the Kariba Access Road contract, which was ahead of schedule, those who wanted to stay with the company were naturally concerned with their futures. Others would move on to work for other contractors in the area and Al was one of those. I was very fortunate to have already been asked to go to the new job; it was just a case of when. There was a lot to do in the office during this time, settling claims, progress reports etc. and showing the other clerk, Jock, all the nuances of meeting a payroll for nine hundred natives and around two hundred whites each month.

During this time, we lost one of our most popular comrades. Not long after the road contract started and we had the Chancer's Arms running, a new mechanic came on the scene. Like Van, Max was a white South African. But unlike Van, Max was a mountain of a man with a huge frame and the strength to go with it. Van and Max teamed up right from the start and were the best of friends. They were told they would be going to the Copperbelt, if they so desired.

One Saturday, after news of the new contract broke, Van and Max decided to celebrate by driving down to the Chirundu hotel, on the Zambesi river for a few drinks. By this time, Van had brought his sister and his two boys to live at the camp. They made it to the hotel, safely, and enjoyed a few beers and conversation with some of the other patrons. An hour or so after dark, Van started to get anxious about leaving his family and they started off back along the main road which led to the Kariba Access Road. They were cruising along at no more than sixty m.p.h., according to Max, when a large articulated truck came up from behind, flashing its lights, indicating that it was going to overtake them. Van, who was driving as usual with his elbow resting on the window sill, edged over to the side of the road to make plenty of room for the truck to get by. The truck roared past at breakneck speed and as the trailer behind the main truck, passed the car, Van swung the wheel over to get back in position on the highway. As he did so, a second trailer, which Van hadn't seen side-swiped the car, hurling it into the bush on the side of the road. The truck driver didn't even know he had hit something and carried on to his destination.

Max managed to crawl out of the wreckage but when he called out for Van, there was no reply. He climbed back up the short embankment to the road and flagged down the next passing car. He explained what had happened, and the other driver, who had a flashlight in his car, helped Max locate Van. He was unconscious, jammed behind the wheel of the wreck, his right arm torn completely off at the shoulder. Without tools, there was no way they could free him from the car, and the other driver decided to go back down the road to the Chirundu hotel and call for the police and ambulance from there. Max stayed with the wreck in case Van regained consciousness. Eventually help arrived, and both Max and Van were loaded into an ambulance and rushed off to the Lusaka hospital, some 60 miles away. During the journey Van woke up and asked Max where they were. Max told him what had happened. Even though he must have been experiencing terrible pain, Van said nothing about it. He just told Max to make sure his two boys and his sister were taken care of as he didn't expect to be seeing them again. He closed his eyes and he was gone. Max came back to camp a few days later, a changed man. He had suffered only a slight concussion, but I never saw him drink a beer again after that.

8.

By the time we were ready to leave the Kariba Access Road project, most of the staff who were not staying with the company, had already left. Few of the natives wanted to relocate as we would be going several hundred miles away from the area and they wanted to stay closer to their home villages. Joseph decided to come north with me and by now he had picked up quite a lot of English, in addition to some of the other tribal languages. He would be a valuable asset, as well as a good friend, on our new contract.

The advance party consisted of Max, Joseph, myself and six natives who hoped to find work in the copper mines when our contract ended. A low-loader with a D8 bulldozer and some supplies had gone ahead of us and with any luck, the crew would have prepared a concrete slab on which we could erect our sleeping quarters. Max and I would have to share the aluminum structure, initially. Joseph would have accommodations in the copper mine's native compound, with the other boys. We had a three ton truck to carry most of our personal belongings, the aluminum panels of our first building and some supplies, with our six workers singing and chanting in the back as if they were going on vacation. Max drove the truck and led the way, I followed in a Land Rover with Joseph and our water and food for the trip.

It was only about four hundred miles north, to the Copperbelt and not far from the Belgian Congo as it was known in those days, but it took all day to get there We left the Lusito camp at dawn, after saying our goodbyes the night before in the Chancer's Arms and by mid-morning we were on the far side of Lusaka headed north. Until the black top road ran out, the going was easy, but then came the fun part. At least we couldn't get lost; there was only one road north from Lusaka, with only the occasional bush track off to either side and no other roads.

Unsurfaced roads in this part of Africa were made of red murram, a type of soil unique to the area. It had the consistency of red clay mixed with sand and gravel and had the unfortunate tendency of forming hard corrugations in the surface, interspersed with occasional bone-shaking potholes. The ideal speed at which to travel varied, depending on the vehicle. I found that, up to about 40 m.p.h. in the Land Rover, the going was rough but smoothed out between 40 and 45. Over 45 and up to 60 was rough, and over 60 it smoothed out again. In the rough spots, the vehicle tended to dance along in short side to side skids, caused by the vibrations. The truck, being heavier and with a longer wheel base, had a slightly wider speed window for the smoother ride. Balancing the speed of the two vehicles to get the smoothest ride possible for both, presented quite a challenge. Add that to the fact that it was a boiling hot day, on a dead straight road, stretching forever it seemed to a distant horizon. The road had wide shoulders which were lined with the exact same vegetation and stunted trees for the entire journey. Boring, was one word for it. It was early afternoon when we reached the half way point, a small village, called Broken Hill. We took a break from driving and ate our lunch. After lunch, the boys and Joseph, stretched out under the truck and took a nap while Max and I went for a walk around town to get some of the kinks out of our bones.

We were walking past a small hotel when I said, "How about it, Max, feel like a cold one?"

He just looked at me and kept on walking.

Nap time over, we re-fueled both vehicles and left Broken Hill, for another butt-numbing ride of a hundred miles to a town named Chingola, on the Copperbelt. It was an incident free ride with no mechanical problems, serious skids or spin outs to delay us and we arrived on site in the early evening. The site was a huge, flat, open area with very few trees, about three miles from Chingola town. Our contract was for the removal of overburden from a very large deposit of copper ore. The Nchanga mining company had estimated that it would be less expensive and safer to dig an enormous pit to access the ore, rather than the traditional shaft and tunnel operation, as in coal mining. This was to be the first open-cast copper mine in the country and would be a new experience for both Max and me.

We soon found the concrete slab for our metal "tent" and a mud and wattle thatched hut that the mine survey crew had left. Inside the hut were two wooden cots with bark- string "springs." After that ride, none of us felt like putting up the aluminum building, so I told Joseph to take the boys and find the mine compound and return at dawn the next day.

Max and I unpacked a couple of blankets and a kerosene lantern from the truck, and as uncomfortable as the cots looked, we were soon "lights out."

We were up at daylight, Joseph had already brewed coffee over an open fire and we felt that we had, at last, arrived. When the rest of the boys arrived, a short time later, they brought another eight men with them. On their recommendations, we hired them right away. We would need more laborers on the job later but there was plenty of work for them to do while we established the camp. We needed the maintenance area with office space for the shop foreman, who would be Max, an office block, a mess hall, store, living accommodations, shower stalls, toilets, etc. Except for the site engineer this would be a single men only contract. The only two females on the site were to be the site engineer's wife, who would work as site secretary, and a middle-aged lady in charge of the mess.

It took a few days to establish a routine and a work schedule but after a week, we were able to send a message back to Lusito, that they could start sending additional staff. They would, at least, have somewhere to sleep when they arrived. The aluminum "rondavel," as it was known, was erected, and Max had moved into it. I chose to stay in the mud hut with the thatched roof. It was much cooler inside, and eventually we constructed a framework of branches, with a one-foot space between it and the metal roof of Max's quarters. After applying a layer of thatch to the framework, his house was much more comfortable. Having the space between the actual roof and the thatched roof, allowed a breeze to blow between them, and it made a huge difference to the inside temperature. Eventually we made this modification to most of the living quarters.

Our top man, the site engineer Henry Smithson, arrived on site without his wife, initially. He wanted to make sure that everything was going to be ready for her and that the house would be adequate. I had a couple of the laborers working around the wrinkle-tin building, making the area look clean and tidy. We couldn't do anything about the furniture, that was standard company issue. The place looked pretty good from the outside and she would have to fix up the inside to her taste, when she arrived.

The next white man to join us was Piet van de Merwe, the site foreman. As soon as he saw the aluminum tent sleeping quarters, he asked who was living in the mud hut. When I told him it was mine he immediately asked if he could share it. I didn't see why not as we could always extend it, if we found it too crowded. Eventually we did add a separate bedroom for Piet. When the actual contract was underway and he was on call night and day, it was more convenient for both of us to have separate sleeping quarters. Joseph liked the idea as he would be making more money, looking after two. Piet was my counterpart at the number-two position under the site engineer, Henry, in the command structure. Piet was responsible for everything technical, and as site accountant, my area of concern was everything administrative. Fortunately we got on very well together, and we soon became good friends. Piet could drink just about anyone under the table, and by that time I was no slouch either, so we started off with something in common.

Keeping to schedule, the heavy machinery we needed to remove several million cubic yards of dirt and rock from the copper ore body, was released from the Kariba road contract and arrived on our site. Max organized the maintenance shop work force, using the few of his old Kariba crew who arrived with the equipment and some of the locals.

They made a really good team, which was just as well. The equipment would be tested to the limit in the months that followed.

Standing at the office door one day, in the shelter of the overhanging roof during a brief but powerful storm, I was watching Max who was crouching down on the tracks of a D8 dozer, doing something to the engine. He was oblivious to the storm and the rain in his efforts to repair something on the machine. Suddenly the sky erupted in a blinding flash and lightning struck the Cat D8 on which Max was working. The shock threw Max into the air off to the side and dumped him into a puddle of greasy red mud, some ten feet away. It was so sudden, I must have been in shock myself as it took me a couple of seconds to realize that Max wasn't moving and needed help. I dashed across the yard, splashing through the mud and bent down to see if Max was still breathing. He wasn't moving at all, and I thought the lightning had killed him.

I was feeling for a pulse in his neck when he suddenly opened his eyes and jumped to his feet. Spinning around with his huge fists raised ready to fight, he screamed, "Who the hell did that? Some bastard knocked me down, and I'll rip his head off when I catch him." He was a scary sight, with red mud and oily water running down his face, and if there had really been an attacker, he would have died of fright just looking at Max.

It took quite a bit of talking to convince him that he had been struck by lightning and not whacked from behind with a two-by-four, as he suspected. Once he had calmed down and had given up on the idea of killing someone, I tried to get him to go and clean up, and I would drive him into town to see a doctor. He wouldn't hear of it. He said he felt no worse than if he had been on the beer last night, and a little headache wasn't worth bothering a doctor over. And I wasn't about to argue with him!

When I first saw the town of Chingola, I immediately thought of an old Western town I had seen in movies. Two parallel streets, one of them called Main which held a row of stores and the Nchanga Hotel at one end. Service industries, like the local garage, doctor's office, a welding shop and hardware store occupied the other. It held all the basic amenities, but nothing fancy. The only bar in town was at the hotel and was rarely frequented by the miners. They had their own bar and social facilities in the mine recreation hall. All the housing in and around town was occupied by non-mine personnel but as the mine was the biggest employer in the area, everyone in town worked indirectly for the mine by providing goods and services to the employees and the mine itself. Housing for the mine employees was provided on the mine property. The mine was called Nchanga and the town was named Chingola; a little confusing at first. And now we were going to add another element; the Chingola Open Pit.

Removing the overburden was an enormous task. Caterpillar D8 bulldozers worked day and night tearing up the ground which was hauled off in huge scrapers. As the pit became deeper, roads were cut into the walls around the edges to reduce the slope angle, which made the towing of the scrapers easier. The soil and rocks removed from the pit were dumped on the outskirts of the property and formed a man-made hill.

In town one day, I was stopped by a young lady on the street and she persuaded me to buy a ticket in her Church Raffle. The first prize was an 8m.m. movie camera. Never having won a prize in any kind of raffle before, I was surprised and delighted when I received a note asking me to come to the Church to pick up my new movie camera. My first stop after collecting the camera, was to the drug store for a film and batteries. I already knew what my first subject would be. I was fascinated by the blasting operations in the pit which took place twice a week. Piet was the man in charge of all the blasting, so I guessed he wouldn't mind. I didn't fill him in on all the details in case he refused. I visited the pit without the camera the following day, to find out the time of the next blasting operation and where the explosions would take place. Piet told me that he intended to stop all work at noon the following day for blasting. He pointed across the pit to indicate that the area in question would be along the base of the wall on the far side of the pit.

Before leaving the pit and returning to the office a few hundred yards away, I took note of where the closest ramp to the bottom was located. A group of large rocks was piled in the center of the pit floor, about a hundred yards from the area to be blown up and that was my target. Piet thought I would be filming from the rim of the pit but I had other ideas.

The next day, about thirty minutes before noon, I made my way to the ramp complete with loaded camera. I could see Piet with some of his men, packing the dynamite in the pre-drilled holes and running the fuses. Everybody was too busy to take any notice of me strolling down the ramp to the bottom and then quietly dashing across to the rock pile in the center. I eased between the rocks and found a place where a gap between two huge boulders would allow me to film the pending explosions in the pit floor. I quietly moved some of the rocks around so that I was fairly well hidden from anyone standing on the rim above. I had a strong feeling that if Piet knew where I was, he would have put a stop to the blasting and I wanted those pictures!

I had just settled down to wait, sweat running down my face, in the mid-day heat in that rather uncomfortable little cave I had built, when the blasting alarm sounded. I checked my watch—twelve o'clock exactly. Within seconds of the alarm ending, the first charge detonated, throwing a plume of rocks and dirt high into the air as the ground shook. I had lodged the camera amongst the rocks of my hiding place and all I had to do was to push the start button and let it run. By the time I reached forward to start the camera, the debris that had been thrown into the air by the first charge was on its way down, and the rocks and dirt from the second charge was on its way up. This sequence repeated itself across the floor of the pit a hundred yards away in a kind of rolling explosion, eight times. A thick cloud of dust, dirt and rocks completely enveloped the pit bottom, including my hiding place. The ground shook as each charge exploded and the sky above seemed to be raining rocks of all sizes. After the first two charges, I could see nothing and just crouched down, huddled over with my arms over my head. The explosions finally stopped but the rocks still fell from the sky for several seconds afterwards. Once all was quiet and I could hear no more impacts on my rock roof, I tried to work my way out. The camera was totally buried and I couldn't even reach it. Jammed in as I was, it took some time before I was able to get an arm through the debris.

Piet was inspecting the blast site with his gang when one of his boys happened to look my way and saw my arm. He shouted for Piet and pointed my way. Piet and the gang dropped what they were doing and ran my way. With everyone working together, it wasn't long before I was free once more. Except for a few small cuts and bruises there was nothing wrong with me, physically. Mentally was a different story according to Piet as, once he was certain I had no broken bones, he proceeded to give me the tongue lashing I truly deserved. He found cuss words in both English and Afrikaans that even he didn't know he had in his vocabulary. All I could do was take it. I knew I had done something stupid again, and I realized how fortunate I was that I hadn't been killed.

Maybe Piet was right, I should stick to the office and the accounting business in future, while I still had a future!

After a while Piet slowed down his tirade, running out of words and spluttered to a stop. He started to smile and then burst out laughing.

"If you could just see yourself right now," he said, "looking all sorry for yourself, streaks of sweat running down your filthy face, you'd probably laugh too, you damn fool. After work let's go into town for a drink and forget this, okay?"

We never mentioned the incident again and a couple of days later, one of Piet's boys brought me the remains of my new cine camera. It went into the trash and was also forgotten.

Piet and I had developed a taste for Black and White Scotch whiskey, and after a night on the town, either at the Nchanga hotel or at the Mine Club, we would come back to the mud hut where a fresh bottle and two clean beer mugs always awaited us. That was our nightcap. With the bottle split between the two mugs, we'd sit and discuss the day's events and make plans for the next day. One of Joseph's tasks was to pick up all the cash we left hanging around the hut, when we emptied our pockets at night, and he would go into town and buy the whiskey for us.

One night we came back to the hut and there was no bottle waiting for us. This was the first time Joseph had ever let me down, and I was a little concerned, but I thought, *I'll just ask him what's wrong in the morning. Perhaps he didn't find enough money around here for the whiskey.* Waking up in the morning, reaching for that first cigarette, there was no smell of coffee and no sign of Joseph. Now I was more than a little concerned. I hurriedly dressed, woke Piet, and told him that Joseph was missing. He suggested I asked Max's boys when they came on duty, as they lived with Joseph in the compound. They should know where he was.

Before work started I was in the Maintenance shop, waiting for the gang to arrive. I told Max about Joseph's absence and he assured me that his boys would know the reason. When they arrived and I asked them if they had seen Joseph, they were very quiet and didn't want to talk about him. Max finally got the head man to talk and he told us that Joseph had been taken away from the compound, by the local Department of Native Affairs. He wouldn't say any more than that. I thanked Max, jumped into my Land Rover and drove off to find out for myself where Joseph was being held and why.

My first stop was at the mine compound office. The man on duty there couldn't tell me much, only that Joseph's quarters had been vacated. He did, however, give me the address of the local Native Affairs office in Chingola, which was where I headed next. When I asked to see Joseph, at first I was told that no one of that name was there. I explained that Joseph was the name I had given him and that he was my houseboy who had been taken from his quarters in the mine compound by their agents. I was getting more and more frustrated with these people when a white supervisor entered the office. Sensing my agitation he asked, "What's the problem here?"

"I'm looking for my houseboy, who also happens to be a friend, and your staff are being less than cooperative. I'm sure they know where he is, but they won't tell me, and if someone doesn't change their attitude soon, I'm about to change it for them," I replied.

He turned to the two clerks and said, "Is this the man we had to send away yesterday, after the doctor had seen him?" They just nodded. Looking at me he said, "I'm sorry, sir. This is going to be bad news, I'm afraid. Joseph, as you call him, was diagnosed with leprosy. Right now it appears that it was caught in time. It hasn't developed into the contagious stage yet, but it's just a matter of time. The law is strict about this; no contact with any other person is allowed. There's no cure for the disease. All they can do is to keep him away from non-infected people, so we had no alternative but to send him to the leper colony. He will eventually die there."

I was shocked. Poor Joseph. I didn't even get a chance to say goodbye to my friend. He was one of the very few Africans I met who I could trust completely. I hated to see him go, particularly under these circumstances; both Piet and I missed him a great deal.

The work continued on the open cast pit on schedule and having a site secretary made my job so much easier. Ellen was very efficient and I was able to pass over most of my paperwork to her. She also took over the Petty Cash and soon all I had left to occupy my time was the wages. With only ten "expats," as we were called, and a native payroll of anywhere from forty to sixty locals, there wasn't much to that, either. I was getting bored and needed a change. The contract was getting close to the end, and there had been no mention of any other work to follow on, so I started looking at the ads in the daily newspaper. Piet would stay on with the company; he would have no problem with his skills. But I felt I had been with them long enough, and I wanted to move on.

"Expat. Male wanted, with accounting knowledge to manage the stores and supply functions of a large construction company on the Copperbelt," the advertisement read. It sounded interesting, so I mailed a brief letter to the box number printed in the paper, requesting more details.

I told Piet about it, and he said, "Don't get your hopes up too high; jobs like that generally go to someone already in the company. You'll be very lucky if you get it." Not very encouraging, but I don't think he wanted me to leave. He'd have to find another drinking partner.

Within a week I had a reply inviting me to an interview at the company's office in Kitwe, another Copperbelt town about thirty miles south of Chingola. The associated mine there was known as Nkana. By then I had my own car, an ancient Hillman Minx and on the suggested date, I took a day off and went south. The office block was about the size of a modern three-bedroom ranch house with a two acre yard at the back. In the rear of the yard was a large warehouse and a workshop area. Most of the remaining space was taken up with parked construction equipment. Robinson Construction had been in business as long as the Nkana mine had been in existence.

I was interviewed by the general manager and the chief accountant. I didn't much care for the G.M. but had no problem with the chief accountant. Initially the job would be to take over the store keeping operation. The elderly man who had been doing the job for many years, had suddenly passed away. I would report directly to the G.M. until a qualified replacement could be found and then I would move to a construction site, unspecified, where I would once again function as site accountant. Then I would be responsible to the chief accountant. I asked how long it would be before I could go on site and was told that they had a contract opening up in another town in about eight weeks' time. This would allow me two weeks' notice for my present employer, four weeks to straighten out the storekeeping function, and two weeks to hand over to the replacement storekeeper. With Christmas only a couple of months away, I reckoned I could put up with the G.M. that long so I accepted their offer right there.

Piet wasn't too happy when I returned to Chingola and broke the news and neither was Henry.

"So what are we going to do about the payroll, Don? Did you think of that?" he said.

"Don't worry, Henry," I replied. "Ellen can take over that, too. She already does most of my work, and she can handle the payroll easily. Just think of it as saving the company my salary. Or else you could just promote your wife to site accountant, pay her my salary, and save hers. Anyway, she's got two weeks to learn it, so there shouldn't be any problem."

Two weeks later, when I left for Kitwe, Ellen was up to speed with all the admin. work and everyone had accepted the fact that I was leaving.

The chief accountant at Robinson Construction had arranged a temporary apartment for me, in a large block in town. One thing I liked about site work was that I could pretty much live where and how I liked. I really didn't enjoy being crowded into a building with many other people, most of whom I didn't know or even want to. But I told myself that it was only temporary and I could put up with anything for just six weeks.

As I expected, the storekeeping records were a mess. For the first four weeks I spent so much time at work I didn't see much of the apartment, but I did manage to get things organized and on an even keel again before the new man arrived. Paul was about my age, another Englishman, and the chief accountant asked me if I would mind sharing the apartment with him for the last two weeks of my stay in Kitwe. As he would be taking over from me, both at work and at the apartment, that seemed only logical. Paul was a fast learner and he soon mastered the record system I had instituted in the stores. I felt confident that he had everything under control when, with just a couple of days left before I moved to the new contract site, we were both invited to the general manager's Christmas party, at his house.

Apparently this was an annual party, thrown by the G.M. for his senior staff. I was told it was a somewhat formal affair and that a lounge suit would be required. I really didn't want to go as I don't enjoy that sort of thing, but I made the effort and bought a smart, dark gray suit for the occasion. A pair of polished, black casual shoes and a new shirt and tie and I was as dressed up as I had ever been! Paul already had the clothes to attend a social function of this magnitude and quite a few heads turned when we arrived at the party, in my recently acquired Morris Minor convertible.

Fully expecting a big, sit-down Christmas dinner, I had eaten very little all day and was very disappointed when it turned out to be a finger-food affair.

"I thought we were going to get food," I said to Paul. "I can supply my own finger!"

He laughed and said, "Well, there's no shortage of booze to make up for it. Did you see the bar?"

This was a self-serve arrangement in the corner of the room, with a grand display of spirits and wine.

"But where's the beer?" I asked Paul, when we made our way there to get a drink.

"It looks like this is a sipping kind of party, not a drinking one," he replied.

"So you're telling me that there's no dinner and no beer! And I bought this outfit for that?" I said. "Well, I'm not sipping anything. I'm going to get my money's worth." and with that I poured myself a large, neat Black and White whiskey. I ate a few of the snacks that were being passed around, but they did little to satisfy me. As the evening dragged on I began to feel like an outsider. I was the one who would be leaving town the next day, and Paul was the new man staying. Everyone wanted to get to know him, and nobody wanted to talk to the departing drunk. I was well into my solitary pity party and the second half of the bottle of Black and White when someone popped the cork of a magnum of champagne. I had never tasted champagne before, and I couldn't wait to try it. And that was the beginning of the end for me. It tasted so good I just had to have three or four glasses of the stuff. I vaguely recall someone suggesting a swim in the G.M's pool in the back yard and saying that there were swim trunks in the changing room. Paul told me the rest when I woke up the following day.

Apparently, I thought a swim might clear my head and weaved my way to the pool. I didn't want to get my new shoes wet, and took them off and carefully placed them beside a seat near the pool. Staggering onto the springboard fully dressed except for the shoes, I bounced once, shouting "Last one in's an idiot" and I jumped in. Guests coming out of the french doors onto the pool surround were soaked in the resulting splash. Some saw the funny side of it, and it wasn't long before several of them were also splashing around in the pool fully dressed. This lasted for a while as husbands tried to retrieve their wives from the pool and vice versa., but it signaled the end of the party, and people started leaving. Somehow, Paul managed to get me into the car and drove us back to the apartment. I was asleep when we arrived, and he couldn't wake me so he left me in the car outside the apartment to sleep it off. By daybreak I was almost dry and sober so I climbed out of the car and entered the apartment. I stripped off all the damp clothes, leaving them in a heap on the bathroom floor and found a clean pair of shorts to put on. Then I crashed out again on my bed.

By the time Paul came back to the apartment at noon I was packed up and ready to go to Ndola, the site of our new contract. According to him, my actions of the previous night were the talk of the company. Most of them thought it was funny and had a good laugh at my expense, except for the G.M. who said that he never wanted to see me at his house again.

"So, from what you're saying, maybe I shouldn't call round at his house on my way out of town, to pick up my shoes?" I asked.

"You're crazy!" he replied, shaking his head.

Ndola, "Gateway to the Copperbelt," as it was called by some of the residents, was a much larger town than either Kitwe or Chingola. It was the commercial center for the entire northern half of the country and located about an hour's drive south of Kitwe. This was the peak of civilization in Northern Rhodesia at that time. It was sadly lacking in one area however, and that was its sanitation system. Our contract was to upgrade their sewerage system by replacing old lines and constructing others. It didn't sound pretty but we really had no contact with anything undesirable. Most of the work consisted of digging trenches for and laying a network of salt-glazed, earthenware pipes throughout and around the town and surrounding residential areas. Pumping stations and a disposal plant were included.

The company had secured a fenced-in area on the outskirts of town for an office, stores, and workshop, and a large space on which to store the thousands of feet of pipes and fittings needed for the project. My office was located on the end of the building overlooking the pipe storage area and this was my prime responsibility. I had to keep records, all by hand, of quantities of pipe and elbows of various angles, design and size. Items were being withdrawn and added throughout the day as work progressed. Until I worked out a system and taught a couple of native clerks what was required, that took up most of my time and I soon became quite an expert on sewer pipes. The site engineer would give me an estimate at the beginning of each week, of what should be required, according to the drawings and his schedule. I would use this information as a budget line and provide him with details of any major variations. Site foremen would be required to explain differences at the weekly meetings. My other duties included the payroll for the hourly paid workers, which was a bit more sophisticated than on previous jobs. All expats were paid by check from the head office in Kitwe.

Once again, the site engineer was the big boss! I enjoyed the number two slot, in conjunction with the site foreman. I was responsible for all administrative functions and Ted, the site foreman, was responsible for just about everything else. Because of the wide-spread nature of the work, two junior engineers were hired to work directly under the boss. When I first arrived in Ndola I stayed in an apartment rented for me by the company and when the two junior engineers came on board, they shared my accommodations.

They were both white South Africans and very easy to get along with. None of us could afford a new vehicle, but each had his own car. Charlie had a ten-year-old Humber Hawk, a mid-range British car, and Terry owned a Riley, of a similar vintage. My ancient Morris Minor made up the fleet. I was never really interested in cars; they were just a means of getting from A to B as quickly as possible without breaking down. I'd fix them when they broke, but cleaning and polishing them was not my thing. When the windshield became dirty enough to block my vision, I would first pray for rain rather than wash it!

On a pretty, sunny Sunday morning, in the courtyard behind the apartment block, Terry and Charlie were cleaning their vehicles while carrying on a loud conversation in Afrikaans. It was disturbing my lay-in, and I thought it might be disturbing other tenants in the building. I couldn't rest, so I got up, put on some shorts and a pair of "tackies," or sneakers, and made my way downstairs to the courtyard. Charlie had both front doors of his Humber Hawk open and was busily polishing the red leather front bench seat. Terry spotted me immediately but I put a finger up to my lips and he said nothing, just watched to see what I was up to. Charlie had been rubbing a pad of mutton cloth across the full length of the seat for several minutes and must have built up a considerable charge of static electricity. I took off my shoes and crept up behind him with my right index finger stuck out, on a level with his behind. He was putting everything he had into polishing the seat, at the same time telling Terry some lengthy and loud story in Afrikaans. I inched closer to him until the gap between his backside and my finger was just right, and a bright blue spark leapt between them. The spark, his yell, and his dive straight across the seat and out of the other side of the car all seemed to take place in the same instant. I got quite a shock myself, but it wasn't so bad for me, as I was expecting it. Charlie jumped to his feet, looking around to see what had happened to him but I had a head start. His face was as red as his hair as he charged after me while Terry doubled over with laughter. Charlie eventually saw the funny side of it too, and we all had a good laugh at it over breakfast. I told him that I hoped I hadn't interfered with any future plans he might have had of being a father!

Charlie got his own back on me a few days later at work. I was doing some work on the engine of my Morris Minor, and I had the hood propped up. The spark plugs needed to be replaced, and I was bent over the engine with the plug wrench in my hand. I wanted the car to be running well when I took it to trade in on a sports car I had seen in a dealership. I had almost finished when Charlie quietly approached me from behind and tossed a dead rat into the engine compartment, almost under my nose. I reacted instinctively and jerked my head up, banging it on the inside of the hood. Cursing loudly, I swung round and there stood Charlie with a big grin on his face. He immediately took off running out of the yard and along the road, with me hot on his heels. When I had almost got my hands on him he ducked, turned and ran back the way we had just come. In my hurry to catch him, I somehow managed to trip over my own feet and went down like a ton of bricks. My left hand hit the road first, and I was aware of a lot of pain shooting up my arm, which completely took my mind off catching Charlie.

When he heard me fall, Charlie stopped running and hurried back to help me stand up. I was feeling a little dizzy from the fall and the pain in my hand and went into the office where there was a first-aid kit. I took six aspirin, and Charlie helped me put a tight bandage on the hand, to immobilize the fingers. I thought something was broken in there, but at that moment I had that sports car in mind; I didn't want someone else to get it before me.

After a cup of strong tea and a few more aspirins, I felt well enough to go to the dealership. I traded in the Morris and drove off in a bright red, ten years old, MG TC convertible, with track-style suspension. I thought it was the smartest thing on the road, even though it was really totally unsuitable for that area. The suspension was so stiff that, with the steel frame top up, I would crack my head into the cross bar every time I hit a bump in the road. Being six feet three inches tall didn't help much either. There was just enough room for me and my little dog, "Twink," who went everywhere with me. But I loved that little car, and not even a broken hand was going to stop me driving it.

Coming away from the dealership, my hand was hurting really bad. I needed it to change gear and it wasn't working too well, the way I had it bandaged. I knew that if I changed my way back to the office, I would be on the road passing the hospital so I stopped and paid a visit to the emergency room. The doctor asked what had happened, and as I was explaining, he examined the hand which by this time had swollen up considerably. Once the x-rays were complete he confirmed the two middle fingers were broken and said that he would have to put the hand in a cast.

"Wait a minute, Doctor," I said, "That could cause me a little problem. I need that hand to drive, and I need to drive to get to work."

"I can't help that, sir," he replied. "Those fingers won't mend correctly if we don't prevent movement."

"Okay, Doc. I understand that, but the truth is, I just bought a MG TC sports car, and I can't get much fun out of it with only one hand."

He thought for a moment, looked again at the x-rays and then asked me, "Does this car have one of those fancy gear levers with a wooden knob on top?"

"It certainly does; why?" I replied.

He said, "Well, if you could unscrew it and bring it to me, I might be able to mold the cast to fit it, like a ball and socket joint. It won't look good, but it should work."

It worked really well, except for the odd occasion when I "crashed" the gears, and then the vibration would really stir up the nerves in the broken fingers.

As the contract progressed, work spread out over an ever widening area. Excavation gangs working ahead of the pipe layers were scattered everywhere it seemed, and keeping up with the location of the work was no easy task. Without cell phones or portable radios, messages had to be hand delivered. One of the larger diameter pipelines was the main conduit between a large residential area and the pump station. This ran through totally undeveloped land on the edge of town with no access roads leading to it. The only vehicles which could get to the these out-of-town sites were Land Rovers and a couple of James 125cc two-stroke motorcycles. One bike was assigned to Engineering and one to Admin.

The rapid increase in payroll size meant that I was spending too much time on time sheets and wage-related issues and not enough time on material management. I requested permission to hire a wage clerk and after advertising in the local newspaper, I engaged a young white, locally born, lady. She was only two years out of high school but was very intelligent and rapidly had the payroll function running like clockwork. The two African clerks were doing an adequate job with the materials issue and receipt documents, and I was able to spend some time on site inspections checking that there were no ghosts on the time sheets, a common trick on contracts as spread out as this, and ensuring that the on-site materials were correctly accounted for. I had a pretty good idea of how to ride a motorcycle, after having had some experience with a small bike in Kenya, when I was in the R.A.F. and the James two-stroke soon became my favorite form of transport for site work. It was never intended for off-road use, but it served the purpose very well. I could get into the narrow alleyways in the residential areas, where the sewer line was being installed in trenches and also easily ride through the bush on the tracks made by the Land Rovers, at the more remote locations.

The only disadvantage I found using the bike was one of my own making. My footwear, like most young people not employed in more formal offices, consisted of a pair of African made, open-toe, flip-flop leather sandals. The soles of my feet were so hard, I could walk barefoot just about anywhere, and I often extinguished cigarettes with my bare foot. The problem was with the length of my second toe on my right foot. It was just a little longer than it needed to be and if I wasn't being really careful when I kick-started the bike, my toe would catch on the footrest, bend backwards and break. It was quite painful and I quickly learned that proper footwear for riding a bike was essential both on and off the track!

As the months passed and work on the contract was coming to an end, the company announced that the work they had been counting on was not forthcoming. We were all advised to start looking for alternative jobs or to start thinking about leaving the country. With the gradually declining security in the country, independence from Britain being imminent, many decided to leave. I really wasn't too concerned about the situation; there were no Mau-mau like incidents as there had been in Kenya. There was a lot of political hot-air on Zambia television but, I guess, that's true for every country in the excitement of an election.

With all the many businesses in Ndola, it wasn't too difficult to find another accounting position. I found myself working for the local GM dealership head office, as one of the branch accountants. The company had branches in each of the Copperbelt towns; Nchanga/Chingola, Nkana/Kitwe and Mufulira/Luanshya. Each branch had its own bookkeeping staff who would forward their records to Head Office every month for us to produce the monthly operating digests, profit and loss statements and balance sheets. This was all done, by hand, on very large, printed spreadsheets, using the GM Cost-of-Sales system of accounts.

Working for a major car dealership suited me very well at the time. I had the pick of the litter, you might say, when it came to the used car stock. It seemed I traded cars every month or so, for a while. Even though I had a fairly good paying position with the Company, that was no way to make money. I still had enough to rent a small house, buy a few beers on occasion and to feed myself, but not a lot more. But the main thing as far as I was concerned was, I was learning a lot more about commercial accounting. GM had developed this system many years before for their dealerships, who benefitted most by having their results compared with similar organizations throughout the country, by GM. Based on the results, both our management team and GM could provide recommendations and suggestions for improvements down to departmental levels. I found it fascinating that all this information could be gleaned from bookkeeping records, all of which were hand written and balanced without the aid of any machines more advanced than hand operated, Olivetti adding machines. It's difficult to believe now, that all that information and depth of detail, could have been produced without a computer.

Now that I was living in "civilized" surroundings, the old interest in model aircraft flared up again. One day I read in the local newspaper of a coming auction of household items, which included a box of assorted model aircraft engines, etc. Just out of curiosity, I thought I'd go along, just to see what was available. The only model shop in the area was in Kitwe, and that was mostly concerned with plastic car, plane and ship models. When I arrived at the auction, early, I was able to find the box in which I was interested, on a table at the back of the room. It contained two complete plastic control-line models with two more spare engines, lines and handles. There was also a small can of fuel and an old starting battery. It didn't look like much but it would at least be a start. I stayed for the auction and when the box came up for bids, no one else was interested and I secured it for ten shillings.

I had never flown control-line models before, so I had to teach myself, and it wasn't long before my little plastic planes were broken beyond repair. But that modeling craze had been re-awakened and I was learning more and more about the hobby from the occasional magazine I found in the local book shop. It was getting close to Christmas one year when I had to make a business trip to our branch in Kitwe and I decided to visit the model shop to speak to the owner about stocking model aircraft supplies. Jack, the owner, also had a part-time spot on the infant Zambia Television station, as the gardening expert. He said he would be interested if I could assure him of enough customers to make it worthwhile and it would be something new to offer the public with Christmas on the horizon. He then made me a proposition; he would order a shipment of model planes and accessories to arrive before Christmas, if I would go on TV and do a few advertisements for him. That sounded acceptable to me. I didn't know what I was letting myself in for.

There was no video recording in those days, so everything done in the studio was live, and I found out quickly, when I went to the studio for a tryout, that speaking to a large TV camera on a mobile tripod was a lot harder than it appeared. The director, an Australian named Bob, immediately sensed my discomfort and suggested a quick visit to the bar across the street. Apparently that was the TV station "hangout" and he said that most of the staff and presenters called in there for a couple of "nerve settlers" before a show. We had a couple of stiff drinks and returned to the studio for another try, which went over very well. That was the beginning of my brief association with TV production and presentation. The shipment of model aircraft arrived two weeks before Christmas, by which time I had read every magazine and book I could find on the subject. The ads were ten minute spots every other day for two weeks, and with the help of John, the bartender across the street, I got through them with no trouble. In fact, on several occasions I ran over the allotted ten minutes and got the cut-off sign from the director. By the end of the ad. campaign, I was really enjoying myself and experienced quite a let down when it was all over.

After Christmas I asked Jack how sales of model aircraft had done and he said he was very satisfied and would continue to stock whatever was needed for the hobby.

One morning, a few days after Christmas, I received a phone call in my office from Bob at the TV Station. He told me that he had been involved in discussions with management about a possible new show for the upcoming season and had been told to contact me. He suggested an evening meeting in the "watering hole" across the street. He didn't say what it was all about but I was intrigued so I went along with it. Later that evening, I met with Bob and two other men from the station management team who told me that they wanted to have a program devoted to the building and flying of model aircraft and they wanted me to present it. They had no budget for this but they would pay me travel expenses, to cover the cost of the gas for my car.

I wasn't really interested in being paid for doing this. It was an ideal opportunity to promote the hobby. I already had plans for a Zambia Model Aircraft Association and was in the process of forming the Ndola Model Aircraft Club. The TV show, even though it was only in black and white, would be a big help. Bob said that I would have complete freedom to run the show as it suited me and they would try to accommodate any direction and production issues I might have. This was going to be fun and I couldn't wait to get started. The first show would be in two week's time at 6.30 p.m. on Saturday, and I would have to be at the studio for a run-through with the camera crew no later than 3.30 p.m.

Driving home to Ndola that night, I was very excited and my mind was totally occupied with thoughts of the up-coming TV show. Bob had said that the title card and music would be the studio's responsibility, so all I had to concern myself with was the content and presentation. I had a lot to learn in a very short time. To start with, I thought I would just talk about model flying as a hobby and mention my ideas about forming clubs and a national association. I wrote a script for myself and included a couple of camera angle suggestions for the operator, trusting the director, Bob, to follow along. I tried memorizing as much as I could of the script, but half an hour's worth of talk was a lot to remember and when the much anticipated Saturday arrived, I was a nervous wreck.

I arrived in plenty of time for the run-through, and had to wait for the cameraman to arrive. I decided which of the two available desks I wanted to use and sat behind it, smoking a cigarette to calm my nerves. The studio was divided into three sections, one for the news anchor and the other two for interviews and other live features. A movie was being broadcast at the time, so the studio wasn't being used until 5.30 p.m. when Children's Hour would be aired. My live spot would follow that. I had dressed in a suit and tie, thinking that it might be appropriate to look a little professional for my debut as a TV personality with my own show, but I soon wished I hadn't. The heat in the studio, with all the lights and poor air circulation from the fans such that I couldn't stand the jacket any longer. The tie came off too and, I rolled up the sleeves of my new white shirt and felt considerably more comfortable. From across the studio, Bob gave me the thumbs-up sign, and I started my presentation. Trying not to read the script, I stumbled and stuttered my way through the first few lines when Bob called a halt.

"Don," he called, "Let's stop this for a while. I have an idea I want to try out and I need to talk it over with you. We've got plenty of time, so how about we stop over at the watering hole for a quick one while we talk about it?"

"Sounds great to me, Bob. Whatever it takes to get this over with," I replied.

At the bar, Bob shared his idea with me. He understood the "beginner's nerves" I was experiencing and suggested that he have one of the news anchors sit in with me and conduct an interview, based on my script. He would ask pertinent questions and give me the chance to expand on the subjects I had outlined. That way, I would be talking to one live person and could forget the camera and the unknown audience. This was totally different from the Hobby Shop commercials. Then I had a large selection of "props" which I could talk about. The end result was that it worked like a charm. The newsman, a well-known figure on ZTV did a great job. He appeared calm but very interested in model planes and his attitude rubbed off on me. I began to regain my confidence and enjoy myself again. Talking about something which truly interested me, to someone who wanted to learn about it, I tended to expand on the script, and when Bob gave the wind-up sign I was only about halfway through.

"Okay, Don," he said, "That should do it. Just try to relax, and do the same thing when we go live." We both thanked the newsman, and Bob asked him to join us for another drink across the street before the live show.

Needless to say, after another drink, the live show went off without a hitch. My nerves had totally settled down, and we had a good first show. We even had compliments from some of the old hands at the station, who had witnessed many successes and failures in the production of live shows at their station. Now that the first show was out of the way, I had to produce something more interesting for the next. Just talking about the hobby wasn't good enough; I had to demonstrate it. This meant building a plane from a kit. Jack, at the hobby shop, supplied the kit, and I started work on it at home. With only half an hour on the show I couldn't actually accomplish much construction. I did most of it at home, in sections, and just glued a few pieces in place in the studio, while I talked about what I had done and was now doing. This format continued for several weeks while the model was being built and by now, being on camera was no strain.

To complement the construction aspects of the hobby, it was also important to discuss the theory of flight or what makes an airplane fly. I needed to demonstrate how the curved surfaces of a wing developed lift. My wife, at that time, had some thin, black elastic amongst her sewing materials, about as thick as 30-lb fishing line. I believe it was called "hat elastic." I borrowed about three feet of it and used it to indicate airflow over a wing airfoil section. I cut the airfoil out of a slab of half-inch-thick balsa, glued a piece of wire to the back, and poked it through a hole in a one-foot-square piece of plywood. By bending the end of the wire over, I made a handle which I could work from behind the plywood base to tilt the airfoil. The elastic was strung in a straight line above and below the airfoil, which, when twisted from behind would indicate the change in the airflow direction and the area of low pressure which was formed on top of the wing.

I know that sounds pretty crude but with no fancy computer graphics and no budget, it was the best I could come up with. I painted the base board white and the airfoil section dark gray. Being black, the elastic showed up clearly. When we tried it out in the studio, we used the close-up function on the camera to just show the airfoil and the black lines running parallel across the top and bottom. The edges of the board and the nails holding the ends of the elastic were out of sight. Twisting the bent wire handle at the back, my hand was also invisible to the audience. It was amazing how much interest that simple little demonstration aroused. I even had a call from the local full-size flying club, asking how it was done as they wanted to use it to teach their students.

Although the airfoil demo. went over really well, the best one was when I was talking about how the elevator on a plane made it climb or dive. I wanted to show how a plane performs a loop in the studio, which would have been really difficult. The ceiling held dozens of light fixtures of different sizes hanging from steel girders and to try flying a model in there was totally out of the question. I puzzled over this for a day or so before I came up with a plan.

There was a glass and mirror supply outfit in Ndola and I was able to purchase a very thin sheet, two feet square, of light weight mirror. I stuck a balsa wood frame around it to protect the edges and made a hardwood stand which would hold the mirror tilted at about 45 degrees. I then made my model plane. That consisted of a fuselage silhouette, cut out of 1/32" thick balsa sheet, about two inches long with a half-wing and tailplane stuck on one side. On the other side I glued a small piece of tin, cut from a coffee can. I already owned a small but powerful magnet, and by placing the plane on the front of the mirror with the tin against the glass, the reflection gave the appearance of a complete plane. Moving the magnet at the back of the mirror, I was able to make the plane appear to fly through a loop. Once in the studio, we set up the mirror on a spare desk and using the close-up feature again, we moved it around until I could fly the plane in a loop around the reflection of one of the large studio light fixtures in the ceiling. This little trick kept a lot of viewers puzzled for some time, until I "let the cat out of the bag"!

Model aircraft as a hobby was catching on well with a lot of people, looking for something different to do with their spare time. It wasn't long before we had clubs in Kitwe and Ndola, and the News department at ZTV studios expressed an interest in getting some footage of our weekend flying meetings. Hardly knowing which end of the camera took the pictures, I volunteered to get some action shots for them, and they gave me a quick lesson on how to use the 16 mm camera, which they allowed me to borrow. As I still lived in Ndola, I chose to do the filming with the Ndola Club. There were some expert control-line, or U-control, pilots in that club who were just starting to get interested in R/C, or radio control, also. R/C was in its infancy in those days, most of the sets were home built and only controlled the rudder on the plane. The range was very short and fly-aways were common.

The usual flying sessions were held on Sunday, and, although I wanted to get some general footage of the modelers and their planes, I had my mind set on something a little more exciting. I arranged for a couple of the best control line fliers to meet me on Saturday afternoon at the club flying field with their models. This system of flying was done with the pilot standing in the center of a 50-feet radius circle, holding a control handle fixed to two steel wire lines, top and bottom. The lines were connected to the model, fifty feet away from the pilot, and were attached through a bell crank to the elevator on the tail, which made the plane climb and dive. That was the only control needed to fly in a circle around the pilot. With just this one control, a good pilot could fly an incredible number of aerobatic maneuvers.

Once they had warmed up their motors and had flown a few practice laps, we got down to business. They were going to fly combat with ten-foot-long crepe paper streamers tied to the back of each plane. Both pilots stood together in the center of the circle, with their models on the end of their lines roaring around at close to fifty m.p.h., trying to score a "cut" on each other's streamer. Evasive maneuvers included horizontal eights, overhead eights, loops, inverted etc., all at top speed as there was no throttle control. In order to get as close as possible to the action with the camera, I lay down on my back in the path of the models and got the pilots to fly as close as they dared. Looking through the view finder it appeared as if they were flying right into the camera. I realize now that it was a very dangerous thing to do and I don't recommend it for anyone else to try. At the time I thought the results would justify the risk.

As it turned out, much of the film was out of focus, but that added to the impression of speed. Naturally the camera had no sound capabilities but the studio engineers dubbed engine sounds in and it made an interesting addition to the usual program content.

Now that we had established model flying clubs, the next move was to arrange competitions on club and inter-club levels. There were three basic classes of models. Free-flight, where the model is allowed to fly on its own with no controls other than a trim tab on the rudder, to persuade it to fly in large circles; control-line, where the model flies in a circle on the end of steel lines around the pilot and R/C, where the rudder was controlled by a push-button on a small hand-held radio transmitter. Even though the latter class was not very reliable, it was rapidly becoming the most popular and new improvements in the radio equipment were constantly being made.

One of the new members in the Ndola club, was a son of the owner of the VW dealership in that part of the country. We became good friends, with our common interest in the hobby. He worked with his father and brother in the business, Pearl & Sons, and their main branch and Head Office was in Mufulira. When their accountant suddenly resigned, Ted offered me the job, which, in addition to a higher salary, would also provide me with a new VW 1500 station wagon as my company car. I accepted the offer with one condition. I wanted to institute an accounting system based on the GM, cost of sales system which worked so well. I had to show them what I was talking about and even had to explain it to their auditor, who was filling in for the accountant until the position was taken. They were impressed and couldn't wait for the system to be installed. It took three months of long hours and hard work to get it up and running but it made a big difference and helped the company in many ways. When the factory rep. from Germany visited, after the system was in place, he couldn't believe that we had only taken three months to make the transition.

Not having had a real vacation for several years, I decided to take a week off and drive the family to our neighbor, Nyasaland, for a week at the beach on Lake Nyasa. My personal vehicle at the time was an eight-year-old Vauxhall Velox, which was a mid-size, comfortable, British, family car. The tires weren't particularly good but the rest of the car was in pretty good condition and I didn't expect to have any trouble with it. I should have been more careful, with children on board, especially as I had no idea of road conditions or even how to get there. I bought a map which showed me how to get to the Nyasaland road and I loaded up the car. The carry-cot I had to tie on the roof.

We set off early in the morning and it wasn't too long before we ran out of black top road and were kicking up a dust storm on the dirt road to Nyasaland, now Malawi. It was a good road, as far as dirt roads in Africa go, not too many pot holes, and we could keep up enough speed to smooth out the corrugations. That is, until we came to the mountains. Through the foothills the road gradually narrowed as it climbed, until it was only wide enough for one vehicle. At intervals along the road, cut-outs in the side of the mountain had been made to enable oncoming traffic to pass. In one respect it was fortunate that this road saw very little traffic but on the other hand, if we had car trouble we would be on our own. The higher we climbed, the more dangerous the road became. There were no guard rails on the tight, blind, bends and nothing to stop a vehicle from plunging over the side into the ravines below. These weren't sand hills like those between Kenya and Ethiopia, but huge solid rock outcrops.

When it was necessary to cross from one mountain to another we found a crude wooden bridge with no guard rails, barely wide enough for the car, crossing over a ravine, hundreds of feet deep. With my fear of heights, this trip was no picnic. Whoever had made the road through the mountains must have found some mountain goat tracks to follow. I was concentrating so hard on the road, or lack of it, that I saw very little of the scenery. I was however, aware that it was some very wild and nerve-wracking real estate and I said a lot of silent prayers, asking that the car wouldn't break down.

At last we started down the mountains and kept going down. I had to put the car in second gear and ride the brakes to keep the speed down. But even then, there were some scary moments when the back wheels would try to skid out from the mountain side, going round a bend. It was a white-knuckle ride all the way. We only met one other car, heading towards us, while we were in the mountains. The other driver, who was alone, did the reversing to get into a lay-by to allow us to get past. Coming down through the foothills on the Malawi side of the border, we were able to pick up a little more speed, and we were soon on the straighter road, heading towards the lake. It had been nine and a half hours since we left home when we arrived at the hotel check-in desk, and I was ready for a beer and a good sleep. The family wanted to go down to the water first so, after unloading our gear into the room, we made our way across the sandy beach to the water's edge. Having been land-locked for so long, it was a rare and beautiful sight. Lake Nyasa, or Malawi, was like an inland sea and at times in rough weather, the waves could be quite dangerous. But when we first saw it, the wind and water were calm and smooth. We kicked our sandals off and waded for a while in the warm water and by then, it was time to eat. The meal provided in the hotel dining room was fresh lake fish, caught that morning we were told. I had a beer with my food and by the time dinner was over, I could hardly keep my eyes open. After a quick shower, I lay on the bed and was out like a light until morning.

I was up and about long before the family the next morning, and wearing just a pair of swimming trunks and my sandals, I went for a walk along the beach. The hotel rooms were in a long row at the top of the beach with a small, shaded verandah in front of each. Opposite the end of the row of rooms, and halfway between them and the water were two wrinkle-tin His and Hers toilets.

There was only one other person in sight, a young chap about my age who was sitting at the table on his verandah, drinking a beer. I had never tried a beer for breakfast before and when he beckoned me over to join him, it felt like a good idea. After all, why not? I was on vacation! He told me that his wife who was still asleep wouldn't approve, and I was certain mine wouldn't either. Not wishing to wake his wife, we spoke in hushed whispers while we drank our beers. A cold beer in the early morning air was very refreshing but after a few minutes, my stomach rebelled. I excused myself and told my companion that I would have to make a quick visit to the "thunder bucket" and would be back to finish my beer in a little while. I hurried across the beach to the toilet marked "His." Inside, I lowered my trunks down around my ankles and sat down. I looked around at the bare, corrugated walls and glanced up at the ceiling which held a dozen or so semi-transparent, white geckos, with large suction pads for feet and big eyes staring back at me. *Oh, my God,* I thought, *please don't fall on me,* and I hurriedly finished what I had to do.

I had just bent over and reached for my trunks when the inevitable happened. "Plop!" right in the middle of my back. With a yell of, "Oh, shit!" which was heard all along the beach, I smashed out of the toilet, door flying off its hinges, still with my trunks only up to my knees. All I could think about was getting this enormous, four-inch-long lizard off my back. It must have been a funny sight I'm sure, but I wasn't seeing it that way at the time. I had my trunks covering what needed to be covered by the time I passed my "beer breakfast buddy," and as I rushed by he waved at me, holding his sides and gasping for breath, he was laughing so hard.

The gecko must have dropped off, somewhere along the dash to my room and I didn't feel clean until I had another shower, just to make sure. I went to the check-in desk and told the clerk what had happened. He also thought it funny and he could barely contain his laughter. He told me that he would get one of the maintenance men to fix the toilet door right away and as I left, I heard him laughing out loud. By then, I could see the funny side of it too, so I ignored him.

It was only later, when I thought about the incident, that I recalled the destruction of a similar toilet door when I had come close to killing an Italian worker by shooting an arrow through a toilet wall, behind the "Chancer's Arms" at Lusito.

The remainder of the seaside vacation was without incident, and at the end of the week we headed back along the road to the mountains. This time we would get through the mountainous portion of the journey closer to the beginning, when I was fresher and knew what to expect. That is until I realized that the brakes on the car were failing and I had to pump the pedal to get any effect from them. That certainly made the drive home a lot more interesting and we were all very relieved to be back on a straight and level road again, after the mountains. My wife made it very clear that neither she nor the children would ever be put through that again.

During the week that followed our return home, I worked on the brakes and by the following weekend everything was working again. Which was fortunate as the Club was hosting a model flying competition on that Sunday. I helped set up the safety barriers and the refreshment booth and, as no one else wanted to go, I drove off to pick up some ice from the ice factory in town, seven miles away on a smooth black top road. I had only gone about four miles when a rear wheel blew out and I stopped to change the tire. Searching the trunk for the tools, I found the jack but no handle or wheel nut wrench. It wasn't long before another car came along and the driver stopped to help me and I couldn't help thinking just how blessed we were that it hadn't happened a week before on the mountain road from Lake Malawi.

As I needed to be closer to my office in Mufulira, I rented a small house on the outskirts of that town and moved my wife and two toddlers into it. I was spending far too much time on my work and hobby and not paying enough attention to my family. There was also another reason for what eventually happened, but we won't go into that here. Let's just say it was all my fault. I came home one day to find that my wife had packed up the children and most of the furniture and had moved out. I eventually tracked them down to an apartment in Kitwe, and when I spoke to her she made it very plain that there was no hope for a reconciliation. It was more than forty years before I would see either of the children again.

Life eventually settled down again to a routine of work and hobby. Now that the management team and bookkeeping staff had become accustomed to the new system and were familiar with their duties, my work load was considerably lighter. I was becoming bored when a newspaper advertisement caught my eye. It was for a position with another, much larger, truck dealership, with branches throughout the Copperbelt. They were looking for an assistant to the chief accountant and it would involve a lot of travel between the branches. They already had a well established system of accounts; the main duties would be of a liaison nature. Once again my curiosity won out and I applied for the job. And got it. I moved back to Ndola, single again and got a room at the local YMCA, until I could find a house to rent. I would have to use my own car for the traveling part of the job for which I would be reimbursed, and I bought a used Simca 1500, which was a sporty type of small sedan. I was enjoying my new position; the chief accountant was easy to get along with and didn't put a lot of pressure on me and I was able to devote more time to the hobby and ZTV. I eventually found a house big enough for me and my hobby, which I could afford. I still had some furniture in storage from the house in Mufulira and I didn't need much more to be comfortable. I hired a houseboy to do all my chores and he lived in the servant's quarters at the bottom of the back yard.

This new company had a branch in Livingstone, a town on the Zambezi river above the Victoria Falls. Part of my introduction to the company was to be a visit to Livingstone with the chief accountant, to conduct a vehicle inventory audit. It was really nothing more than a chance to meet the staff there and for a couple of very enjoyable days out of the office. Victoria Falls was truly a sight worth seeing and I enjoyed the rain forest and the ever-present baboons who would steal the cookies out of your fingers at the outside tables of the local tea room. They would steal a lot more if you weren't careful and quite a few tourists needed new spectacles or sunglasses when they left there.

We spent two days there and after work on the second day, the manager of the branch invited us to go on a river cruise with a friend of his who operated a tourist boat on the Zambezi. I had seen these large pontoon style boats taking visitors for rides on the river above the falls. It sounded very interesting, even more so when he said that the bar on board would be open and free! Larry, one of the car salesmen asked if he could join us and the manager, the chief accountant, Larry and I met the boat owner at the dock on the river. The boat was fitted out to accommodate thirty passengers but this was going to be a private party. I asked why these tourist boats had pontoon hulls and was told that it was a matter of safety. The water was not very deep, but was very fast. A regular mono hull would sit deeper in the water and would be more liable to damage from sunken rocks and debris. It would also have to be a lot bigger to be able to carry the same number of passengers. Although the boat boasted a well-stocked bar, it did have one small disadvantage; there were no toilets. Those of us who needed to made use of the men's room on shore before boarding the boat.

Leaving the dock we headed upstream, away from the falls. We could still hear the noise of the falling water and see the mist hanging over the surrounding rain forest. The owner was an excellent pilot and we were soon cruising between the many islands out in the middle of the river. He gave us a running commentary as we moved along and explained that during the dry season, the river became no more than a stream and many animals would walk across from the mainland and graze on the lush vegetation on the islands. When the rainy season arrived they were often trapped there and had to wait until the next dry season to get home. We were in the middle of the wet season then, so we might get a close-up look at some of the island "prisoners."

As we cruised, we made ourselves at home with the bar. The beers were plentiful and cold and Larry, who had declined to take advantage of the men's room on shore before we left, decided that he just had to relieve himself.

The pilot said, "Okay, Larry, hang on until I get the bow of the boat lodged against that island over there. Then you can get out on the fore deck and pee through the railings."

With that he nosed the boat up against the bank of an island sticking out of the water by about four feet. The top of the bank was covered in six feet tall elephant grass, with no sign of wildlife. The rest of us were sitting and chatting quietly, while Larry walked out on the left side pontoon as far as he could go. Holding onto the handrail with one hand, he was doing what he had to do and enjoying the evening quiet, broken only by the sound of the fast flowing water—his and the river's.

Everything was peaceful when suddenly the mood was shattered by a mind bending screaming bellow. The grass on top of the bank burst apart and there stood, in front of and above us, a huge bull elephant, ears erect and trunk raised high.

The pilot reacted very quickly and the boat was reversing away from the island before Larry realized what was happening. Hanging onto the railing with one hand he managed to zip up his pants without personal injury, but not before peeing all over his shoes.

When he regained his composure, he called to the pilot, "What the hell was that all about? I not only peed on my shoes, I damn nearly fell in the water!"

"Sorry about that," said the pilot. "I just didn't want to annoy that old fellow any more than you already had. Clearly he has been stuck on that island since the last dry season and he didn't take too kindly to you pissing on his little piece of paradise. If that bank had given way we could have been buried under several tons of elephant. Now all you've got to do is get the houseboy to clean your shoes when you get home. It could have been a lot worse, believe me."

Larry saw the funny side of it eventually, and we all had a good laugh at the situation. Another round of cold beers as we made our way to the dock and our little river excursion was over.

At about this time the model flying club organized a trip to the Southern Rhodesian National Championships in Bulawayo. That was as far south that I had been in Africa. It was held on the Founders Day weekend, a four day holiday. There were four cars in the convoy, two modelers in each, one pilot, and one mechanic, with their planes and equipment. This was the first time that any of us had entered any formal kind of competition, and we hoped to gain enough insight into the process to help us organize our own Zambia National Championships. It would take one day to get there, two days of competition and one day to get back.

We left the main North/South highway which ended in Salisbury, Southern Rhodesia, after crossing the Zambezi river, to head towards Bulawayo. This road consisted of a gravel track on which two lines, about two feet wide each, of black top had been laid. Separated by a dirt space, they accommodated most cars. Nobody tried to overtake on this road. The level, between the blacktop and the gravel base was deep, sometimes as much as eight or nine inches. The fun came when a vehicle was approaching from the opposite direction. That was when it took a lot of driving skill and concentration to drop down off the strips, riding on the gravel with one strip running under the car. After the other vehicle passed by, missing by the thickness of an extra coat of paint it seemed, then the driver had to choose his moment and jump the car back up onto the strips. And all of this was done at break-neck speed.

If we were too cautious we wouldn't get there in time to compete. There were several hundred miles of this road to cover and nerves were stretched pretty thin by the time we arrived at a motel outside of Bulawayo where we spent the night.

The motel consisted of a collection of individual circular rondavels with thatched roofs, which were the sleeping quarters, a large rectangular building housing the front office and sitting room and another smaller rectangular building which appeared to be some kind of workshop. We were all too tired when we arrived to do much more than fall into bed.

Early the next morning, after a cold cereal breakfast, we made our way to the flying field. The Bulawayo club had sent us directions when we registered to compete. It was a perfect location with a wide flat field of short grass surrounding a huge, abandoned termite mound which had been terraced, like bleachers, to provide seating for spectators. About 100 yards in front of the mound, was a concrete runway, 20 feet wide and 200 feet long. Between the mound and the runway, a temporary rope barrier had been erected to prevent spectators getting too close to the action.

Practice flights were underway when we arrived at the field and we hurriedly parked the cars and after introductions had been made, we unloaded our models and field equipment. Most of the competition was for R/C planes and that was the only type of model we had brought with us. I had brought two, one was the plane I intended to enter for the competition and the other was a very small bi-plane, which was just for fun. I had built my own radio gear from a kit which I had purchased, by mail, from England. All the Zambian entries were single channel; rudder only. Only one member of the Ndola club had been bold enough at that time, to purchase one of the new multi-channel sets which could control the throttle and control surfaces on the wing and tailplane, in addition to the rudder and he wasn't with us. This arrangement was very complex to operate and expensive to crash! This was well before the introduction of today's fully proportional radio control gear.

The first round of the flying competition started at 10 a.m. Points were awarded individually for takeoff, followed by a set sequence of aerobatics. Each maneuver was scored on accuracy of completion and placement in the sky with regards to the judges' viewing position. Landing quality and accuracy was the final scoring opportunity. By mid-day, the first round of the multi-channel flights were complete, and it was the turn of the single-channel fliers. By then most of the spectators had arrived, and the bleachers had filled up. The area between the base of the mound and the rope barrier was filled with picnic parties sitting on rugs and blankets, spread out on the grass. In all, I estimated that there must have been over a thousand people watching that day. The weather was absolutely perfect, with just a few cotton-ball clouds in an otherwise clear, blue sky and the faintest of breezes to keep the temperature bearable.

Our contingent was towards the bottom of the schedule for flying order, so we were able to see what the competition had to offer. There were some really good pilots ahead of us, some having come from as far away as South Africa. None of us expected to win, being relative newcomers to the sport, but we were learning a lot. Each pilot was allotted ten minutes to start the engine, take off, perform whatever stunts he could and land. Nothing counted outside the ten-minute window. I was second of our group to be called and with my mechanic holding the five feet wingspan model, started the motor and nodded for him to release the model at the end of the runway. With no help on my part, the model raced down the strip and pulled up in a perfect, gentle climb. As I turned the model to bring it round into the wind, a sudden gust came along and pushed the circling plane back over the picnic area. With the only control being the rudder, it was difficult to bring the plane back to the flying area against the wind. Any attempt to make a full turn would just take it further away.

The model was at about 200 feet altitude when the turn to the left suddenly tightened, and I got no response from the radio.

I yelled, "Stick on!"

The commentator, with the public address system bellowed, "Heads up, everyone."

The term, "Stick on," meant that the rubber-band powered escapement in the model had jammed and prevented me from controlling the rudder. With the rudder jammed hard over to the left, combined with the engine torque, the plane tightened into a spiral dive and disintegrated in the middle of a hastily abandoned picnic area. Crashing a single channel aircraft was not an uncommon event, even for the best of pilots, but to do it in front of a thousand or so spectators was particularly humiliating. Having to explain, over and over again, the reason for the crash as my mechanic and I cleared away the wreckage, was bad enough but to have to listen to all the well-meaning expressions of sympathy was almost painful.

It was just a model, and it happens! I thought. *Thank God it didn't hit anybody!*

The evening was spent at the workshop of one of the Bulawayo modelers. He had kindly offered his resources to visiting competitors for any repair work which might be required before the second and final round of flying on Sunday. My model was beyond repair but we all joined in to help where needed. We enjoyed getting to know others with the same passion; it was a good opportunity to share ideas and learn from each other.

On the final day of the competition, the spectator crowd was even larger than previous. I thought I would have to miss my flight but my mechanic reminded me that I still had my little biplane and the judges might allow a substitution. I knew that if the weather was calm I could put on a good show with it but as small as it was, I couldn't see them allowing it. I was pleasantly surprised when the judges agreed that I should fly my sport plane, when it came round to my turn. All the other competitors were flying sleek, streamlined, colorful mono-planes with wingspans in excess of 60 inches. My little bipe had only 18-inch, solid-balsa-sheet wings, a short and fat fuselage, and a very basic paint job. The engine was a Cox.049, one of those I had bought at the auction a long time ago. With the small, built-in fuel tank, it only ran for a little over four minutes.

At last my name was called, and I started up the engine and let the plane go at the end of the runway. In no more than ten feet it was in the air and climbing well. I knew this model like the back of my hand and had been flying it for many months. It was so light that even when it had made a bad landing it had always bounced with hardly any damage. The trouble here was that I needed it to perform aerobatic stunts and it wasn't designed to do that. The best I could get out of it was a spiral dive followed by a loop and a stall turn. The landing approach was perfect and it touched down exactly on the mark on the runway and taxied to a halt. Everybody was amazed and the judge asked me if I would like to have another flight to see if I could do any more maneuvers, as I still had time. I fueled up the little tank and started the motor. This time I gave the model a hand-launch, which really means I threw it up in the air instead of taking off from the ground. I really wasn't looking for points, I was just having fun. I flew the plane around, diving close to the ground and pulling up at the last second and flying really close to the tops of the long grass in the outfield. Then, when I estimated that the fuel was getting low, I put it into a gentle climbing spiral until the engine stopped running.

That little plane would glide like a champion and responded to the rudder control almost as well as when the engine was running. I walked away from the runway, with the plane gliding overhead in long, sweeping, wide circles. When I reached the area of long grass which was about a foot high, I set up the model on a long approach path, directly towards me. It gradually sank closer and closer to the grass and when it was close enough to crash into me, I held the transmitter with my left hand and put my right hand down and caught it. It was something I had done many times before at the club field outside Ndola but apparently, it was a surprise to the local crowd and they even gave me a round of applause!

None of the Zambian team won any prizes that year, but we did learn a lot and promised to return the following year.

That evening at the motel, we were relaxing in the sitting room, watching a little black and white TV when the owner came in and asked if anyone would like a beer.

"I didn't know you had a bar," I said.

Dave replied, "I don't, but I make my own. Would you like to try it?"

"I sure would. And maybe you could tell me how to make it. I'd like to try that too!"

"Okay," said Dave, "come with me, and I'll show you the brewery. If you other chaps want to stay here, that's fine. We'll bring some back for you in a few minutes. Come on, then, Don."

I got up from the easy chair and followed Dave out of the room. Once outside we headed across the grounds towards the other rectangular building I had noticed on our arrival. On the way, Dave explained that his private brewery was partly responsible for the upkeep of the motel. He was able to trade his beer with local farmers and storekeepers for most of the supplies needed to run the motel.

Not only did this save a lot of money changing hands and reduce his taxes, it also overcame the local rule that home-brewed beer may not be sold for cash without paying excise tax to the government. Apparently, bartering was acceptable. Dave led the way into the building which really was laid out as a small brewery. Immediately inside the entrance were stacks of cases of empty beer bottles and close by was a large zinc bath in which the bottles were washed and the commercial brewery labels removed. A second bath sterilized the bottles and a large rack beside that, dried them. Along the far wall stood the brewing vessels, in this case 55-gallon plastic drums. Each had its own gas trap fitted to the lid, which allowed the CO_2 gas to escape through a U-shape tube containing water. This prevented outside air getting in to spoil the contents. Along the opposite side of the building, cases of filled bottles were stacked in date order, the oldest closest to the door at the far end. Dave explained that after filling the bottles, they were treated with a small amount of sugar to start the secondary fermentation process which would cause the beer to have a head when it was poured. Some of this gas had to be released or the bottles might well explode, and this was done gradually as the cases were moved further down the line each day, towards the far door. By the time they arrived at the end, they were ready for delivery. In the center of the room, closer to the door through which we had entered, stood a bench with a drill press rigged with a bottle capper. A similar device was located near the delivery door to ensure that each bottle was securely capped when it left the premises. Dave's brother helped him run this operation and between them they had quite a business going on. I was totally fascinated by the whole thing. Dave shared some of his recipes and a lot of information with me that evening. After we returned to the sitting room with a dozen of his finest, I excused myself and went back to my rondavel. I took the bottle of Black & White whiskey I had brought with me and gave it to Dave, to thank him for his hospitality and the beer.

The beer that we drank that night was some of the best I have ever tasted, and the strongest! It only took a couple for me to start feeling a little light-headed and knowing that we had a hard day's drive ahead of us the next day, we all decided to turn in for the night. We settled our bills before we went so that we could leave early in the morning without disturbing anyone, and said our goodbyes.

Before the sun came up the next day, we were well on our way towards the double strip road, heading north. It was a long, boring, uneventful trip and we only made two stops along the way. Once when we reached Lusaka for lunch and again at the Broken Hill hotel where we had a couple of beers. The rest of the journey after that was a piece of cake. After dropping off my mechanic at his house, I arrived home at eight p.m. With the prospect of work the next day, an early night was called for.

As you may imagine, my schedule was pretty full those days. Apart from the job, I was building models for myself, building and preparing material for the TV show and promoting the club and the pending association. I really didn't need another hobby. But the memory of that home brew I had tasted in Southern Rhodesia just wouldn't go away. I had to try it. I found the notes I had taken from Dave, including his favorite recipe. I had seen two pound cans of malt for sale in a local grocery store, but I had no idea where I could get hops or brewer's yeast. When I was talking to some of the club members who hadn't been able to go south to the flying competition, I naturally told them about the beer. I was telling them that I would like to try making some but I didn't know where I could obtain the two main ingredients. One of the listeners happened to work in the main chemist shop, or drugstore, in town and asked me what I needed. When I told him that all I was short of was hops and brewer's yeast, he asked me to check with him in a month's time when his next stock order would arrive from England. He would order a supply for me. Waiting was no hardship, anything even slightly out of the ordinary had to come from South Africa or England, and sometimes it was quicker from England.

By the time the order arrived I had converted one of the small rooms in the servants quarters to be my brewery. I had swept all the old spider webs and dirt from the floor and had the houseboy wash the walls and floor. I bought a bucket of white-wash and a brush from the local hardware store and the houseboy painted the walls. I gave him the rest of the whitewash so that he could paint his own room, next door. I then built work benches along three walls, on one of the benches I set three five-gallon plastic water containers which would be my brewing vessels. My collection of cleaned, sterilized beer bottles was stacked neatly in cases, under the benches. The room was only eight feet by ten, but that was big enough, I thought, for a one-man operation. I had no intention of selling the beer; the law in Zambia was much more specific than in Southern Rhodesia. But I did put a lock on the door and the keys on my key chain. I didn't want to provide temptation for the houseboy or any of his friends who sometimes visited him.

Following Dave's instructions, I filled the brewing vessels and inserted my version of the gas traps I had seen in Dave's brewery. I drilled holes in the lids of the five gallon containers and epoxied a short length of thin copper pipe in each hole. I then slid lengths of plastic fuel tubing, as used on the models, onto the copper pipes and with weights on the end, dropped them into bottles of water. This allowed any gas created to escape under water without letting air back in.

Three weeks later, I had my first batch bottled. I didn't know exactly how much sugar to add for the secondary fermentation process so I guessed at half a teaspoon full.

Every evening I looked in on the brewery and nothing seemed to be out of place until a loud knocking on the back door woke me up in the middle of the night. It was Phillip, the houseboy, obviously scared and upset.

I said, not too kindly, "What the hell's going on? Do you know what time it is?"

Holding his hands together in front of him, he cried "Bwana, bwana, someone in beer house shooting guns, come quick!"

I grabbed my single-shot .22 rifle and, wearing nothing but my pajama pants, ran down the yard to the servant's quarters, Phillip close behind. Getting close I could hear muffled explosions coming from the brewery, but I knew they were not gun shots. I remembered that sound very well from my days in Kenya. I checked the lock on the door, and it was still in place and closed. The one small window was still intact, so no one had entered the room. Then I remembered what Dave had said about releasing the excess gas from the bottles or they might explode. Sure enough, that was the cause of the explosions, and the gradually widening stream of beer running out from under the door confirmed it.

There wasn't much I could do about it right then, while the explosions continued. I had no intention of walking in on a shower of broken glass and I told Phillip to go back to bed, everything would be all right the next day.

Phillip told me the next day that the explosions had continued all night and that he hadn't got any sleep at all. I gave him the day off but told him that when everything had settled down, he would have to clean the mess up. When I came home from work that day, I went straight down the yard to see how things were going with, what had sounded like my mini war. All was quiet, and I unlocked the door. Cautiously opening the door, I peered inside and could hardly believe the mess. Cardboard cases had been ripped open by the blast of the exploding bottles inside and beer and broken glass was everywhere. Some of the pieces of glass had even stuck into the plaster on the walls. Anyone in that room when it had all started would have been cut to shreds. What was even more nerve-wracking was the fact that not all the bottles had blown. That who remained sat amongst the shattered remains of their friends, just waiting for something or someone to disturb them, or so it seemed. I decided there and then that "discretion was the better part of valor," and replaced the lock on the door. When Phillip asked when he could start cleaning up the mess, I told him to wait another week or so.

I waited for a cool day, when I guessed that the gas might contract and be under a little less pressure. I then put on a pair of long leather welding gauntlets which I had borrowed from work. Armed with a thick blanket held in front of me, I entered the room. Stepping carefully to avoid the broken glass on the floor, I draped the blanket over the shattered cases and backed out. Once outside I told Phillip to get me some towels from the house. He came running back with half a dozen bath towels. Taking one, I re-entered the room. I gingerly reached behind the blanket and wrapped the first intact bottle I found, in the towel. Once I was sure that it was well covered, I carried it outside and dropped it in a steel garbage can, slamming the lid back on before the bottle hit the bottom and exploded. This procedure was repeated until all of the intact bottles had been removed. Phillip let out a big sigh of relief when it was all over, and I wasn't too sorry, either. The rest of the clean-up I left to Phillip. He did a good job, and I eventually turned the room into a workshop, just big enough for building model planes.

During the next nine months, in addition to all my other distractions, I was building an eight-foot-wingspan model from plans that were published in a British model magazine. The designer had intended it to be a free flight model but I wanted to fit it with my single channel radio control outfit. The fuselage was over six feet long and there was plenty of room in the cabin to accommodate the receiver, escapement and battery pack. The trailing edge of the fin, or vertical tail surface, was meant to be a trim tab but I decided that it would work just fine as a rudder, controlled by the radio. It was the largest model that I had ever built and much larger than anything anyone in the club had seen. I intended to power it with a .60-cubic-inch Anderson Spitfire engine, which I converted from spark ignition to run on standard glow fuel.

Everyone in the club was at the flying field on the day of the first flight. The model had already become something of a local curiosity. I had no shortage of helpers when I was assembling the model and readying it for flight. After doing a range check with the radio equipment, I filled the ten ounce fuel tank and started the motor. One of the other modelers hoisted the plane above his head and on my signal, ran a short distance and launched it into the air. From the hand-launch it flew straight into the wind and started a gentle climb and I applied left rudder to bring it round in a turn back over our heads. That was my intention but the plane had other ideas. Instead of dipping the left wing and swinging back round, it slowly started a very wide left turning climb. The radio was working all right. I could see the rudder moving but the dihedral angle of the wings was such that the small rudder, which had only been intended as a trim tab by the designer, was not able to overcome the inherent stability of the plane.

It continued to climb in ever increasing circles until the fuel ran out and then it settled into a beautiful flat glide, heading down-wind over a heavily wooded bush area on the other side of the main road. It didn't matter in which direction I turned the rudder, the model just ignored it. I dropped the transmitter and Mat, my helper, and I took off running, across the road and into the bush, doing our best to spot the plane between the tops of the trees. The bush was so thick that it was getting more and more difficult to keep up with the model. We were also getting torn up ourselves, running through the undergrowth with our attention on the model.

Suddenly we were faced with a large area of elephant grass, over six feet high, and we had to slow down to force our way though it. Mat was following me as I was parting the grass to either side as we progressed. We had only gone about fifty feet when I noticed something in the branches of a tree, no more than twenty feet ahead of us. It was a big male leopard, sunning himself. I immediately stopped, and Mat bumped into me.

"What's wrong?" he asked.

"Hush," I whispered back. "There's a big cat watching us from the tree up ahead. Don't move." He edged around me so that he could see.

"Oh, shit!" he said and started to turn to run back the way we had come.

"I said, 'Don't move!'" I hissed. "Just stare him out for a few minutes so I can get a feel for his intentions. He looks well fed. Maybe he just ate."

It seemed we stood there for a week, hardly daring to breathe, sweat running down our faces and our backs, staring back at the cat. At last he dropped his gaze and appeared to settle down. He started licking his paws and I was sure my guess that he had just had a meal was right.

I whispered to Mat, "Okay, just back up very slowly, and for God's sake, don't run."

I kept my eye on the leopard for a couple of yards as we backed away, and he didn't even look up from his ablutions. He was too full and too lazy to bother with us. We were still very careful about talking or making noise as we slowly backed out of the elephant grass. Once clear of the tall grass we were able to make better speed back to the road. All thoughts of the model plane were forgotten as we raced across the road and back to the flying field.

I was very thankful to get out of that incident alive. The leopard is considered to be one of the most dangerous animals in Africa as, like the buffalo, it needs no provocation to attack. I met a man once, at a bar in Kitwe, who had been attacked by a leopard. He managed to shoot and kill the cat, but not before his left arm was slashed with the leopard's claw. He was wearing a long-sleeved shirt and rolled up his left sleeve to show me his arm. It was nothing but skin-covered bone. The flesh had all withered away from the toxins carried on the cat's claws.

I wasn't too surprised when, a couple of days later, I saw a story with a photo of the missing plane in the local newspaper. There had been a lot of photo taking at the field on the day of the first flight. The reporter had made it sound as though it was a real plane and only revealed that it was a model at the end. Nobody was more disappointed than I that it had gone missing, but as much as I valued the model, it didn't seem worth risking my life a second time to go back in there to look for it. It would have been like looking for a needle in a haystack, anyway; it could have come down anywhere.

For a while afterwards, Mat, who worked as an air traffic controller at Ndola Airport was directing incoming flights to make their approach over the area where the model was lost. The crew was told to look out for a small white aircraft which could be lodged in a tree top and, if spotted, to supply co-ordinates for a recovery team. Meanwhile, a lady pilot from the local full-size flying club offered to take me and one observer, up in her plane to fly over the area. This incident had caused so much commotion that my boss at work had no hesitation giving me time off to conduct the search. That lady pilot certainly knew how to fly. Once over the area where I felt sure the model must have landed, she had us weaving and turning every which way at just above tree-top height. But it was no good, there wasn't a trace of it. My only hope was that someone might find it or the wreckage, who could read English. Inside the cockpit, as a habit and a precaution, I had stuck a label with my name, address and office phone number as well as the offer of a ten-pound reward for recovery. My usual reward figure was five pounds but this one was special.

Six weeks later, after all the fuss had died down and the incident was just about forgotten, I received a phone call at the office from a local farmer. He asked me to describe the missing model and then he told me that he had it in his barn. One of his African workers had found it in a tree when he had been burning grass. He had called his boss and between them they had rescued it, almost intact, and put it in the barn. He got my name and phone number from the label inside the cockpit, when they removed the wing to carry it.

When I put the phone down and told my boss he told to leave the office and go and fetch the plane immediately. I checked my wallet to make sure I had at least ten pounds in it and took off in my car to follow the directions given to me by the farmer. Our flying field was a one acre cleared patch on the side of a 400-acre corn field, seven miles from town. The farmer's directions took me a mile past that and along a dirt track which led off into the bush. A couple of miles along the track I found the farmhouse. Both the farmer and the finder were waiting for me and took me over to the barn. Sitting inside on a small stack of hay bales was a very sooty and dirty model plane in pieces. When I checked, all the parts were there, except for the big, six-inch, inflatable balloon tires. The hubs were in place on the landing gear frame, but the tires had melted in the heat of the grass fire. I asked the farmer about the location of the model and he told me that it was about three miles away from his house and nowhere near the area in which we had been searching.

Repairs to the plane and building a revised and enlarged rudder took most of a month. Many of the seams in the balsa sheet covered fuselage had split in the heat of the grass fire and the nylon covering had to be replaced and re-doped. It was a miracle that the whole thing hadn't gone up in flames. Had there been any fuel left in the tank, that might well have happened. Finally it was ready to fly again. Mat came round to my house on the Saturday before the intended second flight.

We were sitting in my workshop, sinking a few beers as we talked about the Bulawayo trip and modeling in general, when he said, out of the blue, "You're not really going to do it, are you?"

"What are you talking about?" I replied.

"I don't see how you can risk it again after all the work that's gone into it and the chances we took looking for it. I've grown attached to that plane, and I don't want to see it get lost again," said Mat.

This totally surprised me, as I had been feeling similar sentiments but had not said anything. I really wasn't looking forward to flying it again. I opened another couple of beers, and we sat drinking silently for a few minutes.

At last Mat broke the silence. "How much do you want for it?" he asked.

"I hadn't thought of selling it," I replied.

"Look at it this way," said Mat. "You've had the pleasure and fun of building it, almost twice, and we saw it fly better than either of us expected. If you try to fly it again, it could well be lost for ever. If you don't fly it, what will you do with it? It's too big to keep it assembled in your house. It will just rot away in a heap in a corner of this room. It needs to be seen."

"So what are you suggesting, Mat?" I asked.

"Let me have it, and I'll suspend it from a hook in the center of my living room ceiling. It will never fly again in my lifetime, but it will be safe and admired. What do you say?" he asked.

"I don't know. You kind of sprung this on me. I didn't realize you were so fond of the thing. What will your wife say? Did you ask her? She might not want an eight-foot-wingspan model plane hanging from her ceiling," I replied.

Mat said, "It's my ceiling too, you know. She'll like it some day, I'm sure. She'll either get over it, or she won't!" and he shrugged and grinned.

A couple of beers later, I helped Mat load the plane into his car. The wing came apart in the center, so it was easy enough to carry. He laid the back of his passenger seat down flat to make room for the fuselage. He made me a cash offer for the model but I settled for just the reward money, ten pounds. I had my money's worth out of building and flying it. I saw the plane again, a week later, when he invited me to his house for dinner. Mat had removed the ceiling light fixture and replaced it with a hook from which the plane was suspended. He had rigged four small spot lights around the room, to highlight the model. A couple of floor lamps provided the rest of the room's illumination. When I commented on what a great job he had done, I noticed the weak smile on his wife's face. She still had a little "getting over it" to do!

My part-time TV job had started to take up more of my time. After a year of the model aircraft show, I was asked to do a similar but less technical piece for the Children's Hour. This lasted for another year, after which I had my own show again, called "This is how it works!" These were only once a week, 30-minute shows, but the real work was in the preparation. Particularly the last one. The subject matter was so wide and varied, I had to do a lot of study in my "spare" time, to find out how things did work!

Bob was still the director at the studio, and it had become almost a Saturday afternoon ritual for the two of us to spend a little time in the watering hole across the street. On one particular visit, Bob told me that he would be leaving soon to go to South Africa for a bigger and better job in Johannesburg. I think he had been celebrating a little before I arrived that day. When we stood up after our drink he seemed to be somewhat unsteady on his feet.

Setting up for our practice session, Bob wasn't satisfied with the African camera man's handling of the camera on the large mobile trolley. Somehow the camera cables had made their way in front of the trolley. Bob told the camera man to move the cables to the back of the unit, and he would show the African how he wanted it done. I was sitting behind my desk ready with my opening remarks, as the camera man came out from behind the camera and started pulling at the cables on the floor trying to get them out of the way of the trolley wheels. Bob had taken his position behind the camera and was trying to move it closer to my desk and over to one side, to get the angle he was looking for. In addition to the effects of the previous drinks, Bob's patience was wearing thin, and when the front wheels bumped up against a cable, yet to be removed, Bob backed up the trolley and rammed it forward.

At the sound of the bump I looked up from my notes just in time to see the camera, trolley and all, toppling over towards me. I kicked back on my chair which promptly set me flat on my back on the studio floor, while the camera came smashing down, barely missing the desk.

I stood up and called to Bob, "What the hell happened?"

"I don't know," he said. "I think maybe the brake was on when I pushed it forward. Sorry about that. But don't worry; we've still got the number-two outfit."

I was slightly shook up myself, but nobody seemed to be too concerned about smashing a very valuable piece of equipment. After the wreckage was cleared away, the show went on as usual that evening, using the back-up camera.

Once again I was becoming bored with my regular job, and when the position of cost accountant came open at the local brewery, I applied. Northern Breweries was the only brewery in the country, and their product was distributed everywhere there was a store to sell it. By truck or rail, Zambia had to have its beer. Apart from the new job, I also had in mind that I might learn more about the whole brewing process, which still fascinated me.

I had no idea what to expect when I arrived at the office complex. It was situated on the edge of the brewery property, close to the outskirts of town. Behind the building, the ground sloped down to the main brewery, some two hundred yards away. My first meeting was with the existing cost accountant who, I was happy to learn, would be staying on for a month with his replacement, to ensure a smooth transition. Naturally we discussed my past accounting experiences and knowledge of accounting principles with particular reference to costing. He explained that the system used in the brewery was known as Standard Costing, and the monthly operating digests, as they were called, were extremely detailed. He showed me some of the reports and said that these were samples of the reports issued to each department, by the fifth day after the end of the calender month. Even the variances between budgeted and actual figures were broken down under various categories. And still no computers! I was very interested in what he was telling me and I suppose it showed. He was a very personable young man and I could see no personality conflict which might interfere with us working together; at least for a month.

My next interview was with the general manager. He was a large, heavy-set man with white hair and mustache. His complexion indicated that he was no stranger to his company's products. I had no trouble talking with him about the brewery. He was less interested in the mechanics of the cost accounting system and put more emphasis on company policies and rules. He explained that there was a company bar on the premises that stayed open every night until seven p.m., and the beer was free. If my application was successful, he would be happy to drink a beer with me any time we met there. Each employee was also entitled to two free cases of beer per month and another two cases at wholesale price, to take home. This was beginning to sound like a dream come true!

They had several other applicants to interview so I didn't expect to receive a decision on my application for at least a week. When the letter arrived I was very pleased to see that I had been accepted. It wouldn't be easy, learning an entirely new accounting system in a month, in addition to keeping up with my modeling and ZTV commitments, but I had a feeling that it would be worth it.

Carl, the Cost accountant, and I put in many extra hours of work that first month, but by the end of it I had a good grasp of what was required and how to achieve it. I had one cost clerk working for me initially, an African from Southern Rhodesia, named Ben. He was very handy and accurate with the electric adding machine and had a rather rare quality of doing exactly what he was told. Ben soon became my right-hand man, and I felt confident that I could trust him. In fact, during my sixteen years in Africa, Ben and Joseph were the only two Africans that I trusted enough to turn my back on.

The supervisory staff at the brewery were very friendly and I had very little trouble fitting in. I enjoyed socializing with them in the evenings at the pub, as we called it, and I think that my ZTV appearances may have helped there. At first, my hobby was often the subject of discussion. They all knew the story of the model which had flown away, having seen the picture and read the story in the newspaper and I had to tell them about the recovery of it. A couple of them expressed an interest in joining the model flying club and I invited them to come to one of our flying sessions at the field.

Two of them came to the field the following Sunday afternoon. My friend Mat, the air traffic controller, had a new model to test fly and I was acting as his helper. It was a hot day with very little wind and the conditions seemed perfect for the first flight. With the transmitter in hand, Mat walked away the recommended hundred yards to ground test the radio range, while I observed the action of the rudder on the model at my feet. The rudder was responding normally to the signal so it was time to start the motor and see how it performed in the air. Having learned from my eight-foot-wingspan model flight, Mat only half filled the fuel tank. Our flying field surface was too rough for a normal take-off, especially with a relatively small model of only 48-inch wingspan, so I performed the hand-launch by running into the wind, such as there was, and releasing the plane in a level attitude. Single channel models were trimmed to climb under power, and this one performed flawlessly. Responding to Mat's signals, the model climbed in large gentle circles and Mat kept edging it further up-wind to allow for the glide back when the engine ran out of fuel.

It was a beautiful day at the flying field, watching the model gently circling against the clear blue sky. The sun was hot, and the uniform of the day was shorts and sneakers. The plane was high enough that the engine sound was no more than a soft buzzing sound, but everyone noticed it when it stopped. I glanced at Mat who was glaring up into the sky and pushing frantically on the transmitter button. For some reason the rudder had stopped responding to the signals and the model was now in free-flight mode. Luckily the wind was still very light and with the model still flying in a gentle turn and slowly losing altitude, we could make a reasonable guess as to where it was headed. Its flight path led well to the south of the area where the big model disappeared, but still in the bush on the opposite side of the road.

"Not again!" growled Mat, as he put the transmitter down.

"Let's go," I said, "while we can still see it. The rest of you carry on with your flying; it shouldn't take more than the two of us to find it."

The area of bush to which we were headed was familiar ground to us. It seemed to be a favorite place for fly-aways to settle. We had recovered many other planes from this "Bermuda Triangle," as we called it. The undergrowth was fairly sparse and the trees were spaced wider than normal. This made it easier to run and keep an eye on the sky at the same time and I felt confident we would soon return with the model intact.

We were easily keeping up with the model at little more than a jogging pace when we came upon a large clearing in the bush. Keeping our attention on the model, gradually losing height as it circled down towards the short mpani trees, we ran between the trees and into the clearing. I was in the lead and we had only gone a couple of yards when I became aware of something tickling me all over my back and chest. I looked down and shouted out, "Oh, my God! Get these filthy things off me!" I was covered, or so it seemed, with large, black-and-yellow striped spiders.

Apparently the webs had been strung between the trees on the edge of the clearing and concentrating on the model overhead, I hadn't seen them. Mat hadn't been affected, I had cleared the path for him. I was beating wildly at the things and Mat helped get them off my back. At last I was cleared of spiders and their webs. I have always hated spiders, even before that incident and I was suffering a mild case of shock. I also had several welts appearing on my skin where I had been bitten. Finding a handy tree trunk lying at the foot of another tree, I sat down and pulled out my cigarettes. Sweat was pouring down my body and I was panting for breath. Between breaths I gasped out, "It can't be far now, Mat. Why don't you leave me here and go look for it. I reckon it's no more than fifty feet in that direction." I pointed.

"You'll be okay?" he asked.

"As soon as I get my breath back I'll be fine," I replied.

I was only half way through smoking my cigarette when I heard Mat's voice coming roughly from the direction in which I had pointed.

"I've got it!" he called. "It's okay, and I'm on the way back. Wait for me."

Following the trail we had made on the way in, Mat led the way back to the road and then onto the club field where we described our encounter with the spiders. One of our members was a doctor at the Ndola Hospital and he advised me to go home immediately and get into bed with aspirin, after taking a shower. Mat showed no signs of having been bitten but apparently I was allergic to the bites. It wasn't long before, on the seven-mile drive home, I started to ache all over and feel light headed. By the time I parked the car in the driveway and opened the door, I couldn't even stand up. I fell out of the car and crawled to the front door. Hauling myself up, using the door handle, I managed to get my key in the lock and open it. Crawling inside, then using furniture and the walls for support, I made my way to the bathroom and ran a cold bath. It didn't take much to kick off my shorts and sneakers and fall into the bath. The shock of the cold water on my body took my breath away but at the same time it was very refreshing. After a quick soaping and short soak I felt well enough to dry myself off and climb into bed. I had taken some aspirin while I was in the bathroom.

I woke up the next morning, shivering. All my joints seemed to be swollen; my knees looked like small soccer balls and I had a headache I could well have done without! There was nothing to do but lie there and take it. I eventually called the doctor who said that I should just give it time and keep taking the aspirin. There was nothing he knew of that he could prescribe for me, so I just had to suck it up until the poison from the bites left my system. I called the G.M. at the brewery and told him what had happened. Fortunately we had distributed the previous month's results and were in a slow period leading up to the end of month rush. He told me to get as much rest as I could and let him know how I felt in a couple of days.

After that first full day, the swelling started to subside, the headache and the fever eased, and I started to feel human again. Well, enough in fact, that at the end of the second day, I swallowed a couple of stiff drinks of Scotch on the rocks. That made me feel a lot better and reminded me that I was hungry, after only having had soup for two days. I called the G.M. on Wednesday morning with an update on my condition and he told me to stay at home the rest of the day and if I felt well enough, to come into the office the next day.

I made it back to the office on Thursday morning, still walking slowly on stiff and sore leg and ankle joints. Even though I was practically over the incident, I didn't make it to the club field on Sunday and a month after that my ZTV program ended, which took a lot of pressure away.

The brewery was a totally different working environment from that which I had experienced previously. Any time during the day, if I felt like a drink, I could go over to the Head Brewer's sample room and help myself. As long as I didn't abuse the privilege, nobody cared. At 4.30 p.m. the official work day ended, and the company bar opened. Only beer was served there, but there was no charge. The only unwritten rule was, "No inebriation." Any kind of drunken behavior would have been frowned upon by management, and I never once saw anyone under the influence on brewery property.

In order to perform my job properly, it was necessary for me to understand the brewing process and the ingredients which went into the beer. It really is a very interesting subject and I was amazed at the amount of scientific knowledge required to consistently produce a good beer. Although working behind the scenes, the head brewer who is ultimately responsible for the product, definitely holds the future fortune of the company in his hands. His talent is a fine mixture of art and science which is required to create the beer's unique properties initially. Then he has to be able to repeat that magic many times over by instituting strict guidelines, quantity and quality controls, testing and tasting procedures. His office also included a laboratory.

Two of the byproducts of making beer are spent hops and brewer's yeast. After fermentation is complete the beer is pumped through banks of very fine filters to remove the excess yeast. During fermentation the yeast works on the other ingredients to produce alcohol and carbon dioxide gas. Some of the filtered yeast is kept for the next brew but there is always a surplus. This yeast is a very beneficial health supplement and is used in pharmaceutical and some food products.

The other byproduct which interested me was the spent hops. Hops are grown mostly in Southeastern England and Europe. They are small, green flowers which grow on vines and. provide most of the beer's flavor. When the brewing vats are emptied and cleaned, the used, or spent hops are discarded. At this particular brewery and of course, I can't speak for others, the hops were taken to a particular part of the brewery grounds where there was a shallow pit and dumped. They were left there to compost and local plant nurseries would truck the stuff away for fertilizer. By the time it was ready for use, the smell was pretty intense!

One of the perks when I joined the brewery, was the use of a brewery-owned house, rent free. It was a very comfortable, three bedroom bungalow with a large, fenced-in backyard. At the bottom of the yard was another building which consisted of a single garage, a shower room and another small room. Part of the yard had been cultivated by the previous occupant and I saw no reason to change it. I hired a garden boy to look after it and the rest of the outside property and he moved into the room at the back of the garage, next to the shower. He had references which showed he had done this kind of work before and when he suggested that we needed some horse or cow manure in the garden area, I didn't argue. But I didn't put it high on my list of priorities and it was soon overlooked.

At that time many foreigners were leaving the country. Although independence from Britain was now a fact, many felt uncomfortable with the situation. This wasn't made any easier by the wild campaign promises of the politicians, such as—all foreigners would forfeit their weapons, all Africans could have a gun, and African men could have their pick of white women who remained. All of that is forgotten today of course, but then it was very real.

One of my acquaintances at the brewery was an Englishman, with a wife and small daughter and he chose to leave. His daughter had a small, black, pet rabbit and at the last moment he asked me to take it. I didn't really want it, but to prevent his daughter being even more upset, I said I would take care of it. It was a cute little creature: male and pitch black. I cut a hole in the side of a beer carton, lined it with an old towel and some straw and put it in the garage. It was a dirt floor so it was easy to build a small pen around the box with two feet high chicken wire. Buddy had a new home.

The story soon came out at work, that I was an easy touch when it came to animals, and it wasn't long before I became the proud owner of two more rabbits. These were of the Flemish Giant variety, pure white with pink eyes and had been the pets of a child of yet another expat returning home. I took them in, but made it clear to everybody who mentioned them at work that I was not interested in obtaining any more.

"Sally" and "Joan" were beautiful animals but were each more than three times the size of Buddy. That didn't worry Buddy a bit, and once they became used to each other I decided to keep them in separate pens. Buddy must have thought that he had died and gone to Heaven. Not one but two gorgeous, big, white partners all to himself! And he soon learned how to jump over a two-foot-high fence.

Practically all the produce from the vegetable garden was going to feed the rabbits. The garden boy once more reminded me that we needed manure for the garden, especially as we would soon be having babies to feed. I remembered the spent-hops pile at work, and one evening I loaded a couple of large, empty grain sacks and brought them home in the trunk of my car. The gardener wasn't too happy that I hadn't brought manure, but he was willing to try it, if it would help the crop. When he spread the stuff on the ground, before digging it in, the neighbors weren't too happy either. One even threatened me in writing. She was going to report me to the sanitation department! I apologized and had to admit that it was a pretty disgusting odor. Once it had been dug into the ground, it was fairly acceptable, but it took weeks to get the stink out of the car.

We were amazed at the effect that the hops had on the garden. Cabbages, lettuce, beans and carrots shot up as if they were on steroids. Where we had only expected to get one crop we actually got three that year. The weather cooperated too, but the rabbits were jumping over fences and interbreeding until the inside of the garage was seemingly knee-deep in black and white fur balls. They were eating everything we gave them and I was getting concerned about what to do with them. The gardener was also getting concerned about keeping up with the food for them and suggested killing them off and selling them over the back fence for meat to the local Africans. I considered the idea, but not for long. I couldn't kill them; they had become pets and families of pets to me, and by then, I had developed a much deeper respect for other forms of life. It was certainly a problem which I needed to fix, and soon!

During the flying session at the club field, on the following Sunday afternoon, I mentioned my dilemma to Mat. I didn't think he had paid much attention to what I was saying but later in the afternoon he said,

"Hey, Don. About your rabbits. I've been thinking, and I may have the answer for you. How about contacting the farmer who returned your lost model? Maybe he would take them. He's certainly got enough room for them."

"That's a real possibility, Mat; thanks! How about we pay him a visit after flying? We're two-thirds of the way to the farm right here," I replied.

We found the farmer at home and I explained my problem of living in town with an untold number of black and white rabbits of all sizes. He was a little hesitant at first until I mentioned that they would probably interbreed with the wild rabbits which might make for some interesting color combinations, running around. Finally he agreed to take them but they would have to look after themselves in the bush. He didn't have time to look after them in hutches. There was one particular area on his property where there was a concentration of wild rabbits and he said we could release them there.

I borrowed a box-van, the following Saturday, from the brewery, and Mat and I loaded up the rabbits. The two big white does somehow managed to break free between the garage and the van and we had quite a chase on our hands. Between the gardener, Mat and myself we finally managed to herd them into a corner of the garden fence and man-handled them into the back of the van. When we arrived at the farm with our load of rabbits the farmer directed us to the area he had selected for their release. It was a large clear area beneath widely spaced mpani trees. The ground was covered in grass about a foot high, and there was plenty of evidence of other rabbits living there. "This looks perfect!" said Mat, and I had to agree. But as much as I needed to get rid of the rabbits, I still felt sad at letting them go. As soon as the back door of the van was opened, the two "ladies" leapt out and ran around the clearing, overjoyed at their freedom. I lifted down Buddy, and he soon joined his girls. Eventually we had the van cleared of rabbits, who rapidly disappeared down the many rabbit burrows which were all over the area. My fears about them adapting to living in the wild appeared to be groundless.

By the time we returned to the house, the gardener had already swept out the garage and had a pile of straw and rabbit droppings, to which we added the parting gifts that the rabbits had left us in the van. He had wanted manure for the garden; now he had some! He had to keep it for a couple of months in the compost pile, but it was very good when he used it. Not as good as the hops, but a lot more neighbor friendly!

The financial accountant at the brewery was a member of the local theater club and when my TV program ended, he asked me if I would like to help him out with a production. He needed someone to play a small part in *Death of a Salesman.* Being something I hadn't tried before, how could I refuse? I would only have a couple of lines but it might be fun. The theater was a city council property and had everything you might find in a normal theater, except a bar. All amateurs, but the standards were really high. Some of the members had been in professional theater earlier in their lives, and I learned a lot from them. All productions only ran for a week at the most. Each show was well attended by the local white community, but Africans showed no interest. At any one time there were two or more plays rehearsing, play readings, scene building workshops, etc, all in progress. It was a very active and enthusiastic club. Cecil, the brewery accountant, was one of the leading actors/producers/directors having had a lot of experience in South Africa, his homeland. On stage he was a totally different person from his normal shy, quiet spoken, undemonstrative self. Any production with which he was involved, either in an acting or a directing capacity, was almost guaranteed to be a success.

But he was a serious alcoholic. I didn't see that side of him at work; in the office he was just a quiet, polite and efficient accountant, who was never late with his work and never showed any signs of consuming at least one bottle of vodka every day. At the theater club it was different, When he wasn't on stage in a production he was rarely seen without a tall glass in his hand containing, what at first I thought was water. I soon realized what it was when I saw him refilling it from a vodka bottle. Two glasses and the bottle was empty. That was a nightly ritual for Cecil.

After that first performance I was involved in several other plays. A musical version of *Charlie's Aunt* and *The Mikado* were a lot of fun. My part in *The Mikado* was really small, and I spent most of my time running an impromptu bar under the stage. Apart from serving drinks, I had to listen for the cues and make sure the required performers were available to take them. Another play I enjoyed was an old melodrama, *The Monkey's Paw.* The club had entered the production in a nation-wide contest for three-act plays, and we took third place. I played the son.

By this time independence had begun to sink in with the local people, and their attitudes were changing daily for the worse towards us "Colonials." My cost clerk at the brewery was deported to Southern Rhodesia; his only crime was that he wasn't a local. His replacement was totally useless and could barely add one and one. But he was secure in his position, he couldn't be fired. White people walking along the sidewalk in town were expected to step off into the road if locals were walking towards them. African women with exposed breasts, feeding babies, would stand in the gutter, legs apart relieving themselves. Independence might have arrived, but civilization was a long way behind. An article in the newspaper reported Kenneth Kaunda, the president, calling Britain a "toothless bulldog" when he asked for some enormous sum of money as a grant to develop more roads in the country and he only received half of it. None of the money went into road building anyway, but it was said that the President's Swiss bank account grew considerably.

But that's enough of politics; it was obviously getting to be time to leave Africa. I hadn't been home in sixteen years, so I had a lot to catch up on in the civilized world, and my parents weren't getting any younger. I had collected quite a lot of belongings in the way of furniture, car, tools and model plane equipment and if I wanted to get anything for them, I needed to sell them soon while there was anyone left to sell them to. I hated the fact that I would have to buy my own airline ticket to England; that was the first time I traveled on my own money. I had sold just about everything, and the car was the last thing to go. A friend at the theater club had given me a good price for it and allowed me to keep it until the last moment. He had also agreed to take Twink, my little dog and constant companion. When he came to collect the car, Twink immediately jumped into the passenger seat and turned to look at me, wagging his tail. I'm sure he knew that he was going to a new home and that we would never see each other again.

I came away from Africa with little more than the clothes on my back, one suitcase and a lot of memories, some good, some bad. Considering everything, I wouldn't have missed it for anything! What little money I had was transferred to England before the new government put a freeze on all bank accounts. For once in my life I had some money in the bank so I was in no rush to settle down in England. It was great seeing my parents again and telling them some of my stories. They had trouble understanding me and my love for Africa and the animals. We had grown apart and lived our own separate lives for so long that we really had little in common anymore.

9.

My parents lived in a suburb of Southampton, Hampshire, one of the largest port cities on the south coast of England. It was a two-story semi-detached house, and Dad had converted the top floor into a self-contained apartment with its own entrance via an outside stairs. When Dad retired from Hollesley Bay, he had built their own house, close to the village of Hollesley. Several of their other retired friends had moved south and he had a brother, Uncle Ron who lived on the Isle of Wight, a short ferry or hovercraft ride across the Southampton shipping channel. They had sold their house in Hollesley and moved to the house on a main road headed north from Southampton, outside the city.

When I landed in England, I immediately made my way south to see them, and they insisted that I stay in the apartment upstairs, at least until I found my feet and got settled in to being in England again. A lot had changed in sixteen years, and it would take a while. I spent some time in Southampton, amazed by all the huge stores and shops, and visited the zoo to see the animals there. The Public Transport system was very efficient with buses criss-crossing the city and its suburbs every which way. Miss one and wait a couple of minutes and there was another! I spent a few days just riding buses. Get on the first one that came along, ride for five minutes, get off and explore the area, get back on the next bus that came along, and so on. It didn't cost very much, and at that time I had money.

Although I was officially occupying the apartment, I spent a lot of time with my parents, trying to make up for lost time, I suppose and trying to bridge the gap that had grown between us. It was very difficult; their interests were totally foreign to me as mine were to them. I tried helping Dad in the garden but I could never do anything just the way he wanted it done. In fact, nothing I did was quite right. I felt that they still thought of me as the teenager who left home to join the R.A.F. and not as a thirty five year old adult who had already lived a lifetime of experiences, by their standards. It soon became obvious to me, and to my parents I'm sure, that this living arrangement could not continue. They wouldn't take any money from me for rent but they were losing the opportunity to supplement their retirement income by leasing the apartment to somebody else. I started to look for a job, at their request in the local area.

Scanning the want ads one day, in the local newspaper, I found one which might have suited me. A sausage factory was looking for an accountant. That might be interesting, I thought. There were two things at this stage, that I had found I liked about England. One was the pork products; their pork sausages, pork pies, bacon, etc., were the finest in the world, and I still think so. The other was, of course, the beer. There was a phone number with the ad. so I called for an appointment and was invited to an interview with the general manager the next morning. They weren't wasting any time and I got the feeling that there was a sense of urgency about the whole thing but I thought no more about it. I didn't have a suit to wear so I caught a bus into town and bought my first English three-piece suit, white shirt, tie and new shoes at a large department store. At least I would try and look the part.

As usual, I arrived early for the appointment. It was an old service habit that I saw no reason to change. Being early for anything was being on time, being on time was being late. The sausage plant was situated in a fenced compound in an industrial area on the outskirts of Southampton. It was a large, two-story rectangular building. On the ground floor, large overhead folding doors provided access to the shipping and receiving docks and an outside steel stairway led to the office suite on the top floor. I couldn't help noticing, as I approached the stairway, a pungent, obnoxious smell which seemed to be increasing as I got closer. I felt sure that they must be experiencing some problems with their sewers.

The G.M. was waiting for me when I entered the office and we shook hands as I introduced myself. He glanced at the office clock and commented,

"You're early; that's good. Let's get this interview thing over with, and we can get you settled in right away."

Hold on a minute, I thought, *this was going way too fast and the stink is, if anything, stronger in the office than it had been outside.* While he talked, I tried to pay attention, but the smell was making me nauseous.

Finally I asked, "Do you mind if I smoke?" thinking that the smoke might cover the smell.

"I'd rather you didn't," he replied. "We really don't allow smoking on the premises; it's a health thing, you understand."

He carried on talking about the business and their accounting system and how they had been trying to get an accountant for some time, but without success. I was beginning to see why and finally I asked, "What is that terrible smell?"

"Oh, that," he said, "that's just the smell of the raw intestines being delivered and treated in the factory below. They're used for sausage skins, you know, after they have been scraped, cleaned, and washed. That smell is always with us, I'm afraid, but it won't take long, and you won't even notice it anymore."

He quickly tried to change the subject and carried on talking about the job as if I were already hired. I wasn't about to be pushed into the accountant's chair under these circumstances. I didn't need a job that bad, and I told him so. I finished up with, "You know, if smoking in the office, away from any food production, is considered unhealthy, do you call the stink from the food factory healthy? I don't think so! You should be grateful that I didn't have any breakfast before coming in this morning, or you'd have a mess to clean up right about now."

"But you'll get used to it; I know you will, and the salary for this position is excellent, well above average." he pleaded.

"I'm sorry," I said, "I don't think so. This company doesn't have enough money to make working here a viable proposition for me. You need someone with absolutely no sense of smell," and I turned, left the office and hurried down the outside stairs. I held my handkerchief over my mouth as I ran across the compound to the gate, and I could hear laughter coming from the loading dock as I ran.

Nobody wanted to sit next to me on the bus going home. The smell of the factory had permeated my new clothes. All I could think about was getting out of them as soon as possible and getting into a hot bath. It took two visits to the dry cleaners before I dared wear those clothes again. I couldn't imagine anyone wanting that job. He'd have to have a very bad sinus problem, a steel can for a stomach and drive a garbage truck for his personal transport!

If that was an example of local job possibilities, I was not impressed and decided to widen my search area. I paid a visit to the local library where they had copies of regional newspapers from all over the country and after much searching, I came across an advertisement for a cost accountant wanted for a light engineering company in Essex. That wouldn't be so far away from Southampton that I couldn't visit, occasionally; and being realistic, nowhere in England would be. The whole country is smaller than Alabama! I wrote a letter to the company applying for the job and received a letter by return, asking me to attend an interview.

The office/factory of this company was located in Harlow, Essex. This was a new town established specifically to accommodate industrial development. Housing was provided by the local government in the form of apartments which I didn't really like but I reminded myself that nothing lasts forever. It would be a reason to get away and allow my parents to get back to their comfortable routines.

Apparently my lack of formal qualifications, in the form of a degree, didn't concern the general manager and the chief accountant, when they interviewed me. they were interested only in my experience with standard costing and whether or not I thought I could apply that experience to their manufacturing methods which were mainly automated. Their primary product was a range of grease fittings, which were turned out by the million on automatic lathes but they also produced a dynamic wheel balancer for the automotive industry. I was fully confident that I could institute a system which would provide them with all the management information they required and get it up and running within a couple of months.

I returned to Southampton after the interview. The company had several other applicants to consider. I wasn't particularly concerned about my ability to do the job; more so about the impression which may have been made by my description of my previous employment in Africa. I need not have worried about it; I had the job and an excellent salary offer in my hand by the end of the following week. While I was waiting to hear about the job, I bought a used car with some of my savings, and after packing up and loading my few belongings, I said, "Goodbye for now," to my parents and headed towards Harlow New Town in Essex.

I rented a small unit in a government owned housing complex and tried to get familiar with the local surroundings, over that first weekend. The town was quite close to the M4 motorway which led straight into London but I was more interested in getting to know my way around locally. I didn't want to get lost going to work but I found the office with no trouble and was the first one there on Monday morning. I spent the first morning, meeting the staff, touring the facility and stocking my office with the tools and stationery that I would require. It was a neat and compact organization and I had a positive feeling about the prospects of doing a good job.

Once I started work, I found that my reception on the shop floor was a little less than enthusiastic. Rumors had been spread that I was there as a hatchet man. It was a union shop, and I was asked point blank by the shop steward if I was there to make cut backs. I tried to explain that any time-and-motion studies I was performing, were to enable me to create standards for the new costing system and not to get people fired. It took a couple of weeks to gain his support, but eventually he came around, as did most of the other staff. The company already had a formal budget, but this was expressed in fairly general terms. I broke it down into departments and units within departments and showed management how, by careful monitoring of actual performance and making comparison with budget, we could analyze variances. This would provide an element of control at the detail level which would result in a higher degree of overall control.

Once I had settled down in the office, it was time to socialize. I was invited to dinner by the chief accountant at his home. He lived in a private house a short distance from the office. He had a charming wife and a young son at home. The oldest son was away at college but the young one, Kevin, was extremely smart. Computer science was in its infancy in those days, but Kevin was up to date with all of it. I couldn't understand half of what he talked about; it was way over my head. His father, the chief accountant, named Dan, told me that if any of his club's members had trouble with their radio equipment, they always called on Kevin to get it fixed. When he made that remark, I immediately started to take notice.

"What club would that be then, Dan?" I asked.

"Oh, it's the local model flying club. I've always liked building and flying model planes. It takes my mind off office politics and all that stuff, you know," he replied.

"Well, you can fill me in on the office politics stuff later, but first I want to hear about the club. I used to be very interested in models myself. The flying kind, that is," I added, with a smile.

Dan went on to tell me all about the local club and their flying field, which was rented from a farmer outside of town. It was only a small patch in a small field, but then, everything in England is. I told him that I might like to join the club once I had the cost accounting at work under control so that I could devote more time to building a model. When I left Africa I sold or gave away all my equipment, tools, etc., and I would have to start from scratch. He told me that he would be happy to help me get back into the hobby and invited me to join him on the next weekend if the weather was suitable for flying. Now that I think about the weather in England, it's amazing to me that there are so many world-class pilots in Britain. How do they ever find the good weather in which to practice?

As the evening progressed, Kevin decided it was time to go to bed and said his goodnights all 'round.

When he had left I turned to Dan and asked, "Now, Dan, what about these office politics you mentioned earlier? I haven't really had a lot of time in the office to pick up on anything like that, so I'd appreciate any advice you can give me."

He looked sideways at me with a slight smile on his face, and said, "I've been wondering when you would get to that. That's really the reason for this evening. I wanted to let you in on what goes on at the office so that there will be no unpleasant surprises for you. You may have noticed that Mr Learhy, the G.M., spends a lot of time out of the office, 'traveling.' When he's out, I am supposed to be in charge. His secretary, Sandra, takes note of every little thing that happens while he is away and even calls him several times a day. Even though I am supposed to be his deputy in his absence, Sandra relays his instructions to those concerned, completely leaving me out of the loop. This would be fine with me, except that when Sandra gets her messages crossed and something goes wrong in the shop, I get the blame. She also spies on everyone in the office and seems to know everyone's personal business, all of which gets reported back to Learhy. All this causes a lot of uncertainty amongst the staff at all levels and encourages a certain amount of boot licking from some of the employees. Sandra, of course, enjoys that, and takes every opportunity to show that she is the queen bee. Quite honestly, Don, I'm not too happy there. I'm trying to hold my tongue, at least until you've got your end under control, and then we'll have to see. If the situation improves, I may reconsider. Right now, I'm making no promises."

Well, that really was an eye opener for me. I had been so immersed in getting my standard costing system up and running that I hadn't noticed anything wrong in the office. Of course there are always two sides at least, to any story, so until I heard the others or experienced them for myself, I would reserve judgement. It wasn't the kind of situation that I was accustomed to in Africa, so I would need to tread carefully.

'Well, Dan, you've certainly given me something to think about, and I'll definitely keep my eyes and ears open from now on. That kind of atmosphere has to be counter productive, and that, I will not tolerate. I'll wait and see how it goes now that I know what to look for, but if the situation is as bad as you say, I know I'll have to say something. But don't worry; I won't bring you into it."

That ended what had been a very pleasant evening, and I left to return to my apartment.

Over the next couple of weeks, now that I had been warned, I noticed that things were not quite as rosy as I had supposed. None of the other girls in the office appeared to like Sandra. None of them stopped to chat with her as they did amongst themselves, and any time she came out of her office, adjoining Mr Learhy's, all chit-chat stopped. One day I had been speaking to one of the production supervisors on the factory floor, about costing standards. When we were finished and I was about to leave, he suddenly asked, "So, Don, what do you think about Sandra in the office?"

"I really don't know, Stan," I replied. "What's your opinion?"

"I'd tell you, Don, and I'd be speaking for everyone in the plant, I'd say. But I always remember what my old Mum used to tell me. 'If you can't say something good about someone, don't say anything at all!' so it's best if I keep my mouth shut."

I then said to Stan, "Well, look, if she's that bad, why doesn't someone say something to the boss?"

"Nobody wants to lose their job, Don, and Leahry thinks the sun shines out of…well, you know what I mean. She's fire proof. But it would certainly be a lot better around here if she wasn't," said Stan as he turned away.

I felt as though I had been given a message and told Dan about the exchange later, when I was sitting in his office. Mr Leahry was out of the office again, as usual. Where he went and what he was doing was a mystery to everyone, except Sandra, perhaps. I couldn't believe that one woman could be the cause of an entire company being in turmoil like this, but that was how it appeared. I wasn't too surprised when Dan told me later in the day, that he had submitted his resignation to management and would be leaving in a month's time. Dan was a popular man in the office, and nobody was happy to hear of his impending departure, when the news finally came out. With two weeks to go before Dan's final day, Mr Leahry called me in to his office and informed me that I would be taking on the financial accounts and the chief accountant's position, in addition to my own duties. That would continue until he could find a replacement for Dan.

The details of that meeting don't matter here. After explaining to him just what I thought about his system of management by absence and his personal spy network, I gave him my own resignation.

"Now you can look for two new accountants," I said. "I'll give you the letter later this afternoon. Maybe Sandra can fill in for us both until you get someone!"

Two weeks later, Dan left the office. We had arranged a small farewell party for him; Leahry was out of the office as usual, and Sandra didn't attend.

When we shook hands at the door, he said, "I'm sorry we didn't get to fly models together, as we talked about. Maybe we will some day."

He didn't know, right then, how true that would be. But that was much further down the road!

The next two weeks were rather uncomfortable for me. Leahry was rarely seen, and Sandra stayed well out of my way. Neither the factory workers nor the office staff went out of their ways to speak to me, and I had the feeling that they were blaming me for the entire thing. But I knew that I hadn't caused the situation; I had just brought it out into the open. I wasn't the least bit sorry when those two weeks were over. I had my bags packed and in the car when I went into the office for the last time, to say goodbye, and then I headed straight back to Southampton. The apartment over Dad's house was vacant, and this time I insisted on paying rent for the privilege of using it.

My work history wasn't looking too good at this stage, and my resume couldn't fit on one page anymore. Dad started giving me "unrehearsed" talks about the values of tolerance, persistence, a steady job, and settling down. I told him that if I ever found a good steady job, I would settle down, but I didn't think it would be in England. I really didn't like the place, and I knew I didn't fit in.

One of my least attractive qualities I'm sure, as far as a prospective employer was concerned, was my habit of speaking my mind. If something or someone was wrong, I would always say so. I didn't believe in beating about the bush and covering things up, and that did nothing to boost my popularity. A good example of this was when I hit the next bump in my road.

Harris Engineering was a small company located about five miles from my parents' house. The general manager was a large, overweight, self-important kind of man who, for some unknown reason, had the complete confidence of the owner, a true English gentleman. The owner, Mr Green, was an older man, who represented his local area as a Member of Parliament. The engineering company was a family business which he had inherited and which really didn't interest him very much. The G.M. could do no wrong and he made it clear, when I interviewed for the accountant's position that, although the position carried the title of accountant, all he really wanted was a good bookkeeper who would do what he was told. At this stage, I was fast losing hope that I would ever find my future in England and agreed to the terms, thinking to myself that this would be no more than a stop-gap until I could find a real job. The commute was easy, which was one advantage.

There were two locations owned by the Company. One was a manufacturing facility and office complex and the other, which was three miles away, was a fibre glass boat building shop. The main product of the company was a chicken plucking machine. I know that sounds a little ridiculous, but think about it. With all those naked chickens in grocery stores, fast-food restaurants, etc it stands to reason that someone or something has to remove the feathers. And that's a lot of plucking! Anyway that was the number one product and the machines were in use in chicken processing plants all over the country. The other product was fibreglass sailing boats. These were small, two-man day-sailers, which were quite popular on the South coast at that time. None of this really interested me as I was not expected to do more than keep the books using information given to me by the G.M. I tried to mind my own business but when I asked for supporting documents for a travel claim submitted by the G.M., I was told that his signature on the check was good enough and my suspicions were aroused. The G.M. was the only signature required on checks so he had complete control of the bank balance, which was surprisingly low, I found. It didn't take too long to see that something was very wrong with this situation.

A few days after I joined the Company, I asked to visit the boat-building factory as I had never seen fibreglass used for boat building before. When I arrived I introduced myself to the man in charge and he showed me around. I asked him about their stock issuing and receiving procedures and was told that there weren't any.

"So how do you work out how much each boat costs?" I asked.

"We don't," he answered. "The G.M. keeps track of all that stuff. We just build 'em. When we get low on supplies I just call him at the office and, generally the next day, a truck delivers what I ask for."

I really didn't like this, but I didn't say anything. We continued the tour and against one wall I noticed a new yacht tender Because of the large difference between high and low tides around England, most sailing craft, when not in use, are anchored or moored in deep-water harbors. The tender, or dinghy, is used to get from shore to the sailing boat and back again.

I said to the foreman, "I didn't know that we also build tenders. Is this a new product line?"

He looked sideways at me as he replied, "Not exactly, that's a one-off for the G.M.'s son-in-law."

"So the G.M. will be paying for that himself?" I asked. He looked a little uncomfortable when he answered, "I really don't know, but I don't believe the G.M. pays for anything he doesn't want to. No, this is just a little something that we are doing on the side for him. Just a favor to keep on his good side, you know?"

"I think I understand, and thanks for the tour. It was very interesting," I said as I left.

Arriving back at the office, I decided to look at the books a little more closely. Apart from the cash and bank book, I hadn't paid much attention to the other records as, other than making entries of invoices and receipts, they were not supposed to be my concern, according to the G.M. It soon became obvious that something was very wrong here. Practically every account was several months overdue, and no statements or overdue notices had been sent. This represented tens of thousands of pounds, when the company was skating on very thin ice, with only a marginal balance in the bank.

When I pointed the situation out to the G.M. he flushed and spluttered for a bit before growling at me, "That's none of your business. I told you before, I'm running this show, and you're to do what I say. Now, if we need more money, ask Mr Green for some. He'll give you a check, no questions asked. Just write the books and keep your nose out of my business, okay?"

This was not the way to run a business. I had never worked for an openly dishonest man before, and I felt very sorry for Mr Green, who was apparently wealthy enough and too busy with his parliamentary duties to be worried about his business.

The company employed one traveling salesman, who spent most of his time out of the office, touring the chicken farms and processing plants in the north of England, ostensibly looking for new business and delivering replacement parts for those machines already in service. This salesman, Jim, didn't get on very well with the G.M., and a week or so later, when the G.M. took off on a week's vacation to play golf, he asked me if I would like to go with him on one of his trips. That was an opportunity I wasn't going to miss. He told me which customers we would be visiting, and I looked up their accounts in our books. Each one of them was long overdue. During the ride, Jim didn't say much about company business. His conversation centered more on the weather, the week's football scores, and TV programs. I believe he was giving me the opportunity to form my own opinions about the company, and he didn't want to be held responsible.

The weather was the usual for an autumn day, traveling north. Misty, overcast with rain showers and cold. That was normal for most days in Britain as far as I could tell, except for summer, which I believed, happened on a Wednesday afternoon sometime in July. Our first stop was at a chicken farm which also operated a small processing plant. The farmer showed us the plant as I had never seen one before. It was something that I hoped never to see again. It was in a large corrugated iron barn and consisted of an overhead cable with hooks spaced at intervals running on steel supports in a large oval. Workers were spaced along the track at various stations. At the start, the squawking birds with feet tied together, were hung upside down on the passing hooks through a covered in area where their throats were cut. The still flapping bodies were then carried along and immersed in baths of alternate hot and cold water to prepare them for plucking. After the baths they were passed between the rubber flails of the plucking machine and then on to the cutting tables where they were gutted and trimmed. The rest of the preparation, cleaning, packing etc, was done in an adjoining room.

I was really only interested in seeing how the plucking machine worked. It consisted of two lines of upright spindles, one line on each side of the conveyor. Each spindle held rubber fingers or flails which spun round, hitting the chickens. The flails gripped the feathers with their rough surfaces and pulled them off. It was something like a small car wash but a lot rougher. It was a simple enough tool, not exactly rocket science. Once again, in a meat processing facility, the smell was gross. It would have gagged a maggot! I couldn't eat chicken for some time after that. If everyone, at some time in their formative years were obliged to spend a little time in a meat processing plant, there would be a whole lot more vegetarians in this world.

Before we left the farm, I asked to speak to the farmer alone. "Mr Brown," I said, "As you know I'm the new accountant for Harris Engineering, and one of the reasons for this visit is to try to work out something with our customers to try to get their accounts up to date." I looked down at the notebook in my hand and added, "We don't appear to have had a payment from you for the last four months, which is well beyond usual limits. You understand we can't continue carrying all our customers in this fashion. Is there any particular reason you haven't been making payments?"

He looked a little surprised that I should be asking him about his account and said "Well, Don, it's like this. Bob, your general manager, told me that I needn't worry about paying if I couldn't afford it, and things have been a little tight this year. He told me that I could catch up with it some time later, when things improve."

"I'm sorry to hear that, sir," I said, "but the truth is, we can't continue to carry this debt for you. Unless you can make some substantial payment immediately, we will have to suspend shipment of replacement flails for the pluckers and any other spare parts you may need. I'd really hate to have to do that."

I came away from there with a check from Mr Brown, who promised to get his account up to date with regular payments, regardless of what Bob might say. I had also taken note of Mr Brown's new Land Rover sitting in the driveway. Things couldn't have been that bad for him that year.

I wasn't that successful with all the other customers that we visited on that trip, but we still returned to the office with enough checks to prevent me having to ask Mr Green for any more money. Bob was furious! He called me into his office as soon as we drove through the gates. I stood in front of his desk. He didn't invite me to sit, and I stared at his flushed, almost purple, face. Glaring at me he took a deep breath and let me have both barrels.

"What the hell do you think you were doing?" he stormed. "I told you to mind your own business, and who told you to go visiting customers? I didn't hire you to do that; why couldn't you just write the books like I asked you? Now I've got a lot of angry friends who think I've cheated on them and all because you can't keep your mouth shut! Well, as far as I'm concerned, you can just f*** off out of here, and don't look for a paycheck."

He had been sprawled back in his office chair, waving his arms around, while he ranted at me, and as he finished he made as if to stand up.

"Go ahead, you big sack of shit. Stand up," I said. "When you do I'm going to knock you on your fat arse, straight through that window behind you. And as far as the paycheck is concerned, I'd like to ram it down your throat. I don't want any of this company's money. God knows you steal enough of it."

He was speechless and with that I turned and walked out.

When I told my parents about the situation, I had the impression that they thought I was making excuses for leaving another job. My Father had only had one job all his life, and I seemed to be changing jobs as often as I changed my socks. But times were different, and this was England where, no matter how hard I tried, I just couldn't settle.

I didn't tell anyone at first that I was really disappointed in England and that I wanted to get away as soon as I could. Instead of looking for work in the local and regional newspapers, I started looking in the nationals, where overseas positions were more likely to be found.

My Father was having a much better time with his little part time job than I was, looking for possible jobs. At about the time I left Southampton for the cost accounting position in Harlow, he found a job that really suited him. A senior official of the National Coal Board owned a large, diesel-powered yacht, which was kept at Southampton. He also had, as a yacht tender, an inboard-powered, 22-foot, classic wooden launch. Both boats were immaculate and fully equipped for coastal cruising. The Boss was a member of most of the sailing clubs around the south and east coasts and he took great delight in entertaining visiting aristocracy and Coal Board Members on his yacht while cruising the Southern coast line of England. These cruises only took place in summer, so there weren't that many of them each year. Out of season, the yacht was kept inside one of the large boat sheds owned by a local marina. Dad was hired as the skipper. His primary job was to pilot the yacht on these cruises between yacht clubs. Once ashore he was free to do whatever he liked until the party returned to be ferried back out to the yacht. He was paid a retainer to watch over the boats all year, and he would make periodic inspection tours of the boats and their accommodations throughout the year. He also had free access to the launch, which he often used to go fishing in the off season.

One day, after mailing a reply to an advertisement I had seen in *The Daily Telegraph* newspaper that interested me, Dad asked me if I would like to go fishing with him. I didn't have anything else planned for that day so I agreed. I had a feeling that Dad had something in mind other than fishing, but as he didn't say anything, neither did I. He said we would take the launch out for a run and see what we could catch in the shallows on the far side of the Southampton shipping channel, one of his favorite fishing spots. We used his car to get to the marina where the launch was kept and we were soon out in the channel, avoiding the ships in the deeper water. Once we were positioned on the shallow banks, off to the side of the shipping lane, we dropped anchor, rigged our lines and settled down with a flask of hot tea to wait for a bite. It was one of those rare calm and sunny days and quite a few small pleasure craft were out on the water. Several of them recognized the launch and the occupants waved to us as they passed.

By mid-morning we had caught all the fish we needed and kept a couple of the biggest. Dad suggested paying a visit to one of the local yacht clubs to see some of his friends who worked as skippers for some of the local gentry. It sounded good to me, so we set a course for the nearest river where the club was located. Most sailing clubs were located in rivers, near the junction with open water. This provided protection during rough weather and also easy access to open water when the weather was fine. We arrived at the club pier about an hour before lunch time, not that it really concerned us. As non-members we were certainly not allowed inside. Skippers and other boat hands brought the owners and guests ashore in the yacht tenders and then waited for them in the dinghy park, well away from the club. This was typical of the British upper class and was one of their less charming traditions, as far as I was concerned.

There was a small, barge-type craft, beached in the dinghy park and Dad tied the launch up to the far side of it so that it was completely out of sight from the club house. Then we joined the other boatmen who were waiting for their owners who were lunching in the club house. After chatting for a few minutes, Dad asked me if I was up for a bit of fun. I had felt something was in the air; so this was it!

I said, "Of course. What did you have in mind?"

"Well, you're the only one of us that nobody could recognize and the only one who can run, if need be," he said.

At last, I thought, *a little bit of excitement to brighten the day!*

"Okay, let's have it. What do you want me to do?"

"You see that yacht approaching its mooring out there?" he asked.

"Sure," I replied.

"Well," he said, "we want you to take this and walk about half way out along the pier and put it down where it will have to be stepped over to get to the club house."

With that, he brought from his pocket a disgusting-looking dollop of dog poop. It was plastic, of course. He had bought it at a joke shop in Southampton.

"We want to see how the big nobs like that!" He laughed.

"Sounds like a plan," I grinned, as I took the poop and strolled off down the pier like some kind of tourist.

I kept one eye on the approaching tender, which held three ladies, two men besides the owner, and the skipper. When I was sure that they weren't looking my way, I bent down, ostensibly to tie my shoelace, and placed the poop where they would have to step over it on the way to the club house. The original plan was for me to then walk away and leave it there, but I had an idea that I could get it back. I walked out to the end of the pier, as if I was admiring the scenery while the skipper off loaded his passengers at the steps that led up to the pier. They then walked the ten yards to the ramp which led off to the club house where they came upon the poop sitting right in the middle of the pathway.

You would have thought it was the end of the world with all the screaming and shouting that ensued when they saw it! Two of the ladies had handkerchiefs up to their faces, I suppose to keep the imaginary stink away from their delicate nostrils. The men were all red in the face, sounding off in their upper-crust British accents about how they would tell the committee and the club secretary in particular, just what they thought about this disgraceful shock to their sensibilities! Very carefully they stepped over the poop, still fussing and supporting the distressed ladies. They made their way into the club house. As soon as they were inside I quickly picked up the poop, stuffed it in my pocket and strolled casually, back along the pier towards the shore. Seconds later, the club house door burst open and a small man carrying a clipboard, followed by the yacht owner, came running up the ramp to observe the "filthy mess." Of course there was nothing to see. The other members of the party came out of the club house to see for themselves, and one of them noticed me walking away and called out, "I say there, my good chap, could we have a word with you?"

I stopped walking, turned and looked at them. "Of course, what can I do for you?" I asked.

"When you were walking along the pier, did you happen to notice anything objectionable on this ramp as you went by?" he replied.

"D'you mean before you came out of the club house?" I asked. The inference was lost on them.

"Yes, of course," said my questioner.

"I didn't notice anything unusual. What were you looking for?"

The conversation continued in this fashion for several minutes until shaking their heads, they all turned to go back into the club house. As they left, the club secretary, looking considerably relieved, glanced at me, and I raised one hand in a drinking motion and pointed at the boat party. He smiled, nodded, waved his clipboard and gave me the thumbs-up sign!

When I rejoined the skippers in the dinghy park they were still laughing. They hadn't missed a thing and had heard everything that ensued. They kept repeating the conversation over and over, imitating the posh accents and every one of them insisted on shaking my hand.

I guess it's true what they say; every man is still a boy at heart, and I'm sure that piece of plastic dog poop had several other outings while my Dad owned it.

By the end of the week following the yacht club incident, I had the reply from the advertisement. I was invited to attend an interview at a well-known hotel in London. It was going to be a one day event when all the applicants would be considered. This was for the position of accountant for an Automotive business in the British Virgin Islands. Philately, or stamp collecting, was another hobby of mine when I was a child, and I knew where that was and the fact that although it was a British protectorate with the Queen's head on the stamps, U.S.

currency was used there. I recalled that they had very attractive stamps, and I was intrigued by the possibility of going there.

London was about a two-hour train ride from Southampton, so on the designated day of the interview I caught the train from Southampton which left at seven a.m., with all the other commuters. Many people worked in London and lived in the Southampton area. You would have to have an extremely good job to be able to afford to actually live in the city. I didn't think to buy a morning paper before I boarded the train; I thought I would just enjoy the scenery. It was just as well that I had something to interest me, as the other passengers did no more than grunt, "Morning," to their neighbors and then buried their heads in their newspapers, silent for the rest of the journey. It was not the friendliest of atmospheres, but I really didn't care; there was fresh scenery to admire outside the compartment window.

Looking out at the dreary outskirts of Southampton on a gray, misty morning in a steady drizzle didn't hold my interest for very long and I was grateful when we finally left that area and started through some quite pretty, if soggy, Hampshire countryside. On a sunny day it would have been beautiful but on that day, even the cows and horses in the fields looked completely dejected I knew this couldn't be my home for the rest of my life. I didn't want to end up like my fellow passengers, who seemed to be as gray and monotonous as the vista outside the window. I began to regret not buying a morning paper of my own. Eventually I propped my elbow on the window sill, leaned my head on my hand and cat-napped the rest of the way.

I took a taxi from the station in London to the hotel where the interviews were being held. I was directed to a waiting room on the third floor where I sat with five other applicants. Sitting next to me was a young black man. He seemed to be a little nervous so I introduced myself to help him feel at ease. I asked him where he came from and he told me, "The Islands."

"Which Islands would that be?" I asked.

He replied, "The Virgin Islands, of course, where this job is going to be."

He then went on to tell me that he had been living in England with his Aunt while he obtained his education and his accounting qualifications. This was the opportunity he had been hoping for, where he could get back to his home and make a name for himself. It seemed I had chosen the prime candidate for the job, to sit beside. While we waited, I encouraged him to tell me all about his home in the Caribbean and it was interesting to hear the native's point of view. It all sounded idyllic, from the weather to the fishing and I couldn't wait to experience it, if I was given the chance. But that chance didn't look to be very promising if I was competing with a young, formally qualified, native of the area.

We were interviewed in the order in which we arrived. I was last in line and followed the Islander. The man conducting the interview was not an employee of the company but a professional head hunter. He explained what was required of the applicant and gave me a brief run down of the situation in the Islands as he knew it. He had my resume on his desk and asked me a few questions about my experiences in Africa with particular reference to my work in the Automotive business. It didn't seem like a regular interview to me and I supposed that the obvious choice had already been made. The interviewer told me that a short list would be prepared and we would be notified within a week of the results. Those selected would be required to return to be interviewed by the Managing Director of this new company which was about to be formed. I left the interview room feeling disappointed. My Islander acquaintance had left and I made my way back to the train station feeling that I had just wasted my day.

I had almost given up hope of hearing any more about the Virgin Islands when I received another letter inviting me to interview with the managing director. My interest was immediately re-kindled but I wouldn't allow myself to be too optimistic. I didn't want to be disappointed all over again. Once again I caught the early train from Southampton to London, but this time I bought my own barricade, the morning newspaper. The same people occupied the same seats as they did on my previous interview trip, and it felt like a prime example of déjà vu. I followed the same routine when I arrived in London. I took a taxi to the hotel, but this time I was shown immediately to an interview room, where I met the managing director, Mr Giles.

He was a short, stocky Englishman with short, graying hair and penetrating blue eyes. He invited me to sit down and then started to explain the details of his prospective venture in the Caribbean. His was a development company and he had obtained the rights, from the local island government, to develop one of their islands by constructing an airport and tourist hotel. The island was named Anegada and was the only coral type island in the group. All the others were formed by the tops of sunken mountains with very little level ground suitable for such development. He already had a company accountant, his personal friend of many years, Mr Henderson, who would be living on Anegada and would be handling all accounting matters concerning that part of the operation. He explained that he had made his money in supplying gravel for road-building projects throughout Britain and was no stranger to construction projects.

Finally he said that he had been particularly interested in my experience with the General Motors' cost of sales system of accounts and asked me if I thought I could implement something like that for a small company he had purchased on the main island of the British Virgin Islands group, Tortola. I couldn't believe what I was hearing! It looked like I was getting out of England again, at last! I promptly assured Mr Giles that he would have the best and most secure accounting system that he could wish for, if I was chosen for the position and that I was available to go, at a moment's notice.

"What's wrong?" he asked. "It sounds like you can't wait to get away from England."

"You're absolutely right," I replied."Apart from the pork pies, sausages, and beer, there's not much else that I like about it."

He stood up, laughed and shook hands with me. "I have one other chap to see today, and then I'll make my decision. Expect a letter from me in the next couple of days to say whether or not you have the job. Okay?"

"Thank you, sir. I'll be keeping my fingers crossed until then," I replied.

I tried very hard to contain my excitement, but I just knew that the job was mine. The next two days seemed like an eternity and then the letter arrived. I had been chosen for the job in the Caribbean on condition that I was able to obtain a U.S. visa in my passport. Some travel would be necessary between the U.S. and the British Virgin Islands. I immediately mailed back an acceptance letter, informing Mr Giles that I would contact him again as soon as I had the visa. I called the U.S. Embassy in London and was told to apply, in person, at that address.

I think my parents were pleased in a way, that I had been successful with my application but were a little sorry that I would be leaving the country again. I had never been good at writing letters home so they rarely knew what was happening to me. I promised I would try to do better in future, but I could see they didn't hold out much hope on that score.

My usual seat was vacant on the early train to London and this time I took a book with me. I had no interest in the local news and I needed to keep my mind on something else or I might start jumping up and down with joy at the prospect of leaving this cold, gray and damp place for an island in the sun! Arriving in London, I took a taxi to the American Embassy and joined the line for visas. It was a much longer process than it is today and it was mid-afternoon before I was told to come back in a week's time to have the visa stamped in my passport. I suppose that was to allow for a background check. Whoever had that task would be earning his pay that week!

I called Mr Giles when I arrived back in Southampton and told him what had transpired that day. He sounded quite pleased and told me to meet him, with my visa stamp in my passport, at a Lyons Tea Room in London after I had returned to the Embassy. He would have something for me. I had collected very few belongings while I had been in England and everything I felt might be useful on a tropical island would easily fit in one medium size suitcase. I left a box of general things which I wouldn't need, like old papers, photographs, etc., with my parents and sold my car. I was going "back on the road," and I traveled light.

I met Mr Giles in London the following week after getting the visa, and he gave me a one-way airline ticket to the British Virgin Islands and one hundred pounds travel money. He told me to keep receipts where possible as I would be accounting for it later. When I arrived at Tortola, I was to find a Carl Meadows who was the manager of the car company where I would be working. Carl already had a room prepared for me in the rear of the dealership. My flight would leave London's Heathrow Airport in two days which would leave me just enough time to say goodbye to my parents again.

The train ride back from London to Southampton this time was slightly unusual. I had only been seated a few minutes when an attractive young lady asked if the seat next to me was taken. I assured her it wasn't and after hanging her coat on the hook beside the window, she sat down beside me. After the usual pleasantries about the weather, she started telling me all about her vacation travels in the North of England, around the Lake District. I had never been there and it sounded very interesting. The time passed very quickly as we chatted and she told me that she was going to Bournemouth, the next stop on the line past Southampton where she would be staying with friends. As the train approached Southampton, I shook her hand and said,

"Well, it's been really nice meeting you, Sandra. You may have even changed my mind about English people. I've made this trip to London and back several times recently, and this is the first time that anyone spoke to me or even put down their newspapers to acknowledge my existence. It's a pity that more of your countrymen aren't as friendly."

Still holding my hand, she laughed and said, "Well, thanks, but I'm not English you know. I'm Australian, and my friends are further back in the compartment. We're staying in Bournemouth and touring the South of England from there. But it really was nice talking to you, and I wish you all the best of luck with your new job."

So there it was; she wasn't the exception that proved a rule after all!

Two days later I found myself at Heathrow Airport, bound for New York, on the first leg of my journey to the Virgin Islands. From New York I would fly to Puerto Rico, then to St Thomas in the U.S. Virgin Islands and finally to Tortola in the British Virgin Islands. It was going to be a full day's travel and the start of *Bumps in the Road: Part Two!*

CPSIA information can be obtained at www.ICGtesting.com
Printed in the USA
LVOW122012030413

327473LV00002B/121/P